Compassionate Eschatology

Compassionate Eschatology

The Future as Friend

Edited by
TED GRIMSRUD
and
MICHAEL HARDIN

CASCADE *Books* · Eugene, Oregon

COMPASSIONATE ESCHATOLOGY
The Future as Friend

Cascade Books
An Imprint of Wipf and Stock Publishers
199 W. 8th Ave., Suite 3
Eugene, OR 97401

www.wipfandstock.com

ISBN 13: 978-1-60899-488-5

Cataloging-in-Publication data:

Compassionate eschatology : the future as friend / edited by Ted Grimsrud and Michael Hardin.

xii + 294 p. ; 23 cm. Including bibliographical references.

ISBN 13: 978-1-60899-488-5

1. Escatology. I. Grimsrud, Ted, 1954–. II. Hardin, Michael. III. Title.

BT821.3 .C66 2011

Manufactured in the U.S.A.

The author and publisher gratefully acknowledge permission to reprint the following essays:

Jürgen Moltmann, "The Final Judgment: Sunrise of Christ's Liberating Justice," *Anglican Theological Review* 89:4 (Fall 2007) 565–76.

Barbara R. Rossing, "Prophecy, End-Times, and American Apocalypse: Reclaiming Hope for Our World," *Anglican Theological Review* 89:4 (Fall 2007) 549–63.

Barbara R. Rossing, "Hastening the Day when the Earth Will Burn?: Global Warming, 2 Peter, and the Book of Revelation," in *The Bible in the Public Square: Reading the Signs of the Times*, edited by Cynthia Briggs Kittredge, Ellen Bradshaw Aiken, and Jonathan A. Draper (Minneapolis: Fortress, 2008) 25–34.

This book is dedicated to
René Girard
teacher, visionary, prophet

Contents

PART TWO: Toward Compassionate Eschatology

Contributors

ANTHONY W. BARTLETT teaches at Episcopal Seminary, Bexley Hall, and at General Theological Seminary.

RICHARD BAUCKHAM recently retired as Professor of New Testament at the University of St. Andrews. He is currently Senior Scholar at Ridley Hall in the University of Cambridge, England.

NANCY ELIZABETH BEDFORD is Georgia Harkness Professor of Applied Theology at Garrett-Evangelical Theological Seminary, Evanston, Illinois.

CAROL BERRY is an artist and lecturer who lives in Manchester, Vermont.

JAMES E. BRENNEMAN is President of Goshen College, Goshen, Indiana.

STEPHEN FINAMORE is Principal of Bristol Baptist College, Bristol, England.

TED GRIMSRUD is Professor of Theology and Peace Studies at Eastern Mennonite University, Harrisonburg, Virginia.

MICHAEL HARDIN is Executive Director of Preaching Peace, Lancaster, Pennsylvania.

ANDREW P. KLAGER holds a PhD in Ecclesiastical History from the University of Glasgow, Scotland. He is the Director of Research on Restorative Justice and Community Peacebuilding at M2/W2 Restorative Christian Ministries, Abbotsford, British Columbia.

JÜRGEN MOLTMANN is Professor Emeritus of Systematic Theology at the University of Tübingen, Germany.

DAVID J. NEVILLE is Associate Professor of Theology at Charles Sturt University, Barton, Australia.

JOHN E. PHELAN is President and Dean of North Park Theological Seminary, Chicago, Illinois.

BARBARA R. ROSSING is Professor of New Testament at the Lutheran School of Theology, Chicago, Illinois.

J. DENNY WEAVER is Professor Emeritus of Religion at Bluffton University, Bluffton, Ohio.

WALTER WINK is Professor Emeritus of Biblical Interpretation at Auburn Theological Seminary, New York, New York.

Preface

IN SEPTEMBER OF 2008, Preaching Peace sponsored a Conference on Compassionate Eschatology. This was the third of four major Preaching Peace conferences dealing with key aspects of Christian doctrine from the perspective of nonviolence and Rene Girard's mimetic theory. The first one on Nonviolent Atonement resulted in *Stricken by God?: Nonviolent Identification and the Victory of Christ* (Eerdmans 2007, edited by Michael Hardin and Brad Jersak), the second was on Constantinian Christianity and resulted in *Peace Be with You* (Cascadia 2010, edited by Sharon Baker and Michael Hardin). The book in your hands (or on your eBook reader) explores how we might conceive eschatology apart from divine violence or retribution.

These essays from an international collection of writers representing several disciplines and a variety of theological perspectives are united in seeking to understand eschatology as a doctrine that motivates Christians to peaceable living in the present. Most of the essays were written for this book. Key ones emerged from the Compassionate Eschatology Conference, though others came to us in response to invitations to broaden the analysis beyond what was possible in a short conference.

The conference was a great starting point, nonetheless. We enjoyed two days of intense interaction with six speakers, great meals, and comfortable lodging. Barbara Rossing was one of the speakers at the Compassionate Eschatology Conference. Her presentations were published in the *Anglican Theological Review* and the book *The Bible in the Public Square* and are gratefully reprinted here. Jürgen Moltmann was scheduled to attend but due to last-minute health concerns instead suggested his essay from the *ATR* for this volume. John Caputo admirably filled in for Moltmann on very short notice. Rene Girard would have liked to contribute to the book as he did at the conference, but as happens when you pass eighty years, health concerns prohibited him from doing so. Two other contributions from that event are the essays by Ted Grimsrud and

Tony Bartlett. Sharon Baker also presented at the conference. Her contribution is now included in her book *Razing Hell* (Westminster John Knox, 2010). Brad Jersak's *Her Gates Will Never Be Shut*, also published by Wipf & Stock (2009), is an essential companion to this book.

Many thanks to San Francisco Theological Seminary in San Anselmo, CA, for their gracious hospitality. Thanks also to the Raven Foundation for their support of this event.

I (Michael) would like to thank Lorri as always. What a gift she has been to me and to the church. Thank you God! Many thanks to all of those who have contributed to the work of Preaching Peace (www.preaching peace.org). I also want to thank my students from the Monday night class at Landisville Mennonite Church; they are inquisitive beyond measure. We have had great fun together. And where would Preaching Peace be without the financial support of *Imitatio*. As always, thanks Lindy, Bob, and Peter!

I (Ted) would like to thank my colleagues and students at Eastern Mennonite University for making it such a receptive place for constructive peace theology. For encouragement to reflect on the book of Revelation and peaceable eschatology I thank the numerous congregations who have invited me over the past thirty years to join them in discerning the message of scripture on "the end." And, again and forever, thanks to Kathleen for all the great talk and everything else.

July 2010

PART ONE

Interpreting Apocalypse
and Apocalyptic Non-Retributively

1

Biblical Apocalyptic

What Is Being Revealed?

TED GRIMSRUD

Eschatology all too often means judgment, vengeance, the bad guys and gals getting their "just desserts." Probably at least in part because of the titillating allure of violence, and in part because of the attraction of being part of a story when our side wins and the other side loses, eschatology is pretty popular.

But is this kind of eschatology Christian? What might Christian eschatology look like if it is done as if Jesus matters? If we look at Jesus' own life and teaching, we won't find a clearer statement of his hierarchy of values than his concise summary of the law and prophets: You shall love the Lord your God with all your heart, mind, and soul—and, likewise, you shall love your neighbor as you love your own self. This love of God and neighbor is why we are alive. It is what matters the most. The "end" that matters is our *purpose* for being here, not any knowledge we might think we have about future events. Our *purpose* is to love—that purpose is the eschatological theme that is central if we do eschatology as if Jesus matters.[1]

To talk about the "end of the world" biblically points us to our purpose for living in the world. The word "end" can have two different meanings. (1) "End" means the conclusion, the finish, the last part, the final outcome. In this sense, "the end of the world" is something future and has to do with the world ceasing to exist. (2) "End" also, though, means the purpose, what is desired, the intention. "End of the world," in

---

1. Grimsrud, *Theology*, especially chapter 12: "The End Times are Now."

3

this sense, is, we could say, what God *intends* the world to be for. In this sense of "end," the "end times" have to do with *why* we live *in* time.[2]

The book of Revelation is usually seen as the book of the Bible most concerned with "the end times." The book of Revelation has always vexed interpreters. Rarely has it been seen as an indispensable source for Christian social ethics; often it has been seen more as an ethical problem.[3] I want to suggest, though, that Revelation has potential to speak powerfully to twenty-first-century Christians about our purpose in life.

The Bible generally speaks in the future tense only in service of exhortation toward present faithfulness. The Bible's concern is that the people of God live in such a way that we will be at home in the New Jerusalem—not with predictions about when and how the future will arrive.

How do we relate "eschatology" with "apocalyptic"? Let me suggest that *biblical* apocalyptic (which I will differentiate from the genre "apocalyptic literature" that modern scholars have developed) actually is best understood similarly to eschatology. The biblical use of apocalyptic language, like the broader use of prophetic and eschatological language, serves the exhortation to faithfulness in present life.

When I take up the issues of eschatology and biblical apocalyptic, I do so from the standpoint of my commitment to the gospel of peace, and more particularly in trying to construct Christian theology that serves this commitment. I believe that the three main sources for theology—the Bible, tradition, and present experience—all give us mixed signals concerning the gospel of peace and its applicability for our world (which, for example, is why so many Christians in this country support American military actions). For the clarity we need, I think it's important to add a fourth source for constructive theology: hope or vision.[4] Where do we want to go? What do we hope for? And, then, how might we interpret the Bible, tradition, and present experience in ways that serve this hope? That is what I propose to do with the book of Revelation.[5]

2. Grimsrud, "Why Are We Here? Two Meditations on an Ethical Eschatology," in *Embodying*, 179–89.

3. For a full-blown critique of Revelation and its role in the history of Christianity, see Kirsch, *History*.

4. I develop this fourfold approach to theological method more fully in Grimsrud, *Embodying*, 37–53.

5. In what follows I will be drawing on an ever-expanding school of peaceable interpretations of Revelation. The founding text for this school was Caird, *Commentary*.

My essay will test the following thesis concerning biblical apocalyptic in service of a compassionate eschatology: What biblical apocalyptic *reveals* may be seen especially in the formation of communities of faith called to resist imperial hegemony. The power that matters most in biblical apocalyptic is the power of love that sustains these communities in the face of empire.

THE QUESTION OF POWER

The fifth chapter of the book of Revelation begins with a poignant image. The seer, John of Patmos, writes in chapter 4 of an awe-inspiring vision of the throne of God. Surrounding the throne in John's vision, the entire animate creation worships the one on the throne. In chapter 5, though, a shadow falls. John sees a scroll in the right hand of the one on the throne. From how John describes this scroll ("written on the inside and on the back, sealed with seven seals," Rev 5:1) and how he regards it (begging for it to be opened), we get the impression that what he's describing should be understood as, in some sense, history fulfilled, the completion of the project initiated in Genesis one.

The poignancy enters when John sees the scroll but is overcome with grief at the thought that it may not be opened. Who can open the scroll? "No one in heaven or on earth or under the earth was able to open the scroll or to look into it" (5:3).

This account provides us with a metaphor that speaks to much of human history. How can history be redeemed? How can the human project be redirected from brokenness and alienation toward healing and wholeness?

Human beings tend to think of power in terms of the ability to control events, to force others to do one's will even if that means coercing them. Political power is often linked with the ability to use violence. We are most likely to answer the question of how to open the scroll by asserting the need to "force" it open, to open it by our firepower.

In Revelation 5, John, like most people, seems to assume the scroll will be opened by firepower, power as domination. He weeps bitterly when he thinks no one can be found to open the scroll. However, John

---

Some of the other important contributions to this approach to Revelation include: Bauckham, *Theology*; Blount, *Revelation*; Boring, *Revelation*; Bredin, *Jesus*; Ellul, *Apocalypse*; Kraybill, *Apocalypse*; Maier, *Apocalypse*; Rossing, *Rapture*; Rowland, "Book"; Sweet, *Revelation*; and Yeatts, *Revelation*.

then hears an audacious claim. One of the elders immediately comforts John. "Do not weep. See, the Lion of the tribe of Judah, the Root of David, has conquered, so that he can open the scroll and its seven seals" (5:4). These images evoke a mighty warrior *king* (or Messiah) who will open the scroll with the use of force.

John's vision continues, though, with a shockingly different claim. He may have *heard* the promise of a warrior king to open the scroll, but he actually *sees* something altogether different. "Then I saw between the throne and the four living creatures and among the elders a Lamb standing as if it had been slaughtered, having seven horns and seven eyes, which are the seven spirits of God sent out into all the earth. He went and took the scroll from the right hand of the one who was seated on the throne. When he had taken the scroll, the four creatures and the twenty-four elders fell before the Lamb" (5:6–8).

According to the next few verses, the creatures and elders, and ultimately the rest of creation, worship this Lamb as the one who does have the power to open the scroll.

BIBLICAL "APOCALYPTIC"

How does this claim for the power of the Lamb correspond with the claim that power-as-domination is the only way to address the huge problems of human history?

To answer this question, we need to reflect on the message of the biblical materials known as "apocalyptic." If we focus primarily on the biblical language of "revelation" (from the Greek *apokalypsis*) and consider this language in the context of the rest of the Christian Bible, we will find that power according to biblical apocalyptic does cohere with John's vision in Revelation 5. The power that biblical apocalyptic understands to be decisive in human history, the power that will "open the scroll," is the power of suffering love and communal faithfulness, not the power of weapons of war and coercive force.

The term "apocalyptic" as a label for a genre of ancient Jewish and Christian literature comes from the first several words in Revelation: "The revelation (*apokalypsis*) of Jesus Christ." The linking together of apocalypse with Jesus Christ provides our first essential clue for understanding power in biblical apocalyptic. The power of biblical apocalyptic is the power of Jesus Christ.

Most contemporary writing on biblical apocalyptic in general, and Revelation more specifically, does not generally self-consciously link "apocalyptic" with "Jesus Christ." We don't allow "Jesus Christ" to shape our understanding of "apocalyptic." General approaches to apocalyptic may be divided into three general categories, each of which by and large shares with the others the same general sense of what "apocalyptic" conveys.

To think apocalyptically, it is said, is to think in terms of visions of fire from the sky that judge and destroy. The "apocalypse" is a time of catastrophe, of dramatic change, the end of what is and the birth of something drastically new and different. Apocalyptic power, it is implied, is top-down power, the power of might and coercion, vengeance and judgment. As a consequence of God's exercise of such power, every knee is forced to bow before God—either in joyful submission or in defeated submission.

The three general responses to apocalyptic (all understanding apocalyptic in roughly the same way) include (1) avoidance, (2) historical literalism, and (3) futuristic literalism.

1. *Avoidance.* Many Christians have simply ignored apocalyptic. It has been seen as the literature of extremists. Many in the early church disputed the acceptance of Revelation into the canon. Much later, John Calvin wrote commentaries on the entire Bible, *except* Revelation. Martin Luther also considered Revelation to be sub-Christian and taught its avoidance.

More recently, many "mainstream" Christians continue to avoid Revelation, willingly giving over the discussion of this part of the Bible to the prophecy purveyors. Revelation is seen as a book of fear and violent judgment that reinforces many of the most uncivilized tendencies of religious people—and thus is best avoided as much as possible.

2. *Historical Literalism.* Beginning with the publication of Albert Schweitzer's *The Quest of the Historical Jesus* (1906), the consensus view for most biblical scholars in the historical-critical vein has been to accept the apocalypse-as-world-catastrophe-and-divine-judgment view as being what Jesus, Revelation, and the rest of earliest Christianity literally expected to come very soon. However, obviously they were wrong. Since Schweitzer, the question of how thoroughly this apocalyptic view should be applied to early Christian thought has been vigorously debated. But

the general sense that biblical apocalyptic concerns violent power and judgment has not been contested.[6]

Neither the avoiders nor the historical literalists themselves see biblical apocalyptic as valid for our present. The third approach shares a similar sense of what biblical apocalyptic's perspective was, but this view affirms that this perspective *does* remain valid for today.

3. *Future Literalism*. Throughout the past two thousand years, at least a few Christians have understood the visions of biblical apocalyptic writings, especially Revelation, to be predictive of actual future events in human history. This future prophetic view found powerful expression in the writings of a nineteenth-century British reformer named John Darby who formulated a thorough system of interpretation called "dispensationalism" that has shaped countless perspectives on biblical apocalyptic.[7]

In recent years, dispensational theology has gained wide currency through the phenomenally popular science fiction novels in the Left Behind series. These books articulate a theology of future judgment, of apocalypse as destruction and recreation, vengeance and reward. Though presented as fiction, in many ways the vision of these books is believed to be an articulation of the kinds of things that their writers (and many of their millions of readers) expect literally to happen.[8]

In all these three approaches, then, the assumption that biblical apocalyptic understands power in terms of force, coercion, and top-down impositions of God's will has remained unchallenged. However, turning back to Revelation chapter 5, we may ask whether these assumptions about power accurately capture the sense of what John the Seer believes allows the Lamb to open the scroll. And, in light of our long history of wars and rumors of wars, we must ask whether all our "myths of redemptive violence"[9] might not be utterly counter-productive in relation to the universal human longing for the scroll to be opened,

6. For two contemporary Schweitzerian interpretations, see Ehrman, *Jesus* and Allison, *Jesus*.

7. The authoritative history of this movement is Boyer, *When*.

8. The by-now classic text on popular dispensational theology and likely still the best introduction is Lindsey, *Late*. For a sample of many volumes critiquing this popular movement see Guyatt, *Have*; Rossing, *Rapture*; Shuck, *Marks*; and Standaert, *Skipping*.

9. This term was coined by Walter Wink to refer to the essentially religious belief people have in the efficacy of violence—Wink, *Engaging*.

brokenness to be healed, and wrong-doing to be dealt with in ways that bring genuine redemption.

APOCALYPTIC POWER IN REVELATION

Clearly, the book of Revelation does mean to convey a sense of crisis. It envisions impending catastrophe, along with a polarized view of reality. We see clearly separated forces of good and evil at war with one another and demanding absolute allegiance. Life and death themselves are at stake in relation to the choice of people's loyalties. However, we need to pay close attention to the way power is construed in the book in order to have a better sense of how John envisions the scroll to be opened and the conflicts to be resolved.

What characterizes "apocalyptic power" according to the book of Revelation? Let's look at four themes.

(1) First, the book's self-designation as a "revelation of *Jesus Christ*" (1:1) reminds readers of the gospel message of Jesus' persevering, self-giving, transforming love as the truly creative power of the universe—in direct contrast with the type of power characteristic of the Roman Empire and all other human empires (signified in Revelation as the "Beast").

This *contrast* reflects Revelation's agenda. The "revelation" of Jesus correspondingly reveals the nature of the empire that demanded Christians' loyalty. John's visions *disillusion*. To see through eyes of faith in the Lamb and his way undercuts the Beast's hegemonic demands. The power to perceive the character of the true God and the contrast between that character and the true nature of the Beast stands at the heart of biblical apocalyptic.

The story of Jesus continually portrayed Jesus' message as a challenge to *sight*. *See* the world and your place in it in light of Jesus' good news of God's love. In the context of the rest of the New Testament, John's attempt to convey the message of Jesus as a "revelation" most of all underscores how "correct sight" was at the heart of the Christian message.

Revelation's urgency stems from John's concern about the *perennial* struggle of people of the promise to worship God aright and not trust in idols. Just as the first Hebrews faced the choice between believing in the inevitability of the domination of Pharaoh's empire or trusting in Yahweh, just as later Israelites faced the choice between the Babylonian

and then Persian Empires and Yahweh, just as Jesus challenged his followers to choose between God and Caesar, for John of Patmos, a key
choice his audience faced was who would be the object of their trust—
the God of the Bible or almighty Rome. To respond appropriately to this
challenge, John's audience (he believed) needed to have clear sight. They
needed a reminder—a revelation of the true message of Jesus.

The book of Revelation came into being in the late first century.[10]
Though traditionally, Revelation has been seen as set in the context of
intense persecution from the Roman Empire, more recent scholarship
has tended toward understanding overt, widespread persecution not to
be the likely environment. Certainly, the book indicates spots of persecution among the seven churches, though only one direct case of martyrdom is mentioned. However, among the seven churches, John fears
the conformity of his fellow Christians to the surrounding culture much
more than immediate persecution.

John seems mostly concerned with emphasizing choices between
following the way of Jesus and seeking to fit in comfortably with the
imperial Asia Minor environment. The vehemence of John's rhetoric and
the drama of his visions challenge the imaginations of his readers to
recognize the deep-seated dangers of making wrong choices more than
they speak to obvious and extreme cases of overt persecution.

The power of the Roman Empire stemmed from its control over
cultural religious practices that reinforced the popular sense of the
Empire's status as blessed by the gods, inevitable, and all dominating.
Dissent from these practices would lead to the threat of sanctions, including overt violence. These cultural religious practices lent legitimacy
to the entire socio-historical arrangement of the first-century Roman
Empire. The empire had a strong presence in each of the seven cities
mentioned in Revelation 2 and 3; several of these cities, in particular,
were centers of imperial religion, hosting major temples.

The key "revelation" in John's text is not actually about particular
events that literally are to come. The key "revelation" has to do with per-
ceiving the importance of this fundamental choice of loyalties.

Why would John have been so certain that Rome's vision for human
life was incompatible with Jesus'? Obviously, many of the achievements
of the empire served human well-being—the cessation of the many civil

---

10. For what follows, I draw heavily on an excellent study of Revelation's historical
context: Howard-Brook and Gwyther, *Unveiling*.

wars and other violent conflicts that had plagued the Mediterranean world, the development of secure transportation routes that allowed commerce to flourish, the development of a common language that allowed people from all over the empire fruitfully to share life together.

Yet, in John's view, the order of the empire rested on a fundamental core of violence and injustice (the word for "injustice," *adikia*, is also translated "wickedness").[11] John feared that Christians' acceptance of the empire's construal of reality would actually separate them from the God of Jesus. He refers to the empire's dependence upon violence and coercion as its basis for authority. He understood the expansion of the practices of commerce to be resting on oppression, even trafficking in the exploitation of human souls (18:13). The empire ultimately links with the spiritual reality of the powers of evil that in some sense held responsibility for all the murders of authentic prophets and saints throughout the years (18:24).

So, the book of Revelation presents "apocalyptic power" as directly linked with the revelation of *Jesus Christ*, whose way stands in direct contrast with the empire's way.

(2) The second characteristic of power according to biblical apocalyptic may be seen in the *fruit* of God's "apocalyptic intervention." This intervention does *not* turn out to lead to the catastrophic end of human history, *nor* the massive and violent punishment of God's human enemies. Rather, God intervenes to create and sustain faith communities that stand over against Rome—in *this* world, not in some "after-world."

John seeks to foster a sense of crisis, presenting visions and proclamations of impending traumas and great conflicts. Chapter 12 conveys first a war in heaven. "Michael and his angels [fighting] against the dragon" (12:7). Then the dragon is thrown out of heaven and takes the war to earth, making war on the children of the woman, "those who keep the commandments of God and hold the testimony of Jesus" (12:17). The surrounding chapters contain many more images of conflict, trauma, intense struggle, and suffering.

From these visions, we get Revelation's stereotypical "apocalyptic" sense of unimaginable and world-ending catastrophes. However, when

---

11. "What John sees, for the first time, is that the primordial Dragon has come to represent the spiritual power behind empire. . . . Now evil is represented, not as the threat of anarchy, but as the system of order that institutionalizes violence as the foundation of international relations" (Wink, *Engaging*, 90).

we read more carefully, we will see something else actually going on. These visions do not mean to predict literal events. Rather, they clarify the *importance* of the churches for God's purposes in the world, and they push those churches to embody a genuine social alternative to Rome.

Chapter 5 has already made clear (as, indeed, have comments from the very beginning of the book) that there will in reality be no *future* war. The decisive battle is past. When the Lamb was slain and rose back to life, the victory was won.

The pictures of crises and catastrophes serve a different kind of purpose than predicting some future, wide-open battle. They portray the continual struggle to *perceive* that the Lamb's victory is genuine and worth shaping Christians' lives around. They contrast the Lamb's claims with the competing claims from Babylon concerning the nature of power and the outcome of history.

These visions, this sense of crisis, intend at their heart to empower the community of the followers of the Lamb to stay together and resist the powers of Babylon. God's "apocalyptic" intervention to bring salvation through the Lamb's faithfulness creates and sustains communities of resistance. God's apocalypse (revelation) empowers these communities for the long haul of following the Lamb wherever he goes and living as faithful witnesses who "conquer" through suffering love rather than violence and the sword.

The revelation of Jesus Christ that constitutes this book most of all reveals that those who worship the Lamb embody within their common life and faithful witness the same kind of power that enables the Lamb to open the scroll. "Apocalyptic power" finds its paradigmatic expression in the formation and sustenance of these communities. In making this point, Revelation continues in the biblical apocalyptic tradition as seen in Paul's writing, Jesus' proclamation, the visions of Daniel, the prophesies we call Second Isaiah, and the exodus story: God intervenes in the midst of catastrophic events most fundamentally by creating and sustaining communities of resistance.

So, God's apocalyptic intervention bears fruit: communities of resistance empowered to follow the Lamb wherever he goes and witness to the ultimacy of suffering love as the fundamental rule of the universe.

(3) A third characteristic of "apocalyptic power" may be seen in *how* it provides sustenance for those communities of resistance. John writes to encourage the actual communities he describes in chapters two and

three. And his message is not simply, hang on tight for a short time, the end of history will soon come. Rather, John encourages his readers to establish ways of being that will sustain them over time.

We may list ways Revelation emphasizes the sustenance of the community of faith:

a. The book begins with the affirmation that *Jesus* is "the ruler of the kings of the earth" (1:5). Given what follows in the book, this affirmation instills in John's readers a sense that *right now* the churches' "ruler" is supreme over all other rulers. John goes on to emphasize the *present* fruit of Jesus' work: he "loves us and freed us from our sins by his blood, and makes us to be a kingdom (or, 'empire'), priests serving his God and Father" (1:6). It is through the common life of the followers of Jesus in their faith communities that they share in Jesus' rule, exist as an alternative "kingdom" to the Roman Empire, and freely serve God.

b. Later in the first chapter, John relays a vision of Jesus ("one like the Son of Man," 1:12) walking among the "seven golden lampstands," that is, among the churches (1:20). This vision encourages John's readers with Jesus' presence among them as "the living one" who has come back from the dead and has "the keys of Death and Hades" (1:19).

c. The part of Revelation that most clearly underscores John's use of apocalyptic exhortation as a means to sustain the life of the communities of faith over time (rather than prepare them for an immediate end of history) may be found in chapters 2 and 3. These seven messages anchor the book as a whole in the world of actual congregations facing actual challenges to faithfulness.

d. The vision of the slain Lamb standing victorious as a present reality based on past action in chapter 5 underscores that the congregations are challenged to walk faithfully with the one who already holds the outcome of history. This sense of the definitive triumph of the Lamb serves to encourage the congregations that their embodied suffering love coheres completely with the true power of the one seated on the throne who creates, sustains and brings to fulfillment.

e. One of the more ambiguous visions in Revelation comes right after the vision of the triumphant Lamb. Chapter 6 begins, "then I saw the Lamb open one of the seven seals . . ." Then follows the first of several series of catastrophic plagues. Conquering, war, famine, martyrdom, and the like erupt as the seals are broken.

We may understand the vision of the Lamb opening the scrolls as a statement of how even the terrible events of human history are not able to overcome the history-transforming work of the suffering love of the Lamb. The portrayal of the Lamb revealing the contents of the scroll, a revelation that ultimately unveils New Jerusalem as the destination of all who allow themselves to be transformed by the Lamb's love (including "kings of the earth," 21:24), means to encourage the congregations with the sense that the traumas they experience and see in the course of human history do not mean that God's transforming work is null and void.

f. Throughout the book John slips in visions of multitudes of the Lamb's followers worshiping, offering thanksgiving, reiterating their commitments to the Lamb and the one seated on the throne as the true sovereigns of human existence. These worship visions model for believers the spirit of worship that should continue to characterize their common life. They also remind believers that no matter how overwhelming the plagues may seem, the God of Jesus remains the true God and worthy of their trust.

g. Chapter 13 gives striking visions of the immense power of the Beast. But rather than intimidating the believer, these visions must be read in the context of the entire book and the triumphant Lamb. When read thus, their role is not so much to fill the reader with fear as to help the reader discern the true character of the empire. With such discernment, John's readers will be empowered to clarify their loyalties and resist the tendency to accept the empire's claims to be their true "benefactor."

h. The flip side to the visions linking Rome with the Beast, the Great Harlot, and Babylon the Great may be seen in the celebration of the marriage of the Lamb in chapter 19. The "bride" is none other than the community of faith John has been exhorting throughout this book. The possibility of joining this celebration follows from the bride having "made herself ready" (19:7) through her faithfulness.

i. A final example of how Revelation seeks to sustain the life of the community of faith over the long haul may be seen in the final contrast of the book—between two very different communities, Babylon and New Jerusalem.

John begins chapter 17, the vision of Babylon's downfall, with these words: "Then one of the seven angels who had the seven bowls came and said to me, 'Come, I will show you the judgment of the great whore. . . .'" (17:1). Then, in chapter 21, the vision of New Jerusalem's emergence is introduced with the same words: "Then one of the seven angels who had the seven bowls . . . came and said to me, 'Come, I will show you the bride, the wife of the Lamb'" (21:9).

The book reaches its conclusion with the contrast being drawn. In which of these two communities will you all find your home? The answer to this question is not simply a matter of intellectual assent; one's citizenship follows from the shape of one's entire life.

So, the apocalyptic power of Revelation serves the purpose of encouraging the faith communities—God *will* sustain you.

(4) The fourth characteristic of apocalyptic power may be seen in the contrast between the two ways of conquering portrayed in the book. These two ways of conquering characterize the difference between citizens of Babylon and citizens of the New Jerusalem. John does see a spiritual struggle defining human existence. It is either "conquer" or "be conquered." But, for those who would be conquerors, the question centers on the *nature* of the conquering.

The ones in the messages to the churches in chapters 2 and 3 who will receive rewards are labeled "conquerors." Most of the rewards in those messages anticipate later visions in the book, underscoring the unity between the exhortations to the actual faith communities and the visions that follow. That is, the purpose of the later visions serves the exhortations to the actual communities.

What kind of power gains one a reward as a "conqueror"? Chapters 2 and 3 provide hints. Hold fast to love as definitive of your life as God's people (2:4). Listen to Jesus (2:1, 8, 12, 18; 3:1, 7, 14). Remain faithful unto death in the face of persecution (2:10). Reject the teachings of those who advocate giving loyalty to the Beast (2:14; 2:20). Actively commit yourselves to following the Lamb (3:10). Chapter 5 makes the basis for conquering absolutely clear. It is the Lamb's persevering, suffering love, validated by God's bringing him back to life.

In contrast, the Dragon, Beast, and their allies "conquer" with violence, force, deception, intimidation, and domination. This kind of conquering seems overwhelming—"who can stand against it?" Even as John asks that question, though, he supplies the answer. Those who follow the Lamb wherever he goes (14:4) *conquer*, celebrating their victory with worship of the true God even amidst their trials and tribulations.

The ultimate "battle" scene underscores the nature of the conquering of the Lamb and how that contrasts with the power of the Beast that seeks to conquer through force. Chapter 19 provides the denouement to the scene set up at the end of chapter 16. The allies of the Dragon gather "for battle on the great day of God the Almighty" (16:16). However, in chapter 19, when this "battle" is described, it turns out not to be a battle at all.

The rider on the white horse comes forth for battle, the imagery clearly identifying this rider as Jesus. Crucially, prior to any engagement with the enemy, we read of the rider being "clothed in a robe dipped in blood" (19:13). The rider simply captures the Beast and false prophets and dispatches them to the lake of fire without an actual battle. The "robe dipped in blood" alludes to Jesus' victory through suffering love, the only victory needed.

The two kinds of power for conquering in Revelation correspond with the two cities, the two objects of loyalty vying for adherents.[12] The Beast's power for conquering, characteristic of Babylon, rests on violence and domination, top-down power that enforces its will by crushing its enemies. The Lamb's power for conquering, characteristic of New Jerusalem, rests on resistance through love and adherence to peace that seeks to convert its human enemies. According to Revelation 21, the very "kings of the earth" who join the Beast in facing the white rider at the great "battle" end up bringing their glory into New Jerusalem, as transformed people.

John does not intend his readers to be passive observers of God's transformative work in creation. In fact, he portrays God's expectations of them as being quite rigorous and demanding. Follow the Lamb wherever he goes. Live in the Lamb's empire right now; his type of power *is* authentic. Turn from the trust in idols and idolatrous ways of exercising power. And in doing so, you will actually play a crucial role in God's work of *transforming* the nations.

12. See Rossing, *Choice.*

John's visions, in their imaginative power, reveal both that the establishment of the promised transformed heaven and transformed earth will be God's work without obvious cause and effect in relation to human efforts *and* that human faithfulness nonetheless plays a crucial role in this transformation. That is, we can not say precisely *how* following the Lamb will turn the Beast's domain into the Lamb's, but we are shown that such following is important.

The fruit of faithfulness in following the Lamb is genuine "victory." This victory contributes both to the destruction of the personified powers of evil (the Dragon, the Beast, the False Prophet) and, correspondingly, to the healing of the nations and the transformation of the kings of the earth. The power of apocalyptic in Revelation is much, much bigger than simply the power to destroy or coerce. It is actually the power to heal.

THE LAMB'S WAR

The controlling metaphor in Revelation is the Lamb, the one who indeed does open the scroll of Meaning and ultimately moves history toward a peaceable resolution. In this resolution, even the kings of the earth find healing. Revelation 5 powerfully portrays the Lamb's power when it evokes messianic hopes for an all-powerful savior and answers those hopes with a slain and now standing Lamb, worthy to be worshiped by all creation.[13]

Revelation portrays the Lamb's love manifesting God's power bringing victory and ultimate salvation. We need to hold on to the *first* part of Revelation 5's vision, though, as we discern the relevance of its answer to John's lament about how the scroll will be opened. It is love, indeed, but it is still powerful. The Lamb is one with the "Lion of the tribe of Judah." The messianic, or kingly, element of his identity remains.

The way the Quaker tradition has emphasized the Lion-ness of the Lamb is through the term, "the Lamb's War." This Lamb is a fighter. This Lamb does take on the Beast and his minions. This Lamb does conquer, does win victories, is a royal figure. Two elements must be held *together*—suffering love and genuine, conquering power.

---

13. On the Lamb as a peaceable metaphor, see Johns, *Lamb*.

In two key places near the end of the book, Revelation holds together the images of the Lamb and of warfare—the Lamb's War: chapters 17 and 19.

In chapter 17, John sees one of the most striking of his visions of the Beast, here portrayed as a "great whore" who "is drunk with the blood of the saints" (17:6). The vision goes on to allude to ten kings who "are united in yielding their power and authority to the beast; they will make war on the Lamb." But this war will result in their defeat. "The Lamb will conquer them, for he is the Lord of lords and King of kings, and those with him are called and chosen and faithful" (17:14).

How does the Lamb do his conquering, how does he and "those with him" win this war? We have already been given the answer back in chapter 12: "Now have come the salvation and the power and the kingdom of our God and the authority of his Messiah [his king], for the accuser of our comrades has been thrown down, who accuses them day and night before God. But they have conquered him by the blood of the Lamb and by the word of their testimony, for they did not cling to life even in the face of death" (12:10–11).

We need to keep these words in mind when we look at the second allusion to the war of the Lamb. In chapter 19, the stage is set for the final battle. Our images switch and we see here a great rider on a white horse. But this is clearly the same character as the one symbolized by the Lamb. He is "called Faithful and True" (19:11). He "judges and makes war." But what kind of war? He rides forth "clothed in a robe dipped in blood" (the "blood of the Lamb") and "from his *mouth* comes a sharp sword" (the "word of testimony"). This rider "wages war" with no other weapon than his willingness to die and the word of his testimony. But these weapons are enough. The forces arrayed against him are simply captured and judged—and in the end, the kings find healing as they are freed from the powers of evil that hold them in bondage.

So, this is the Lamb's War: the followers of the Lamb banding together, forming communities of resistance, following the Lamb's way of self-giving love and sharing in the Lamb's word of testimony—the gospel of God's healing mercy for all the nations, even for the kings of the earth.

THE BIBLE IN LIGHT OF THE LAMB'S WAR

This Lamb's War constitutes the central revelation of the Christian Bible's paradigmatic apocalypse. The book of Revelation shows us and tells us in wild and crazy ways something very simple: trust in Jesus and follow in his ways, do this together in communities of resistance. In doing so, you work with God in healing creation, in bringing in the eschaton. Compassionate eschatology indeed.

Now, I want to suggest that the revelation of the last book of the Bible is best understood in full continuity with the rest of the Bible. We don't have anything new here, just a new kind of packaging. But in this new kind of packaging, I think we may be given a special urgency and sense of inspiration that can stimulate us to look back at the rest of the Bible with some new insights. So, I suggest a reading strategy for the Bible as a whole in light of the Lamb's War. Understanding what is revealed in the book of Revelation may help us better understand what is being revealed in the rest of the Bible.

One way to read the Bible in light of the Lamb's War is to recognize how times of conflict and crisis, even near extinction, are times of *revelation*. What is revealed in such times? In Revelation, we have an almost overwhelming sense of crisis. However, we too easily let this sense of crisis obscure the actual *content* of Revelation's revelation. The revelation is not about cataclysms, the chronological end of history, raptures, Armageddon, and unprecedented future trauma. The ultimate message is simply this: band together, hold fast to the way of Jesus, cultivate communities of faith that will sustain the way of the Lamb over time. God creates communities of people who will know God's transforming love and by their testimony to that love transform the world.

So, let's consider some other times of crisis in the Bible and reflect on what is revealed in those contexts.[14]

The Calling of Abraham and Sarah

At the end of Genesis 11, we are introduced to the genealogy of the descendents of Noah's son Shem. At the end of the list, without fanfare, we first see the name Abram, one of the three sons of Terah. We meet Abram's wife, Sarai, and we are told, "Sarai is barren, she had no child" (Gen 11:30).

14. For more detail on my reading of the Bible as a whole, see Grimsrud, *God's*.

This short statement belies a major crisis in the lives of this now elderly couple. Without children, their footprints will fade away at the time of their deaths. The fate of Abram and Sarai seems to symbolize the dead end of the human project at the end of the eventful first eleven chapters of Genesis—creation, fall, brotherly murder, the judgment of the flood, the scattering at the tower of Babel, then Sarai's barrenness.

Out of this time of crisis comes a new revelation directly from God. "The Lord said to Abram, 'Go from your country and your kindred and your father's house to the land I will show you. I will make of you a great nation, and I will bless you, and make your name great, so that you will be a blessing. . . . In you all the families of the earth shall be blessed" (Gen 12:1–3).

This foundational revelation makes large claims. The childless couple will, via God's gift, bear children and become the parents of "a great nation." This nation will ultimately bless "all the families of the earth." God has not given up on the human project. Sarai's barrenness does not symbolize a dead end; rather, it symbolizes the revelation of God's healing strategy.

God will enter history and bring forth a people who will serve as agents of God's healing love. The old strategy of punitive judgment seen in the story of Noah and the flood will be replaced by a new strategy. This gift of a future to Abram and Sarai stands as the paradigmatic biblical revelation. This unveiling of God's transformative work in a broken world governs all the future unveilings revealed in the biblical story.

We see a great deal of continuity between this revelation in Genesis 12:1–3 and the "revelation of Jesus Christ" described in the final book of the Christian Bible. We have God entering human history in a time of crisis and providing a direct word, a word of comfort, of transformation, of hope. This new revelation results in the formation and empowerment of a community of peace—meant to transform the nations and their kings with their witness.

Might we not see this pattern as the paradigm for reading the biblical story as a whole? "Biblical apocalyptic" does not have to do with catastrophic interventions of drastic change and judgment and an end of history nearly so much as God's creation of communities of faith that will know shalom, witness to this knowledge, and help transform the world. Let's look at several other key biblical moments.

Exodus

As with other contexts that brought forth divine revelations, in the time of exodus the community of faith found itself in crisis. The story tells of God's direct intervention—to sustain a faith community.

Abraham's descendents find themselves enslaved in Egypt, with little sense of identity and certainly little sense of shalom. The Pharaoh seeks to eliminate the Israelites by murdering every newborn boy. Then comes the crucial moment. "The Israelites groaned under their slavery, and cried out. Out of the slavery their cry for help rose up to God. God heard their groaning, and God remembered his covenant with Abraham, Isaac, and Jacob. God looked down upon the Israelites, and God took notice of them" (Exod 2:23–25).

We go on to read of the consequences of God taking notice of the Israelites' plight—an extended dance with Pharaoh that ultimately results in the liberation of the Israelites, their escape through the Red Sea to new possibilities of life together as the newly invigorated community of God's chosen people.

The basic responsibility of the Hebrews was to be still and see the victory of God. The exodus story directly repudiates the imperial coercive power of Egypt. The Hebrew community does not include militarism in any sense. The effect of the liberating work of God was to establish a counter-cultural community that witnesses *against* the ways of empire.

If we extend the exodus story to include the gift of Torah (beginning with the Ten Commandments in Exodus 20), we see even more clearly the counter-cultural nature of the new community intended by God to resist. God intervenes in order to provide for the long-term sustenance of the community. Torah, as presented in Exodus through Deuteronomy, self-consciously *counters* Egypt's politics. Torah places priority on care for the vulnerable members of the community and places God's justice as mediated through the weaponless prophet at the center, not the human emperor or general.

Second Isaiah

The central catastrophe of the Old Testament story for the children of Israel came when the Babylonian Empire conquered the southern Hebrew kingdom of Judah, destroying the temple, exiling the ruling class, and bringing an end to Judah as a nation-state. In the rubble of the destruction a new vision found expression in the prophecies of Isaiah 40–55 ("Second Isaiah"). The bearer of salvific power here is the "suffering servant," a community that brings light to the world through the vocation of power as persevering love.

The fruit of God's intervention that Second Isaiah emphasizes is the emergence and sustenance of the servant community. And this community will carry on the saving work of God in the world (Isa 42:4—the servant "will not grow faint or be crushed until he has established justice in the earth"). The saving work of the servant community does not share in Babylon's conquering coercive tactics but conquers through suffering love and God's vindication of that love. The vision of the suffering servant definitively *delinks* the revelatory community from the nation-state—a delinking crucially essential for the ongoing revelation of God's shalom community, especially as seen in Jesus.

With the fall of Judah at the hands of the Babylonians, the temple, kingship, and the possession of the land all end—three pillars of the community's identity. But a fourth pillar remains—Torah. Stemming from Torah, Jeremiah calls to the scattered communities separated from Zion: seek the peace of your new homes—while also sustaining your sense of peoplehood. Torah was just the ticket. And, as we see in Second Isaiah, Torah consciousness provides the amazing insight that this peoplehood may still fulfill the promise to Abraham of descendants who will bless all the families of the earth. The catastrophe leads to the intervention of God with a new revelation. This new revelation sustains this community of the promise *in history*.

Daniel

The book of Daniel emerged out of trauma and ferment faced by second-century BCE Israel. The community struggled to sustain its identity in face of the battle for the domination of Palestine among the Egyptian Empire, the remnants of Alexander the Great's Hellenistic empire, and the emerging Roman Empire. In this battle, all interests converged in seeking to eliminate the Jewish nation as a distinct faith-based community.

Revolutionary Jews took up arms to resist the empires, with significant short-term success. They saw the chaos as an opportunity to gain political autonomy. The book of Daniel articulates a different option for the sustenance of the faith community: not absorption into the Hellenistic culture—nor into the Roman or Egyptian ones; and not violent revolution. Either absorption or violent revolution inevitably would lead to the loss of the core of Torah. Such a loss would negate the reason for Israel's existence as elected by God to be a light to the nations.

Israel's peoplehood has been sustained even through great trauma. This sustenance was not to be based on violence but on God's persevering love, and the embodiment of that love in Torah-centered faith communities. To fight the empires with violence, even if successful, would transform the Hebrew community into something just like the empires. It is impossible to fight monsters with monstrous means and not become a monster oneself.

The book of Daniel challenges the either/or of absorption versus violent revolution by drawing on folk tales (such as Daniel in the lion's den) in the first part of the book and describing dramatic and highly symbolic visions in the second part of the book. The book of Daniel as a whole is united on the theme of portraying God's court in conflict with human courts. "God as sovereign is an idea intended to challenge the idea of the emperor as sovereign. Daniel the visionary in chapters 7–12 is also a courtier of the true king; the tales in chapters 1–6 serve to highlight the difference in loyalties between one who lives in one court, serving one king, while actually being obedient to the other king, his God."[15]

The book of Daniel as a whole advocates cultivation of knowledge of the truth as its central strategy of resistance and sustenance. "The most revolutionary act under Antiochus IV, according to Daniel, was for one to *be* Jews and to teach others to be Jews." Seeking truth must be done nonviolently. "The revolution of truth must arise from education and conviction by the truth, and never by coercion. Coercion always demands empty exercises in false discipleship and obedience to idols, because both are necessary to the rule of the armed few."[16]

The ultimate weapon for followers of God (called the "wise") according to Daniel is their knowledge of the truth. The wise indeed are "warriors"—not warriors using the sword to kill but warriors wielding the sword of the truth of God. They trust in God, counting on God's vindication of their faithfulness. The wise sustain their faith and peoplehood by resting in this trust. They turn from both the assimilation that

15. Smith-Christopher, "Book," 150.
16. Ibid., 151–52.

giving loyalty to one of the empires would involve and from the assimilation that making violence central to their identity would involve.

Daniel shows that indeed the people do live in times of profound
crisis and trauma. The revelation here sustains resistance in the *here and
now*, trusting in God's truth in communities of resistance and in this way
keeping the promise alive. The world will change, God will vindicate the
wise, and healing will come. So remain strong, remain loyal to Torah.

Jesus

The accounts of Jesus' life and teaching in the gospels support the account of apocalyptic power we have found in the rest of the Bible. Jesus,
like the others, saw himself living in a time of crisis, days that were "trying people's souls." However, his response to the time of crisis was not to
seek to escape history but to *change* it—over the long haul.

Jesus proclaimed, and then embodied, a message that the kingdom
of God is entering history, effecting the transformation of the here and
now. I quote a summary from John Howard Yoder, *The Politics of Jesus*,
the book that shapes my thought in significant ways:

> The Kingdom of God is a social order and not a hidden one. It
> is not a universal catastrophe independent of the will of human
> beings; it is that concrete jubilary obedience, in pardon and re-
> pentance, the possibility of which is proclaimed beginning right
> now, opening up the real accessibility of a new order in which
> grace and justice are linked, which people have only to accept. It
> does not assume that time will end tomorrow; it reveals why it is
> meaningful that history should go on at all.[17]

The community Jesus established reflected an intent to work for
change in the world, over time—not an expectation that the world will
end. This community included: "a visible structured fellowship, a sober
decision guaranteeing that the costs of commitment to the fellowship
have been consciously accepted, and a clearly defined life-style distinct
from that of the crowd."[18] Jesus' community sought to exist as a counter-
cultural alternative within history to the politics of empire.

Jesus' proclamation of God's kingdom would not have been understood "as pointing 'off the map' of human experience, off the scale of time"

17. Yoder, *Politics*, 105.
18. Ibid., 39.

in announcing "an end to history." Jesus would have been understood in continuity with past deliverances of Israel that happened *in* history and centered on sustaining the faith community.[19]

Understood in this way, Jesus apocalyptic message makes all the points we have seen elsewhere in the Bible. God's "empire" stands in stark contrast with domination-based empires such as Rome. Followers of Jesus must choose to give their loyalty to one or the other. God's "empire" has revealed in new ways the nature of God's own rule—and established communities meant to live according to that rule. These communities live as "lights on a hill," witnessing to God's rule for all with eyes to see. For members of these communities, life lived in coherence with the rule of God takes the shape of suffering love, nonviolence, and restorative justice.

Matthew's gospel concludes with a clear statement of Jesus' purposes with his apocalyptic message. He meets with his disciples, the core of the new community he has formed to embody his vision for humanity. "All authority in heaven and on earth has been given to me. Go therefore and make disciples of all nations, baptizing them in the name of the Father and the Son and of the Holy Spirit, and teaching them to obey everything that I have commanded you. And remember, I am with you always, to the end of the age" (Matt 28:19–20).

Jesus reveals not that history will soon end. No, Jesus reveals why history continues and why history is meaningful. The end of history is the fulfillment of the task given to Abraham's descendents—bless all the families of the earth, make disciples of all nations, know God's shalom and witness to that shalom to all the ends of the earth.

Finally, let's look at Paul's apocalyptic message in the book of Romans.

Romans

Paul also writes in a time of crisis—addressing Christians living in the belly of the Beast. At two key points in Paul's portrayal of the gospel in Romans, he writes of saving work of God being *revealed* ("apocalypsed") or "disclosed" to human beings.

In introducing the message of his book, he writes: "I am not ashamed of the gospel; it is the power of God for salvation to everyone who has

---

19. Ibid., 85.

faith, to the Jew first and also to the Greek. For in it the justice of God is *revealed* through faith for faith" (1:16–17). Then as the culmination of the argument he develops in chapters 1–3, Paul writes, "Now, apart from law, the justice of God has been *disclosed*, and is attested by the law and the prophets, the justice of God through the faith of Jesus Christ for all who believe" (3:21–22).

Paul says that the work of God to bring salvation to the world has been disclosed in the life, death, and resurrection of Jesus Christ. God's apocalyptic power is the power to bring salvation—through the "revelation of Jesus Christ."[20]

The nature of the world-defining character of the gospel as revealed in Jesus requires that those who trust in him reject trusting in idols (Romans 1); that is, reject the call to loyalty to Caesar instead of Jesus. At the heart of Paul's gospel, he reiterates the Bible's call to trust in God and God's mercy in contrast to trusting empires, coercive power, and human constructs that vie with the true God for our loyalty.

For Paul, a central *fruit* of the revelation of the justice of God is the formation of a new kind of community bringing together Jew with Gentile. God's "apocalyptic" action brings forth not an end of history but the establishment of a community of faith charged with embodying a transformed way of life, a "kingdom of priests" (or, an alternative "empire") that serves to counter the way of life characteristic of the mighty human-centered empires such as Rome.

CONCLUSION

Let's conclude by turning back to Revelation. The "War of the Lamb" in that book has to do with people of faith striving against Rome's hegemony as communities of resistance, who understand their identity as God's people, who know God's transforming mercy themselves, and who witness to that mercy even in the face of hostility and rejection. This "war" is not limited to the book of Revelation. We have seen it throughout the Bible. In fact, the War of the Lamb is a useful rubric for characterizing the entire plot from Genesis through Revelation.

Revelation uses the language of warfare, conflict, victory, and conquering to characterize consistent, persevering love—even for enemies. Conquering happens as a consequence of a quality of life that follows the

20. For a more detailed discussion, see Grimsrud, "Against."

same pattern that Jesus' life followed: visible and concrete acts of mercy and rejection of power politics, leading to conflict with the powers that be, leading to suffering (even in Jesus' case death), leading to vindication through God's ongoing commitment, resurrection and transformation in history.

When we understand biblical apocalyptic as the revelation of this pattern of communal life, symbolized in Revelation as celebration and worship amidst the slings and arrows of historical living, then we may see that biblical apocalyptic and compassionate eschatology refer to the same kinds of things. Apocalyptic and eschatology both have most centrally to do with clarity of purpose, perceptive vision about what matters to God and in life, and trust in God's ongoing intervention through the social healing effected within faith communities (the dividing wall of hostility broken down) and the social healing the flows out to the nations as a consequence of the witness of the faithful.

So, wherein lies our hope? According to biblical apocalyptic (and compassionate eschatology), it lies in the inherent meaningfulness of life lived in the Lamb's way (not in blueprints about the future). The Lamb shows us the way into God's heart—to life that truly rests in God's hands.

2

The Language of Warfare in the Book of Revelation

RICHARD BAUCKHAM

HOLY WAR

THE IMAGE OF WARFARE is evoked frequently in Revelation.[1] Conquest and war are among the plagues that afflict humanity in history and intensify as the end of history approaches (6:2, 4, 8; 9:14–17). But also, much more importantly for the overall theme and message of Revelation, there is the war between God and the forces of evil, a war in which evil is to be defeated and the rule of God is to prevail throughout the whole of creation. While this war is of greater-than-human dimensions, humans play important parts on both sides. Jesus Christ and his followers are in conflict with the dragon, the beasts and their minions. In fact all people must, in the last resort, either throw in their lot with the forces of evil or acknowledge the sole sovereignty of the true God. The book of Revelation situates its readers within a situation of escalating conflict that is on course to reach a decisive climax at "the battle of the great day of God the Almighty" (16:14).

The general background to this way of representing the world undoubtedly lies in the Jewish apocalyptic tradition, but more specifically in the Hebrew Bible's notion of a holy war in which God is portrayed as a Warrior engaging and defeating his enemies, usually the enemies of his

---

1. I discussed this topic in Bauckham, *Climax*, chapter 8; and *Theology*, chapter 4. In the former, some more detailed argument for my views, together with references to the secondary literature, can be found. Besides commentaries, relevant studies published since I wrote my two books on Revelation include: Friesen, *Imperial*; Maier, *Apocalypse*; Bredin, *Jesus*; Johns, *Lamb*; Thomas, *Revelation*.

people Israel. The paradigm example was the exodus, and it is therefore noteworthy that among the various clusters of images and ideas that Revelation deploys to depict the present and future activities of God within human history the theme of the new exodus is prominent.

Notably, at the exodus God's people did not themselves fight: God alone overthrew the Egyptians while Israel looked on (Exod 14:13–14). Other biblical examples of this ideal kind of holy war, in which the divine Warrior required no human assistance, are the deliverance of Jerusalem from Sennacherib (2 Kgs 19:32–35) and the great victory in the reign of Jehoshaphat (2 Chr 20). This kind of holy war, in which sometimes the heavenly hosts of angels fight but God's human people do not, is the kind that predominates in biblical and early Jewish expectations of the future (Isa 59:16; 63:3; Ezek 38:17–39:6; Joel 3:11; Zech 14:1–5; 1 Enoch 56:5–8; T. Mos. 10; Sib. Or. 3:657–99).

However, besides the ideal kind of holy war that is fought by the divine Warrior alone, another kind, in which the armies of Israel wage military campaigns and annihilate their enemies, is prominent in the Hebrew Bible, especially as the kind that was waged, by divine command, against the Canaanites (Deut 7:1–6; Josh 6–11). But as an expectation for the future, as the war that will finally and decisively deliver Israel from her pagan oppressors, this kind of holy war is surprisingly rare in the Hebrew Bible and early Jewish literature (Zech 9:11–15; 12:6–9; 1 Enoch 90:19; 91:12). The one outstanding example is the War Scroll or War Rule (1QM) from Qumran, which purports to be a kind of manual giving instructions for the eschatological war of "the sons of light" against "the sons of darkness," with angelic forces fighting along with humans on both sides. Very probably it was composed in expectation of a holy war to be fought against the Romans, and it illuminates the ideological background of at least some of the groups who actually took up arms against the Romans in the great revolt that began in 66 CE.

It is likely that the sort of militant messianism that inspired both that revolt and the second great revolt of 132 CE was reflected in apocalyptic literature that has not survived. Significantly, in the two great Jewish apocalypses that were written in the wake of the disastrous failure of the first revolt, the apocalypses of Ezra (4 Ezra) and Baruch (2 Baruch), the expected victory of the Messiah over Israel's pagan enemies features prominently, but the idea of victory by judicial sentence takes precedence over military images (4 Ezra 12:31–33; 13:9–11, 37–38;

2 Bar 40:1). Especially in 4 Ezra, where human participation in the messianic war is pointedly excluded, there seems to be a reaction against the militant messianism that had proved so disastrous.

Against this background of holy war in the Hebrew Bible and early Jewish literature, it is notable that in Revelation the exodus is the model of divine victory that is the most prominently evoked, but at the same time human participation in the defeat of evil is envisaged. While the victory is ascribed primarily to the Lamb (Jesus Christ), one of the major purposes of the book is to call on the Lamb's followers to play their part in the defeat of evil. Most strikingly, whereas the Song of Moses at the time of the exodus celebrated a divine victory in which Israel played no active part (Exod 15:1–18), those who sing "the song of Moses . . . and the song of the Lamb" in Revelation are humans who have themselves "conquered the beast" (Rev 15:2–3). Evidently the prophet envisages the new exodus as a holy war in which, unlike the old, God's people have an active part to play.

It is worth observing carefully the way Revelation uses the vocabulary of war. The expression "to make war against" or "to fight" (expressed in Greek either by the verb *polemeo* or by the phrase *poieo polemon*) occurs with Christ as its subject (2:16; 19:11), with angels as its subject (12:7), with the dragon as its subject (12:7, 17), with the beast as its subject (11:7; 13:7), with the ten kings as its subject (17:14), and with the beast and the kings of the earth as its subject (19:19).

The people of God are sometimes the object of "war" (11:7;[2] 12:17; 13:7; cf. 19:19), but never its subject. On the other hand, they are sometimes depicted as an army (7:4–8; 14:1–4 [on these passages, see below]; 19:14, 16), and they are the subject of the verb "to conquer" (*nikao*), both when it is used without an object (2:7, 11, 17, 26; 3:5, 12, 21; 21:7) and when it has either the dragon (12:11) or the beast (15:2) as its object. Christ is the subject of this verb, both without an object (3:21; 5:5) and with the ten kings as its object (17:14). Christ himself is never the object of this verb, but his followers are twice said to be conquered by the beast (11:7; 13:7).

Finally, only Christ wields a sword (*romphaia*: 1:16; 2:12, 16; 19:15, 21), described as "the sword of his mouth." Neither his enemies nor his

---

2. I understand the two witnesses of Rev 11:3–13 to be the church fulfilling its prophetic vocation.

followers are said to use weapons.[3] Thus military language is employed largely to refer to the war between Christ himself and the forces of evil. Its use with reference to the people of God is more restrained, but it is notable that, unlike Christ, they are said to be defeated by the powers of evil as well as to defeat the powers of evil. What exactly constitutes their role in the messianic war is certainly not immediately apparent.

As we have noticed, even in the Jewish apocalypses the language of holy war is not always to be taken literally. When God or his Messiah fights, military language is often mixed with judicial language, and the latter often predominates. God does not literally slay his enemies on the battlefield, but pronounces judicial judgment against them. This is probably one reason that participation of God's people in the holy war is not considered appropriate: judgment is God's prerogative. As we shall see, Revelation also mixes military and judicial images, especially in the case of Christ's end-time victory over the beast and his armies (19:11–21), but it also gives his followers a role that is depicted in both military and legal language. The former is the language of victory (*nikao*), the latter is the language of witness or testimony. The saints do not pronounce judgment,[4] but they do bear witness.

The book of Revelation is a work of visionary imagination in which almost everything is conveyed in symbols and figurative language and very little is to be taken literally. The contention of this essay is that, while the book does envisage a cosmic conflict of good and evil in which Christ and his followers take part, the language of warfare is always figurative. Just as the chief combatants are not literally a lamb and a seven-headed monster, so there are no battles fought by armies wielding physical weapons. We need to consider carefully both how the book transmutes the language of warfare into a figurative sense and also why it does deploy the language of warfare, rather than substituting other terminology that would not suggest military engagement.

---

3. Most other references to swords (6:4; 13:10, 14) use a different word (*machaira*), perhaps in order to mark out Christ's sword as different, though *romphaia* is used in 6:8. In the case of the sword that inflicted the beast's fatal wound (13:14), the reference is to the dagger with which Nero killed himself.

4. In 20:4, "judgment" (*krima*) is used in the sense of "rule." For the rule of the martyrs, see also 2:26–28; 5:10.

THE CALL TO CONQUER

The seven messages to the churches in chapters 2–3 of Revelation are a series of introductions to the rest of the book, providing each of the seven churches with its own individuated introduction to the rest of the book. Each message contains a prophetic discernment of the condition of the church in question and offers either warning or encouragement. Towards the end of every one of them there is a promise of eschatological blessing for "the one who conquers." Evidently the exhortations to repent or to remain faithful are designed to enable the members of the churches to "conquer."

Another such promise to the one who conquers occurs in the final vision of the book, when the New Jerusalem descends from heaven, and God himself announces that the one who conquers "will inherit these things" (21:7). Many of the blessings promised to the conquerors in the seven messages are depicted in the description of the New Jerusalem in chapters 21–22. From this point of view, the intervening chapters of the book (4–20) depict what must happen if those to whom the promises are made in the seven messages are to enter the New Jerusalem. They provide readers with prophetic insight into what is really at stake in the situations in which they find and will find themselves, and thereby enable them to fulfil the call to conquer.

In the seven messages the readers are not told whom or what they are to conquer, a fact that underlines the sense in which these messages are not self-contained oracles but introductions to the rest of the book. What conquering means is still to be revealed, but in the last of the seven messages there is an important indication: "conquering" is what Jesus Christ has already done (3:21). It is not long before this victory of Christ becomes the center of attention in the heavenly vision that follows the seven messages.

THE LAMB'S VICTORY

In heaven John sees a sealed scroll in the hand of God. It contains God's plan for the coming of the kingdom, the plan that John, as a prophet, will later reveal in the part of his book that imparts new revelation. But only one person, he hears, has the authority to open the scroll: "See, the Lion of the tribe of Judah, the Root of David, has conquered, so that he can open the scroll and its seven seals" (5:5).

The two messianic titles evoke a strongly militaristic and national-istic image of the Messiah, son of David, a figure who would deliver the people of God from their oppressors by armed victory. (While the use of these phrases precisely as messianic titles is not attested in Jewish lit-erature, the passages on which they are based [Gen. 49:9; Isa. 11:4] were favorite messianic texts, interpreted militaristically.) But there is a strong contrast between what John has heard and what he now sees, standing on the throne of God: "a Lamb standing as if it had been slaughtered, having seven horns and seven eyes, which are the seven spirits of God sent out into all the world" (5:6). This Lamb (which becomes the over-whelmingly dominant image of Christ in the rest of the book) takes the scroll and will subsequently open it.

The contrast between the Lion and the Lamb is impossible to miss. But it would be too simplistic to suppose that John simply replaces the two images he hears with the one he sees. After all, the Root of David is a title Jesus himself claims at the end of the book (22:16). Moreover, it is clear that the Lamb has done what is said of the Lion and the Root: he has conquered and thereby has authority to open the scroll. What John has done by the juxtaposing these contrasting images is to forge a new symbol of conquest through sacrificial death. The Jewish messianic hopes evoked by the images of the Lion and the Root are not repudiated: Jesus really is the expected Messiah of David (22:16). But insofar as the latter was associated with military violence and narrow nationalism, the role is reinterpreted by the image of the Lamb. The Messiah has certainly won a victory, but he has done so by sacrifice and for the benefit, not only of Israel, but also of all the nations, as we soon learn (5:9).

The image of the Lamb certainly belongs, in part, to the pervasive imagery of new Exodus. He is the Passover Lamb of the new exodus. When the inhabitants of heaven celebrate his victory in "a new song," they say that "by his blood" he has "ransomed" people whom he has "made to be a kingdom and priests" (5:9–10). These words allude to the exodus, in which God "redeemed" or "ransomed" his people (Exod 6:6; 15:13) and made them "a priestly kingdom" (Exod 19:6).

However, in a way characteristic of Jewish exegesis John has seen a link between the Passover lamb and the description of the Servant of the Lord whom Isaiah described as "like a lamb that is led to the slaughter" (Isa 53:7). This allusion to Isaiah may seem unnecessary to explain the text, since, after all, the Passover lamb was slaughtered (Exod 12:21), but, since (as we shall see) there is a further allusion to Isaiah 53 in Rev 14:5 (Isa 53:9), the double allusion in 5:6 seems likely. Moreover, Isa 53:12 uses language of military victory to refer to the exaltation of the Servant after his death (the phrase "to divide the spoil" is common in the Hebrew Bible, referring to what the victors in a battle do), a connection that could have suggested to John the notion of victory through sacrificial death.

This passage is programmatic for Revelation's refunctioning of the language of warfare and victory. John does not, of course, simply use "conquest" to mean "sacrificial death." But he deprives the term of its usual connotations of violence and suggests that suffering death could actually be the means of overcoming evil. Power is still involved, but it must be a quite different sort of power from that of armies. It is worth noting again that this shift in the meaning of victory is accompanied by a shift from the national people of God to an international people. The war against evil can no longer be conceived as a nationalistic one, pitting one nation (God's) against others, and therefore it cannot be militaristic either.

We should not miss the significance of the fact that in John's vision the slaughtered Lamb is on the throne (that the obscure language of 5:6 means this is confirmed by 7:17). The heavenly throne is one of the most pervasive and important symbols in Revelation: it evokes the universal sovereignty of God over creation. That the slaughtered Lamb is on the throne makes the sacrificial death of Jesus Christ the key to how God rules the world.

The description of the Lamb continues: he has "seven horns and seven eyes, which are the seven Spirits of God sent out into all the world" (5:6). The reference to horns has led some to suppose that the Lamb is, after all, a violent warrior, but the attempt to identify a pre-existing Jewish image of a warrior lamb must now be said to have failed. Rather, the horns are certainly an image of power, as frequently in the Hebrew Bible, but as the horns of this Lamb they refer to the sort of power that might be released into the world by sacrificial death.

Since the Spirit of God is often understood as the power of God at work in the world, we should take the clause "which are the seven Spirits of God sent out into all the world" as an interpretation of both the seven horns and the seven eyes of the Lamb. In the Hebrew Bible, the eyes of the Lord indicate not only his ability to see what happens throughout the world, but also his ability to act powerfully wherever he chooses (Zech

4:10; 2 Chron 16:9). In Rev 5:6, the number seven (horns, eyes, and Spirits) indicates the universality of the power of the divine Spirit that goes throughout the world, whereby the Lamb's sacrificial death takes effect. The power of God is now the power of that death.

THE MESSIANIC ARMY

Readers of Revelation know from the seven messages to the churches that Christians are called to "conquer," but chapter 5 has depicted only the victory of the Lamb himself. That this Messiah has an army is first revealed in 7:4–17. Just as in chapter 5 there was a contrast between what John heard (the Lion and the Root) and what he saw (the slaughtered Lamb), so in chapter 7 there is a similar contrast, this time with reference to the Lamb's followers. John hears a census of twelve thousand persons from each of the twelve tribes of Israel (7:4–8), but what he sees is an innumerable multitude from all nations (7:9). In the Hebrew Bible the purpose of a census was to reckon the military strength of the people, and so we can recognize the 144,000 as the Messiah's army, linked with the Lion of Judah (5:6) by the fact that the tribe of Judah is listed first (7:5). The innumerable multitude, on the other hand, is linked with the slaughtered Lamb by the facts that they come from all nations (7:9), are victorious (7:9: white robes and palm branches) and "have washed their robes and made them white in the blood of the Lamb" (7:14).

We should note that, just as the Lamb does not simply replace the Lion and the Root, but transmutes their military power into a different mode of victory, so the innumerable multitude does not simply replace the 144,000, who reappear in 14:1. They are the people of God who win a victory by following the Messiah, but their limitation to one nation has been transcended (as in 5:9–10) and the way they win the victory is determined by the nature of the Messiah they follow. The starkly paradoxical language of 7:14 means that they have won the victory (made their robes white) by following the Lamb in his way even as far as death (the blood of the Lamb). They too have given their lives, as he did, but their deaths do not have autonomous value. By imitating his death their deaths help to put the power of his death into effect in the world.

The messianic army reappears in 14:15, this time along with the Lamb himself. Their "new song" is parallel to the "new song" of 5:9, which celebrated the Lamb's victory. Presumably the new song the 144,000 sing (14:3) celebrates their own victory together with the Lamb's. This passage also contains another element of military imagery which, when not recognized as such, has been persistently misunderstood. The 144,000 appear to be all celibate men (14:4). The reason is that in the biblical tradition of holy war soldiers were required to avoid the ritual defilement incurred through sexual intercourse (Deut 23:9–14; 1 Sam 21:5; 2 Sam 11:9–13). (The language of defilement in 14:4 is not derogatory towards women, but the technical language of ritual purity.)

This language of non-defilement is no more to be taken literally than the more obviously militaristic language used of the Lamb and his followers. In fact, John goes on to translate it into terms of moral purity (14:5). Just as the holy wars of biblical Israel required combatants to be ritually undefiled, so the war against evil Revelation depicts requires its combatants (men, women and children!) to be undefiled by untruthfulness. The phrase "no lie was found in his/their mouth" is a scriptural one used both of the Servant of the Lord in Isaiah 53:9 and of the remnant of Israel in Zeph 3:13. Like other Jewish exegetes of the time John is adept at noticing where two biblical texts use the same words and bringing them together. Since the 144,000 "follow the Lamb wherever he goes" (14:4) it is appropriate that they should be as free from untruthfulness as he is. There is a hint here that their truthfulness is connected with the death to which they follow the Lamb. As we shall see, it is their truthful witness that leads to their deaths and explains their effect.

WARFARE AS WITNESS

So far we have seen that the victory won by the Lamb and his followers is, in both their cases, won not by violence but by sacrificial death. They shed no blood but their own. It remains for us to see that in both cases what leads to their death is faithful witness to the truth of God. Jesus himself is "the faithful witness," a phrase whose position in the threefold description of him in 1:5 ("the faithful witness, the firstborn from the dead, and the ruler of the kings on earth") implies that it characterizes him as the one who bore faithful witness even to the point of death. Similarly, Antipas the martyr is called by Jesus "my witness, my faithful one, who was killed among you" (2:13).

The word "witness" (*martys*) does not yet have the technical meaning of "martyr" but is well on the way to it. It refers to verbal witness to the truth, but with the implication that, in the circumstances John's prophecy envisages, such witness to the truth of God is liable to lead to death. Faithful Christians are those who bear "the witness of Jesus" (12:17; 19:10), meaning that they bear the witness to God that Jesus himself bore. They share in his sacrificial death because they share in his faithful witness.

The language of conquering comes together with the language of witness in 12:11, according to which the martyrs

> have conquered [the dragon, Satan] by the blood of the Lamb
> and by the word of their testimony,
> for they did not cling to their lives even in the face of death.

The dragon is "the deceiver of the whole world," but the martyrs have conquered him by maintaining their truthful witness and thus exposing his deceit.

This is the first text in Revelation that provides an object for the verb "to conquer" when the Lamb or his followers are the subject. This is because John only introduces the forces of evil in a comprehensive way in chapters 12–13, where we meet the "satanic trinity" of the dragon, the beast (after a brief trailer in 11:7), and the second beast (also called the false prophet). As well as conquering the dragon (12:11) the Christian martyrs also conquer the beast (15:2), while on the other hand they are said to be conquered by the beast (11:7; 13:7). It seems that the same event—the deaths of those who bear the witness of Jesus at the hands of the military-political power of Rome—can be said to be either a victory of the beast over the martyrs or a victory of the martyrs over the beast. It all depends from which perspective it is seen. From the perspective of the inhabitants of the earth (13:7–8, 12) it looks as though the beast has won, but from the perspective of heaven (where the martyrs stand in 15:2) it is the martyrs who have defeated the beast. The contrast poses the crucial question: Is the world a place in which military and political might carries all before it or is it one in which suffering witness to the truth prevails in the end?

The beast's way is that of violence and deceit. Because his sheer brute force seems invincible, people worship him (13:8), but their worship also depends on the elaborate deceit that the second beast practices to make the beast appear divine (13:12–15). By contrast the martyrs practice nonviolent resistance to the beast and witness to the truth even though they must die for not relinquishing it. The beast appears to defeat them because he puts them to death, but he is not able to make them retract their witness and worship him. The contrast is between the power of deceit and violence, on the one hand, and the power of truth and suffering witness on the other. The beast and the martyrs fight with radically different weapons and win radically different victories. John's visions serve to open up the heavenly perspective that shows the beast's victory to be illusory and temporary while the victory of the martyrs is what will prevail in the end.

THE FINAL SHOWDOWN

The theme of holy war in Revelation climaxes in 19:11–21, where Christ appears, not as a lamb, but in a new guise as a mounted warrior riding out of heaven and leading his army to war against the beast and his allies and armies who have gathered to fight him. The upshot is that the two beasts are captured and thrown alive into the lake of fire, while all the humans in their service are slaughtered, becoming food for the birds is a grizzly parody of the messianic banquet. At first sight it may look as though the slaughtered Lamb has finally turned into a slaughtering Lion. Does the nonviolent witness of the Lamb and his followers here give way to violence? Must the beast in the end be defeated by his own means of victory? To answer such questions we need to unpack some of the profusion of symbolic imagery in this passage rather carefully.

First, although the Rider comes "to make war" (19:11), it appears that he and his army are already victorious. He rides a *white* horse, emblematic of victory, and his robe has been dipped in blood, showing that he comes from the victory he won through his death. His army comprises the martyrs (cf. 17:14), who have already washed their robes white in the blood of the Lamb (cf. 7:14), signifying their victory through martyrdom. The success they now achieve in battle is entirely consequent and dependent on the victory they have already won by the way of nonviolent witness as far as death.

Secondly, the only weapon employed is the sword that comes from the Rider's mouth (an allusion to Isa 11:4), previously in Revelation described as a two-edged sword (1:16; 2:12). This sword is the one with which all the opposing armies are slain (19:21). The martyrs themselves carry no weapons and play no active role in the battle. The fact that the Rider's name is "the Word of God" (19:13) is clearly connected with the fact that his only weapon is the sword that issues from his mouth. He is the very embodiment of God's powerful and effective word that slays the wicked purely through its own utterance.

Thirdly, the imagery combines the military with the judicial. The Rider "judges and makes war" (19:11). The sword by which he slays the wicked is also the judicial sentence he pronounces on them. Of special interest here is the information that he "is called faithful and true" (19:11), echoing the description of Jesus as "the faithful and true witness" in 3:14. He remains truthful but is no longer a witness. Now he is the judge.

Witness to the truth is double-edged. On the one hand, it is the only means of winning people from lies and illusion to the truth. But, on the other hand, witness that is rejected becomes evidence against those who reject it. Those who love lies and cling to delusions in the face of truth can only be condemned by truth.

While the dragon and the beast reign, the earth is the sphere of deceit and illusion. Truth is seen first in heaven and then when it comes from heaven to earth. In 19:11, heaven opens and Truth himself, the Word of God, rides to earth. This is the point at which the perspective of heaven prevails on earth, finally dispelling all the lies of the beast. It must now finally be evident to all that God, not the beast, is truly sovereign, and so, although the Rider has several names, the one that is visible to all, emblazoned on the side of his blood-drenched robe, is "King of kings and Lord of lords" (19:16).

It is the truth of God, to which Jesus and his follows have borne costly witness, that finally prevails over those who would not be won by it, condemning them to perish with their lies. The purpose of their witness was salvific, intended to liberate people from untruth, but it must in the end condemn those who reject it. The two beasts, we should remember, are systems, not persons. The people who perish in this last battle are those who have finally chosen to be identified with these evil systems and thus to perish with the systems.

NEW MEANINGS FOR OLD LANGUAGE

A Jewish apocalypse nearly contemporary with Revelation—4 Ezra—carefully repudiates all trace of messianic militarism, no doubt in reaction to the failure of the Jewish revolt of 66–73 CE. Not only is there no element of human participation in the Messiah's triumph over the Roman Empire and the Gentile nations that gather to make war on him. Military language is also avoided in the depiction of the Messiah's destruction of them, which takes place by judicial sentence, not weapons of war (4 Ezra 11–13).

By comparison, Revelation makes quite lavish use of military *language* while refunctioning it to refer to non-military means of overcoming evil. Even the vision of the Rider on the white horse (19:11–21), while sharing with 4 Ezra 13 the concept of the Messiah's victory by his *word*, nevertheless *depicts* the event, not only in judicial, but, more prominently, in military terms. As we have seen, human participation in the messianic war is not, in Revelation, rejected but emphasized and, again, *depicted* in terms drawn from the traditions of holy war, which are then careful refunctioned to refer to faithful witness to the point of death. The distinctive feature of Revelation, among the ancient apocalypses, seems to be, not its repudiation of messianic militarism, striking though this is, but its lavish use of militaristic language in a non-militaristic sense.

So why did John not simply drop the language of warfare and refer straightforwardly to faithful witness even in the face of death? There is probably more than one reason. First, in the whole book of Revelation John is engaged in a reading of Old Testament prophecy, gathering up all unfulfilled prophecies into his own great vision of the coming of God's kingdom. Since the language of holy war played a part in those prophecies (e.g. Ps 2; Joel 3:9–12; Zech 14:1–5), he chose to echo this language while at the same time refunctioning it. That there is evil to be overcome and that God, perhaps with the collaboration of his people, will overcome it and bring his kingdom to fulfillment, John agreed with the prophets of old. But the victory of the slaughtered Lamb put the matter in a wholly new light, and so John, while retaining the language of holy war, turned it into a way of speaking of victory by nonviolent witness.

Secondly, in advocating nonviolent witness John certainly did not envisage it as "passive" resistance. There is nothing passive about bearing the witness of Jesus in Revelation. It is as active as any literal warfare. It is a form of active and (John wishes to convey) effective action in the context of a real, though not military, conflict between powers of good and evil. John uses holy war imagery to recruit his readers into active engagement in this conflict.

Finally, the militaristic language enables John to use the same words (especially "to conquer") to refer both to the beast's strategy of violence and to the Lamb's and his followers' strategy of nonviolent witness. In this way he is able to pose the issue: whose is the true victory? We should remember that John's first readers or hearers could easily be drawn to the way the inhabitants of the earth view this matter: the beast, in his military-political might, has proven himself to be supreme and invincible, and so should be worshipped. This was the dominant ideology in the contexts of the seven churches. John's prophecy aims to challenge this view, exposing it as a delusion, by the light of the heavenly perspective that the prophecy provides.

3

Between Babylon and Anathoth

Toward a Theology of Hope in Migration

NANCY ELIZABETH BEDFORD

THERE ARE APPROXIMATELY TWELVE million undocumented migrants living and working in the United States. Many, though by no means all, are from Mexico and Central America. They tend to carry on their backs the weight of cheap labor by preparing food, cutting grass, cleaning homes and offices, harvesting vegetables and fruit, taking care of children and the elderly, packing up meat in processing plants, and providing a wide array of vital services without which the whole country would freeze up.[1] Though their contribution to U.S. society is extraordinary, they are subjected to suspicion, violence, and indeed are increasingly being targeted as scapegoats, blamed for many different societal ills. In this essay I would like to suggest that taking seriously the experiences of undocumented migrants can help point us toward the construction of a theology of hope in migration, that is, an eschatology illuminated by the hope in a God who is no respecter of borders.

The reasons for the presence of undocumented migrants in the United States are complex. It would be a mistake to read the dynamics of undocumented migration as the result of a simplistic desire for the "American way of life," isolated from geopolitical realities, such as the freedom of circulation allowed for goods and money in contraposition

---

1. They also pour money into the coffers of Social Security; about two-thirds of undocumented workers will not benefit from Social Security, because they have no valid papers. This amounts to a subsidy of Social Security by undocumented workers of about seven billion dollars a year. See Chomsky, *They Take Our Jobs*, 36–38.

to the barriers to circulation put in the way of human beings desirous of finding viable work.

Certainly, for many, to cross borders into the global North generally, and into the United States in particular, is a survival strategy: one that allows for the maintenance of family back home by way of remittances.[2] This motivation trumps fences and walls, and leads migrants to risk mistreatment, rape, and death to get to a place where they can find work sufficient to provide for their loved ones. But economic and political dimensions are so interconnected in a globalized capitalist market system that many so-called economic migrants are for all practical purposes expelled from their places of origin, while at the same time the motivations of asylum seekers or exiles often cannot be disconnected from the economic interests that cause persecution or war to begin with.

In the 1980s, for example, the United States did not recognize Guatemalans and Salvadorans as political exiles, though they fled to the United States to escape paramilitary violence in their countries— ironically enough, a violence that was partially funded by Washington. The same thing happened with Haiti: the United States refused Haitians' right to asylum because they were supposedly "economic migrants," when in reality political persecution and economic survival were closely linked in Haiti.[3] More recently, the great migratory waves of Mexican farmers leaving the land as a result of cheap, subsidized grain imports from the United States are directly connected to the implementation of the North American Free Trade Agreement (NAFTA) as of 1994. Mexico lost over two million agricultural jobs because of NAFTA. Most of the persons who lost their livelihood were formerly mostly small, independent family farmers.[4]

For undocumented migrants, the physical, economic, and emotional cost of crossing borders is becoming ever greater, as the borders become more militarized. Their presence in the wealthy countries that benefit from their cheap labor is increasingly criminalized, and they are often treated as scapegoats, while their voices are silenced. An example of this

2. See the reports collected by the Pew Hispanic Center, such as the article by Robert Suro, "Remittance senders and receivers." The present crisis, which has slowed down remittances to a trickle in many cases, is felt very deeply in countries whose poor depend on the help of family abroad.

3. Cf. Justin Akers Chacón; Davis, *No One Is Illegal*; and Chomsky, *They Take Our Jobs*, 64–74.

4. See Olson, "NAFTA's Food and Agriculture Lessons."

44   COMPASSIONATE ESCHATOLOGY

in the United States are the documents put out by the anti-immigrant organization FAIR, which describes itself as "non-partisan" and "non-racist," that is, as reliable and serious, even while it clearly targets Latinos and Latinas with its discourse about "anchor babies," "non-assimilation," "chain migration," and its explanations about the "contrast" between European immigration in the past and the present-day waves of migration, wherein Mexican immigration is particularly to be feared. It even depicts Mexicans as more likely than others to be the perpetrators in hit-and-run accidents.[5]

Other organizations, such as the so-called Minutemen, are even less subtle in blaming migrants, particularly those who are not coded as "white," for a number of economic and social ills.[6] The scapegoating of undocumented migrants also directly affects U.S. citizens and documented migrants who are thought to "look like," "sound like," or "act like" undocumented migrants.[7] As Marielena Hincapié points out, the real problem facing the United States today is not an invasion of immigrants, but an invasion of fear—a fear that for many seems to justify scapegoating.[8]

The particular case of Latino and Latina migrants is significant at more than one level, because the treatment and scapegoating of migrants is a symptom of how violence, symbolic and otherwise, continues to function vis-à-vis Latin America. Although U.S. thinkers, including theologians, often speak of U.S. majority culture in terms of "Western" culture or "Western" modernity, presumably in continuity with Europe and in contraposition to the "Orient," they normally neglect to perceive that Latin American history and culture is effaced by their discourse.

The Americas, both "Latin" and otherwise, have for over five hundred years, since the European invasion, existed not as the "other" of

5. See for instance the articles "Current Immigratin in Perspective" and "Unlicensed to Kill."

6. For documentation on how the mainstream media misrepresents undocumented migrants, see the "Immigration" section of *Media Matters for America* (Online: http://mediamatters.org/topic/immigration/?tab=all).

7. I am focusing here on undocumented migrants from Latin America, particularly from Mexico and Central America, because that is the reality I know best. There would clearly be much to write as well about the scapegoating of Muslim immigrants and Muslim citizens in the United States, especially as the Cold War waned, beginning with the 1991 Gulf War and increasingly after September 11, 2001.

8. Hincapié, "Aquí estamos y no nos vamos," 95.

the West, that is, of Europe, but as its extension.[9] To circumscribe what is "Western" to the North Atlantic is to obscure the relation between Western modernity and colonialism. Such a limited perspective also too easily misses why the presence of Latino immigration is symbolically bothersome to many "white" U.S. Americans and can be used skillfully to flame the fires of nativist populism. As René Girard points out in his analysis of myths having to do with the foreigner banished from the community or assassinated, "the victim is a person who comes from elsewhere, a well-known stranger."[10] Said otherwise, the scapegoat is not a total stranger. As Girard adds: "Religious, ethnic, or national minorities are never actually reproached for their difference, but for not being as different as expected, and in the end for not differing at all."[11]

Latinos and Latinas, the "well-known strangers" *par excellence* in this country, have the capacity to show that they are as human and as deserving of justice and civil rights as any other person living in the United States. Such treatment should not depend on fully assimilating the mores of "white" hegemonic culture. It is worth noting that a majority of Latinos and Latinas are hard-working, family oriented, and consider themselves Christian, and because they are for the most part not coded as "white," they reveal clearly that it is not necessary to be "white" in order truly to be "Christian," "hard-working," or "family oriented."

Arguably, this is one reason that they are suppressed with such vigor by groups closely tied to militias and "Christian" white supremacy: they symbolically undermine the "white" monopoly on such values. They are depicted as "monstrous" (in Girard's sense), and made responsible for internal and external disasters such as unemployment, violence, poverty, or gang activity in order to preserve the illusion of a stable, safe system (such as that of "white" middle-class families) as the only ontological manifestation of what is "Western" or indeed "Christian."[12]

The relevance of this question to eschatology might not seem immediately obvious, but it is quite simple. Undocumented migrants can

9. On this, see Castro-Gómez, "(Post) Coloniality for Dummies."

10. Girard, *Scapegoat,* 32.

11. Ibid., 22.

12. On the "monstrous," cf. Girard, *Scapegoat,* 34. The supposed regard for "family values" dissipates in organizations such as FAIR, when the families in question are Mexican or Central American families. In reality, so-called "family values" tend to be a code for "androcentric white family structures," the same sort of symbolic structure that was behind the lynching and repression of African Americans not too long ago.

point to the "truth of reality" and help us exercise "honesty with the real."[13] Said otherwise, a close look at the reasons why they leave their countries and why they are singled out as scapegoats, functions as an "unveiling" of reality that can help the scales fall from the eyes of theology. Positively speaking, undocumented migrants also teach us about the dynamics of embodied hope. When they become scapegoats, both the "truth of reality" and the contours of embodied hope are obscured. Migrants carry with them dangerous memories about the reality of borders and of the way global power is exercised, that hegemonic forces—powers and principalities, to use biblical language—would prefer that we forget.

Migrants also carve new channels for the circulation of knowledge; they take and bring symbolic, religious, and cultural baggage with them, in their luggage and in their hearts.[14] They remember what was and imagine what might be. In the midst of tensions and contradictions, they begin to forge new subjectivities, and this opens up possibilities for change, for though migrants are *subjected* to globalization, they are also *subjects* of transformation.[15] They show both how particularities of culture, language, or customs can be embodied, and how that embodiment of particularity does not cancel out a common humanity, but rather reinforces it.[16] The reality of migration from the perspective of the undocumented can therefore function as a heuristic tool for eschatology: on the one hand, it illustrates how the mechanism of scapegoating serves to hide the sins of a given system, and on the other, it illuminates an embodied striving toward what is hoped for, with imagination and openness for the new—and that is indeed the stuff of eschatology.

BABYLON AND ANATHOTH

The question of hope as it relates to migration is clearly a complex one. For many migrants from the global South, reaching the global North is

13. In Latin American theology, both of these factors are important epistemological principles; see for instance Sobrino, *Terremoto*, 67–126.

14. Ramírez, "Call Me 'Bitter,'" speaks in this sense of "religious remittances."

15. Cf. Belsey, *Poststructuralism*, 37f. and 114f.

16. Christologically speaking this is very important: it is not as a "generic human" that the Son becomes incarnate, but as the particular, historically and culturally constrained man Jesus of Nazareth, whose life and death are vindicated in the resurrection and in whose particularities are represented all of the manifold particularities of humanity. The Christian faith has never seriously been able to uphold that his particularities (young Jewish man, unmarried, carpenter, Aramaic speaker, etc.) are in themselves ontologically superior to other human particularities.

not simply a moment of triumph and joy, or an event to celebrate with a joyful dance such of that of Miriam after crossing the Red Sea. A more appropriate metaphor may be that of crossing over to Babylon.[17] The biblical text that comes to mind when I think of the reality of many Latinos and Latinas in the United States, is that of the letter written by the prophet Jeremiah to the exiles in Babylon, sent most likely in the decade of the 590s BCE, a little after the first deportation from Judah. The prophet writes precise instructions, which were likely difficult to hear, and even more difficult to live out, even though that particular group of exiles had the equivalent of what today in the United States would be a "legal permanent resident" status.

Speaking in the name of YHWH *sebā'ôth*, Jeremiah writes: Build houses and live in them; plant gardens and eat their fruit. Marry and have children. Seek the *shalom* of the city where I have put you and pray for it, for in its *shalom* you shall also find *shalom* (paraphrase of Jer 29:5–7).[18] This message, with its dose of realism, must have shaken the exiles, because it implied that there would be no short-term solutions. The text encourages them to carry out positive actions: to plant, to build, to marry, and to have children. [19]

To pay attention to God's message allowed the exiles to liberate their creativity, which in the long term permitted them to gather up the traditions connected to the Torah, the prophets, and Deuteronomic history, and reinvent themselves as Diaspora Judaism, able to sustain its existence all the way to the present.[20] To plant, to build, or to bring children into the world in this context is, then, not necessarily a simple assimilation into hegemonic culture, but rather a form of resistance and negotiation that allows the recreation of a culture and of belief in a new situation.[21] It could even be argued that to seek the *shalom* of Babylon is a creative form of nonviolent resistance, which is perhaps one reason why the instructions in Jeremiah 29 don't lead to the cultural suicide of

17. See the moving essay by Bundang, "Home as Metaphor," where she uses Jeremiah 29 as a clue for interpreting the Filipino experience in the United States.

18. It would seem that verses 4b–7 are a unit that Jeremiah may have included more than once in his letters; cf. Büsing, "Ein alternativer Ausgangspunkt zur Interpretation von Jer 29."

19. Cf. Torreblanca, "Continuidad para el futuro del pueblo de Dios," 28.

20. Cf. Bundang, "Home as Metaphor," 92.

21. Ibid., 96.

the exiles—as it might appear at first glance—but rather to a new cultural and religious flourishing.[22]

People of Latin American origins in the United States today are doing something similar in this new Babylon: they marry and build and plant and have children while resisting full cultural and religious assimilation. Within and without their Catholic parishes and their Protestant congregations they recreate their ancestral religious traditions and integrate practices that allow them to live in several cultural worlds at once.[23] The spaces constituted by faith practices can help migrants contribute positively to the transformation of the Babylon to which they have been pushed by the forces of globalization. However, neither the struggle to survive in a strange land, nor the construction of new subjectivities, and least of all the transformation of hegemonic structures are easy. It is important not to idealize or to overburden the figure of the migrant. Gayatri Chakravorty Spivak points out correctly that to fall into easy praise or idealization of migrants is a way to hide and legitimize the cruel dynamics of capitalist globalization.[24]

For Latino and Latina migrants in the United States, life in Babylon does not entail forgetting home or severing ties with its "good people, its dignity," as the tango puts it.[25] Here also, the book of Jeremiah sheds light on migrant realities as they relate to the people left behind in the "old country." In chapter 32, God asks Jeremiah to buy a field in his hometown of Anathoth, despite the Chaldean siege, the massive exile of his people, and the imminent escape to Egypt of most of the remnant in the land. God orders Jeremiah to take the deed of the land once he has bought it and to put it into an earthenware jar, in order that it might last for a long time, for—as God promises—"Houses and fields and vineyards shall again be bought in this land" (32:14–15).

When everything seems to be crumbling, God reminds Jeremiah that the desolation and the abandonment of the land he loves are not the end of the story. Jeremiah follows God's instructions and buys the field. In Jer 32:27 we read that God tells him: "See, I am YHWH, the God

---

22. See Smith, "Jeremiah."

23. For this argument, see Badillo, *Latinos and the New Immigrant Church,* 204. Of course, not all Latinos and Latinas are Christian or practitioners of a religious faith.

24. Spivak, *Critique,* 382, 398, 402 *et passim.*

25. *Vuelvo al Sur* (1988), lyrics by Fernando "Pino" Solanas and music by Astor Piazzolla.

of all flesh; is anything too hard for me?" This is not merely a rhetorical question, but a serious invitation for Jeremiah (and for us) to continue exploring the ways of God and to try to understand what things are and are not possible when we respond to God's call.[26] In other words, God also invites Jeremiah to exercise imagination, creativity, and nonviolent resistance, even as one who does not migrate to Babylon, despite having been offered excellent conditions in which to do so (see Jer 4:4–6). He will, instead, eventually go into exile in Egypt (see Jeremiah 33–34), leaving Anathoth far behind, yet surely not forgetting it.

This tension between the irremediable loss—be it through physical migration or be it through the ravages of time—of places we have loved, and living in the place where we have been sent by forces we cannot fully control, is a deeply human experience. It is symbolized by Anathoth and Babylon and embodied today—among others—by undocumented migrants. The way to make sense of that tension is not only to remember the past, and to live the present as peacemakers, but also to be open to a "future with hope" (Jer 29:11).

ESCHATOLOGY IN THE FLESH

There are many different images that might shed light on this matter of lives that are lived in hope at the intersection of many cultures and identities, between the foreignness of Babylon and the familiarity of Anathoth, among them exile, diaspora, and pilgrimage. One intriguing philosophical account of human movement is the work of Rosi Braidotti, who proposes the notion of the nomad as "figuration," that is, a "politically informed account of an alternative subjectivity." She desires to use this figuration in order to think in a way that is on the one hand embodied, and on the other neither monological nor dualistic, two rather bad habits of the European philosophical tradition.[27]

Braidotti's challenge is suggestive. It is worth exploring whether the concrete figuration that she proposes, that of the nomadic subject, is able to shed light on a theology of hope in migration. Her emphasis on the bodily dimension of subjectivity is both healthy and necessary. The nomadic subject as imagined by Braidotti, however, is not meant to be a direct reference to actual nomadic cultures or people (such as Bedouins,

---

26. On this, see Fretheim, "Is Anything Too Hard for God?"

27. Braidotti, *Nomadic Subjects*, 1–2.

for example), but rather refers to "the kind of critical consciousness that resists settling into socially coded modes of thought and behavior." She in fact thinks "some of the greatest trips can take place without physically moving from one's habitat." The nomadic subject as she understands it, then, need not actually traverse political borders, but rather is someone who can think in certain ways.[28] Moreover, for Braidotti the "nomadic" condition is superior to that of the migrant.[29] At times she seems to be referring to a kind of superior consciousness obtainable by the few.[30] In this sense, her description of the "nomadic subject" begins to appear quite distant from the harsh material reality of undocumented migrants from Latin America living in the United States.

Nomadic subjects, for Braidotti, are "beyond classification," a "sort of classless unit"; they constitute a prototype of the intellectual and enact transitions "without teleological purpose."[31] Braidotti's nomads are not knocking at the gates of the city to be let in; they are camping outside the city, ready to cross the next desert. Braidotti's prose is evocative, but her project lacks any sort of "thick description"; she doesn't make use of ethnography to check whether or not her generalizations (for instance about migrants) have any material warrant.

Moreover, Braidotti's figuration of the nomad is weakened by its intrinsic individualism; one cannot imagine that a "nomad" of the sort she describes would ever participate regularly in the rhythms of communal worship or even have children enrolled in school. From a theological perspective, it seems to me that it is precisely what she calls the "teleological" impetus of migrants that makes them so suggestive for eschatological reflection: they are living "on the way" between the remembrance of things and places past and their hope for a future that cannot fully realized in this "evil age" but can be anticipated, quite concretely, in hope. Migrants are sustained by hope; a hopeless person would never have the energy to embark upon such a difficult journey.

Admittedly, all figurations—indeed, all theoretical frameworks—can be abused and transformed into abstractions that have little do to with the material experiences of those who cross borders as migrants. When this happens, the figuration loses its subversive potential and is

28. Ibid., 4–5.
29. Ibid., 10.
30. Ibid., 8–15.
31. Ibid., 22–23.

domesticated. Paula Moya shows this in her astute analysis of how Judith Butler and Donna Haraway (two "white" North Atlantic feminists) use the concept of difference as developed by Chicana theorists. Moya rejects that idea that some identities are more advanced or liberated politically just because they are transgressive or indeterminate. She reminds us that it is important to keep in mind the consequences of being situated materially and concretely in a given place, rather than simply to celebrate the crossing of borders, whatever those borders might be. To that end, Moya reintroduces the notion of "theory in the flesh" developed by Chicana theorist Cherie Moraga.[32] It seems to me that this is a very helpful insight for theology. We might ask: To what extent is our eschatology a theory in the flesh? Because migration is a bodily process, tied necessarily to material changes and linked to physical space, perhaps it can help eschatology to "get a grip" on thinking about our hope in God more concrete and embodied ways.[33]

One way for theology to become a "theory in the flesh" is to be reminded of its grounding in praxis. For instance, affective and effective links to migrant women and men can readily be developed in the context of churches, and of other networks, such as NGOs, support groups for women affected by domestic violence, parent groups at schools or even conversations at the park. One advantage that confessional theologians often have over many theorists not involved in faith communities is that we have an organic link to a concrete space for praxis and reflection, beyond the academic realm, but that is demanded by the kind of construction of knowledge in which we are involved.

Our communities of faith are places where we can give some concrete traction to theory. The latter is lacking in Braidotti's figuration of the nomadic subject, who ends up seeming like a fictional character without too many inconvenient obligations, who can cross ideological and political barriers, but who seems to lack flesh. As it turns out, it is precisely in the patient and persistent encounter with migrants in their familiar otherness that flames of hope and renewal are often fanned in communities of faith and elsewhere, and that resistance to scapegoating can be cultivated.

32. Moya, "Postmodern, 'Realism.'"
33. On "getting a grip," see Silvey, "Power, Difference, and Mobility," 501.

NO FACILE HOPE

There is a tendency in the social sciences, and perhaps also in theology, to celebrate the crossing of borders in itself as something purely positive: as an example of resistance and courage. This happens especially when the figure of the migrant becomes more of a metaphor or a figuration than a person who has a body, a name, a sex, a history. Although I try to keep particularity in mind, as a theologian I find that the lure of abstraction and generalization is right around the corner. The temptation to celebrate and perhaps rhetorically to inflate the positive possibilities of resistance, change, and transformation in the experiences of migration is always present, for I find much to admire in the tenacity and the creativity of many migrants, and because I myself have learned so much by living in migration. However, it would not be just to forget the "tales of disillusionment" that are also part of the experience of migration, as María de la Luz Ibarra reminds us, who has documented the stories of many Mexican women who have crossed the border alone or with their children.

For undocumented women, the human cost of crossing the border toward the North can leave deep wounds: rape by the *coyotes* who are supposed to get them across, solitary deaths, sexual trafficking, humiliations, debts that seem to have no end, separation from children.[34] Out of respect for all those who have suffered in migration, it is not advisable to think of migration only in terms of the epistemological doors that it opens. There is much to denounce in the social and economic structural injustices that lead people to leave their home and migrate in order to allow their family to survive. At times it may be necessary also simply to be silent and to exercise a ministry of presence with those who have suffered horribly along the way. Not everything can be fixed with words, and that is good for theology to remember. What we do know, on the basis of the cross and resurrection of Jesus, and from the "hope against hope" of so many lives in migration, is that death and suffering will not have the last word. And we also know that we find glimpses of God's own face in the face of migrants.

Irenaeus loved the image of growth in relation to human beings made in God's image and likeness. According to him, our growth and development as human beings is designed by the Father, molded by the

34. Ibarra, "Buscando la vida."

Son and nurtured by the Spirit: we are both gardeners made in God's image, and ourselves a garden of unexpected flowers and fruits.[35] As the second creation account (Gen 2:4–9) suggests, we belong to the earth (*adamah*) and our home is a garden. We therefore can't think of the matter of the human being created in the image of God without considering also our deep solidarity with the earth and with all the creatures that live upon it.[36] And yet, in a fallen world, the tending of the earth is no easy matter.

Despite the highly mechanized and industrialized character of contemporary U.S. agriculture, for instance, many crops (asparagus, artichoke, cabbage, cilantro, lettuce, berries and peas, among other fruits and vegetables) continue to be human labor-intensive, and this work is most often carried out by migrant laborers, many of whom are undocumented. Only about one in ten farm workers in the United States are U.S. citizens. Much of the work, such the harvesting of strawberries, is literally backbreaking, since it requires a constant posture of bending over. Indeed, though the wages paid to farm workers are very low, farm work is one of the most dangerous industries in the United States. The loss of fingers, back injuries resulting from falls, and daily exposure to toxic pesticides are common, as are molestation and rape, all exacerbated by a lack of access to health care.[37] To keep this concrete reality of migrant farm workers in mind can help us avoid sanitized and romantic ideas about God's "gardening" on our behalf, or of our work in God's vineyards and fields as some sort of pastoral idyll.

The work that these migrants carry out is both difficult and necessary for the harvest. In this matter of hard and continuing work, we again see glimpses of the face of God. When the Johannine Jesus says "My father is still working, and I also am working" (John 5:17), his statement causes a disagreeable impression in some of his hearers, for they think that to say such a thing is blasphemous. The Son, however, is not only involved in the *creatio continua* by which the universe is upheld, but invites us also to join in God's creative work as coworkers with God. In the same way that migrants set out to look for work, we are sent out to participate in the work of God's reign. Migrant agricultural workers, by

35. Cf. *Adversus Haereses* IV.38.3–4. Ireneaus speaks here also of God's imagination as an artisan who gives shape to humans (IV.39.2).

36. See Clifford, "When Being Human Becomes Truly Earthly."

37. See López, *Farmworkers' Journey,* 107–45.

virtue of their labors, are a poignant reminder of the difficulties of living out our vocation as we work in an unjust world.

Those of us who are walking in the way of Jesus are involved in a never-ending journey "toward" God that at the same time is a journey "in" God. In Phil 3:12–14, Paul speaks about pressing on toward the goal and about "straining forward" to what lies ahead. Later, Gregory of Nyssa builds on this idea in order to posit his notion of *epektasis*, that is to say, the way in God without end that is our end. Gregory says of Moses: "Once having set foot on the ladder which God set up (as Jacob says), he continually climbed to the step above and never ceased to rise higher, because he always found a step higher than the one he had attained."[38] Gregory is speaking of our journey in God, which as it happens, is not at all like Braidotti's nomadism without teleology, but is more akin to the journey of migrants between Anathoth and Babylon, in which we are both at home ("in my Father's house there are many dwelling places," John 14:2) and continue on our journey. Here also the experiences of migrants help us sense some of what a constant journey might be like, while at the same time they attune us to that longing for home that can only be quenched by God.

My own experiences of migration and border crossings (though not laced with the hardship of an undocumented status) remind me that the way of Jesus described in the gospels crosses many borders besides the political ones: religious, economic, sexual, ethnic, cultural, class borders. That is why he—unlike most of his male disciples—is comfortable sharing a drink of water and a theological discussion with a Samaritan woman. Jesus seems to point us to the realization that many of the existing borders (both social and political) serve to protect the interests of the most powerful and to contain and control the weak. That is why transnational capital rarely comes up against impermeable borders, whereas undocumented migrants (who carry in their bodies the marks of what the economic system does to the weakest) cross borders stealthily, with hearts pounding, putting their lives on the line. Perhaps Jesus experienced some of this in his infancy, if Matthew's account of the escape to Egypt is to be taken literally.

On the other hand, not all borders or barriers are in themselves bad: our skin, which is porous, is also a barrier that protects us; walls provide privacy when we get home, if we have the privilege of not being

38. Gregory of Nyssa, *Life of Moses*, § 227 (page 115).

homeless; yet walls without windows or doors would form not a home, but a dungeon. Any sort of border, even one that from some perspectives may seem necessary, can become toxic and must be considered with a question: Who benefits from the existence of this border, and who is hurt by it?

In the end, from a theological perspective, hope for change in the face of the difficulties experienced by undocumented migrants is anchored in the conviction that God is no respecter of borders. As the Epistle to the Ephesians puts it, Jesus himself, in his flesh, broke down the enmity that separated us and knocked down the wall of separation (2:14–15). The way of this same Jesus, actualized by the Spirit, has the potential to unmask borders that have become demonic, reinforcing an economy of death and an idolatry of national security, as is clearly seen in the wall being built between Mexico and the United States, which puts the lives of undocumented migrants at risk, and is increasingly disrupting animal migration as well. The dynamic of breaking down the walls of injustice, of hate and of inequity, by the Spirit and without mirroring the violence of the strong, is what—according to the logic of Ephesians—permits us to be "no longer strangers and aliens, but citizens with the saints and members of the household of God" (2:19).

It would seem that we have by no means yet realized the extent to which our expectation of a "future with hope" may put us at odds with the ways borders and barriers are drawn in our societies. Unmasking the mechanisms that lead to the scapegoating of undocumented migrants and resisting the logic of borders drawn by fear and greed—be it by the nation-state or by each of us personally—might be a good place to start. An eschatology of hope in migration encourages the migration of eschatology away from the violence spawned by fear and toward the peacemaking empowered by love (1 John 4:18).

4

Faithful, True, and Violent?

Christology and "Divine Vengeance"
in the Revelation to John

DAVID J. NEVILLE

THE COLLECTION OF AUTHORITATIVE writings for Christians begins
and ends with visions of *shalom* (harmonious wholeness). Taken
together, the two visions in Gen 1:1—2:3 and Rev 21:1—22:5 witness to
God's will and purpose for the created order. Creation neither emerges
from violence nor is violence constitutive of it. If, for Christians, creation
and restored creation mark the alpha and omega points of the biblical metanarrative, the mission of Jesus forms its normative midpoint.
From a peace-oriented perspective, there is consonance and coherence
between beginning, middle, and end of the canonical story, which attests to divine proneness to *shalom*. Conversely, however, the collection
of peculiarly Christian writings known as the New Testament begins
and ends with texts in which the imagery of eschatological vengeance
features prominently. Both the Gospel according to Matthew and the
Revelation to John apparently envisage God's creative purposes being
realized through divinely authorized eschatological vengeance.[1]

Is it possible for peaceful ends to be realized by violent means? "For
God, all things are achievable," Jesus is remembered as teaching (Matt
19:26; Mark 10:27; cf. Luke 18:27). But this is less a question of moral
logic than of theology in the strict sense, namely, human reasoning about
God's "nature" and will for the world on the basis of scripturally mediated divine disclosure. In view of what is conveyed about God in the

---

1. On Matthew's gospel, see Neville, "Toward a Teleology of Peace."

creation story in Genesis, the vision of the New Jerusalem in Revelation, and the story of Jesus in the canonical gospels, might depictions of eschatological vengeance be aberrations deserving of deconstruction or vital pieces of the puzzle concerning who God is and how God relates to the world? If the latter, the specifically Christian conception of God as One most fully revealed in the person, mission, and message of Jesus is jeopardized. If the former, on the other hand, what interpretive resources might there be to deconstruct, faithfully and legitimately, this dark aspect of the biblical depiction of God?

ORIENTATION AND PERSPECTIVE

There are those who envisage a "nonviolent coming of God,"[2] but such an eschatological prospect is not generally associated with the Apocalypse of John, which has been lambasted for its violent imagery, its vindictive tone, and, for some, its sub-Christian or morally dubious theology. Toward the end of the first of three essays that comprise *The Genealogy of Morals: An Attack* (1887), Friedrich Nietzsche punctuated his argument decrying the rancorous Jewish inversion of the aristocratic morality of triumphant self-affirmation (pre-eminently embodied by classical Rome) by describing Revelation as a "book of hatred," indeed, "the most rabid outburst of vindictiveness in all recorded history."[3] D. H. Lawrence, although also antagonistic toward Christian faith, nevertheless devoted time to studying Revelation, which both fascinated and repelled him.[4] He ultimately repudiated the book in its present form, a repudiation well captured in this description of Lawrence's viewpoint by Arthur Wainwright: "It is the 'Judas' among New Testament books, that [*sic*] speaks for people who fail to attain their inward desires and seek satisfaction by wishing destruction on the life they cannot attain."[5]

Similarly negative appraisals have been expressed by biblical scholars. C. H. Dodd regarded the Apocalypse of John as the epitome of "futurist" eschatology reconstructed from pre-Christian Jewish sources as the early church tried to make sense of the delay of the consummation of

2. See, e.g., Douglass, *Nonviolent Coming.*

3. Despite his anti-Jewish invective, Nietzsche later expresses admiration and respect for the Old Testament, at least by comparison with the New. See section xxii of the third and final essay.

4. Lawrence, *Apocalypse.*

5. Wainwright, *Mysterious Apocalypse*, 200.

the eschatological process proleptically fulfilled in the mission of Jesus. Regarding Revelation, Dodd wrote:

> With all the magnificence of its imagery and the splendour of its visions of the majesty of God and the world to come, we are bound to judge that in its conception of the character of God and His attitude to man the book falls below the level, not only of the teaching of Jesus, but of the best parts of the Old Testament. . . . The God of the Apocalypse can hardly be recognized as the Father of our Lord Jesus Christ, nor has the fierce Messiah, whose warriors ride in blood up to their horses' bridles, many traits that could recall Him of whom the primitive *kerygma* proclaimed that He went about doing good and healing all who were oppressed by the devil, because God was with Him.[6]

More recently, Marcus Borg's "re-reading" of Revelation still leads him to conclude:

> The God of Revelation sometimes has more to do with vengeance than justice, and the difference is crucial. Though John cannot be blamed for all the meanings that Christians have sometimes seen in his book, Revelation supports a picture of God as an angry tyrant who plans to destroy the earth and most of its people.[7]

Finally, John J. Collins, widely acknowledged as one of the foremost interpreters of apocalyptic literature, has this to say about Revelation:

> The expectation of vengeance is . . . pivotal in the book of Revelation. The coming fall of Rome is heralded in gloating terms in chapter 18. In chapter 19, Christ appears from heaven as a warrior on a white horse, from whose mouth comes a sharp sword with which to strike down the nations, and who will tread the wine press of the fury of the wrath of God.[8]

These remarks by Dodd, Borg, and Collins crystallize central concerns of this study. First, is John's theology deficient? Is his depiction of God's "character" incompatible with what Jesus revealed? Second, given that the Apocalypse is written in symbolic language, might it be possible, legitimately, to interpret John's visionary language in such a way that his theological and christological imagery is more congruous with the

6. Dodd, *Apostolic Preaching*, 40–41.
7. Borg, *Reading*, 291.
8. Collins, "Zeal of Phinehas," 16.

theology and Christology implicit in the gospel accounts of the historic mission of Jesus? And third, even if one were to accept that there is a disjuncture between the historic mission of Jesus and what John displays concerning God and God's Messiah in Revelation, does Dodd's implicit appeal to Jesus' teaching and mission provide the interpretive means by which one might grapple creatively with this (apparent) discrepancy?

Read from the perspective of its history of reception, Revelation is a text that has generated violence and vindictive vengeance.[9] According to Loren Johns, "The Apocalypse of John is arguably the most dangerous book in the history of Christendom in terms of the history of its effects."[10] This is not simply a matter of reader-response. One of the most evident features of John's Apocalypse is its grotesquely violent imagery. One thinks not only of the "second death," envisaged as a lake of seething fire and sulfur (Rev 20:14–15; 21:8), but also of the calamity and devastation accompanying the series of seven seal-openings, trumpet-blasts, and bowls of God's anger, or of the vision of the winepress of God's blood-letting wrath in 14:17–20, or of the feast of flesh following the victory of the Word of God in 19:11–21, which is especially disconcerting because it follows hard upon the beatitude of 19:9, "Blessed are those invited to the Lamb's marriage feast."[11] This may be one of the main reasons why Revelation has been either disparaged or neglected by so many scholars down through the centuries or, on the other hand, embraced by Christians with a retributive-apocalyptic mindset.[12]

Apart from the incongruity between a retributive-apocalyptic mentality and the historic mission of Jesus, at least as depicted in the biblical gospels, such a mindset has morally corrosive ramifications, whether passively quietist or violently sinister. Even though violent texts *may* foster vengeful attitudes and violent behavior, however, my concern is with the theology of John rather than his ethical exhortation, which consistently advocates nonviolent perseverance on the part of believers. John nowhere calls on believers to use violence against opponents; in

9. See, e.g., Rowland, "Revelation," 528–56. (This is not to say that the violent imagery of John's Apocalypse *necessarily* inculcates a vengeful attitude or violent behavior.)

10. Johns, *Lamb Christology*, 5, 186.

11. This is the fourth of seven unevenly distributed beatitudes in Revelation (1:3; 14:13; 16:15; 19:9; 20:6; 22:7; 22:14).

12. For a survey of various scholarly assessments of the significance of violence in Revelation, see Skaggs and Doyle, "Violence."

fact, 13:10 seems to reject violence out of hand—at least for believers: "If you are to be taken captive, into captivity you go; if you kill with the sword, with the sword you must be killed. Here is a call for the endurance and faith of the saints."

As David Barr notes, "John does not call for violence but for endurance."[13] Likewise, commenting on interpretations of Revelation that have provoked violence, Ian Boxall retorts: "Yet it remains the case that not a single passage of the book bids its readers to take up arms or resort to violence against their fellow human beings. Despite the dominance of the language of warfare, battle and victory, vengeance is firmly placed in the hands of the Creator and Judge of the world."[14] Here John seems to stand with Paul and the writer of "To Hebrews" in restricting to God the entitlement to exact vengeance (Deut 32:35; Rom 12:19; Heb 10:30).

However, there is a further question—whether vengeance is actually *exercised* by the world's creator and judge *as depicted in Revelation*. The picture John *seems* to paint is that once God's patience wears out, God's judgment is described in the same violent terms used of the violence of God's adversaries. It is as though God must ultimately resort to retribution and violence to achieve divine ends. If that is the case—or if this is what Christians believe to be the case—violence is ultimately determinative and "might makes right."

In view of the violent imagery that pervades Revelation, is a peace-oriented interpretation possible? One might like to think that John's gluttonous use of such imagery was intended to cause moral nausea, as when overindulging on rich food. Unlikely as that is, it is nevertheless possible to show that at crucial junctures in the visionary drama John relates textual details in close but conflictual relationship to each other to create a level of dissonance that serves to subvert the surface imagery of violence. Moreover, this subversion of violence and vengeance is in keeping with the Christology of Revelation, which in key respects resonates with the historical mission of Jesus as displayed in the gospel narratives.

Although certain texts in the gospel accounts have been understood to suggest otherwise, most scholars accept that Jesus' mission and teaching, as presented in the canonical gospels, were essentially non-

13. Barr, "Doing Violence," 99.
14. Boxall, *Revelation*, 125.

violent. Jesus applied nonviolent solutions to the problems of his day, and he taught his disciples to emulate his example in this respect. But is the nonviolent conception of Jesus' identity and mission presented in the gospels replaced by a militant perspective in Revelation, as John Dominic Crossan contends in *God and Empire*?[15]

Helpful in this connection is Mark Bredin's discussion in *Jesus, Revolutionary of Peace* of alternative interpretations of Revelation with respect to violence and vengeance. He documents two basic positions on whether the depiction of Jesus in Revelation is significantly different from the nonviolent Jesus of the gospels. The dominant view, according to Bredin, is that Revelation is to be read as a text that both anticipates and endorses divine vengeance. "Revelation, in this perspective, does not call believers to take up arms. But it does call them to believe that God will carry out his [*sic*] vengeful acts against their perceived oppressors."[16] Such a response reads with the grain of the text, taking the imagery of eschatological vengeance at face value. Moreover, among representatives of this interpretation such as Adela Yarbro Collins and Elisabeth Schüssler Fiorenza, John's anticipation of divine vengeance serves to emphasize the present disparity between justice and oppression and makes it, for that reason, justifiable.[17] Such a reading cannot be too easily relinquished. If an alternative reading dispenses with a concern for divine vindication and restoration of those whose lives are marked by pain and suffering caused by injustice and oppression, it must be judged to be seriously deficient.[18]

Bredin associates an alternative reading with G. B. Caird, William Klassen, John Sweet, Eugene Boring, Wilfrid Harrington, Richard Bauck-

---

15. See Crossan, *God and Empire*, 141–42, 191–235. Crossan indicts John for betraying the nonviolent conception of God revealed in Jesus by depicting the returning Jesus as avenging Slaughterer. While I am in basic agreement with Crossan's theological and moral concerns, I am less inclined than he to denounce John as a betrayer of Jesus' vision of God's fair reign.

16. Bredin, *Jesus*, 28.

17. So Bredin, *Jesus*, 27. But Schüssler Fiorenza also calls for theological critique of John's violent rhetoric. See Schüssler Fiorenza, "Words of Prophecy," 19: "While one could argue, as I have done, that the basic theological paradigm of the Apocalypse is not holy war and destruction but justice and judgment, not prediction of certain events but exhortation and threat, it is nevertheless necessary to engage in theological ideology critique and to assess critically the violence proclaimed by the Apocalypse in the name of G*d."

18. Cf. Rowland and Corner, *Liberating Exegesis*, 131–55.

ham, and Richard Hays.[19] For such scholars, and also for Loren Johns and Willard Swartley,[20] the image of the Lamb is the hermeneutical key to interpreting the imagery of vindictive vengeance in Revelation. As Bredin summarizes:

> The war metaphor is rebirthed in the light of suffering witness. Revelation offers another way of perceiving and resisting the world. It implores people to confront the dominant power, but in such a way that seeks their conversion rather than their destruction. Nonviolence is the essence of Revelation's understanding of God and his creation.[21]

Any such interpretation must be grounded in sound exegesis of Revelation. Here the point is that, although not dominant, there is a relatively strong interpretive tradition of reading Revelation from a peace-oriented perspective. An overview of John's Christology followed by an attentive reading of two key texts, Rev 4:1–5:14 and 19:11–21, confirms that this minority tradition cannot be written off lightly.[22]

THE CHRISTOLOGY OF REVELATION

"Nowhere in the New Testament are christological perspectives more decisive than in the book of Revelation," avers Sarah Alexander Edwards.[23] But for Edwards, following in the footsteps of John Whealon,[24] John's christological perspectives serve the source-critical purpose of confirming that Revelation in its canonical form is the result of editorially embracing a (non-Christian) Jewish apocalyptic text (Rev 4:1–22:7) within Christian "parentheses" (Rev 1:1–3:22; 22:8–21). Even if one were to accept such a source-critical conclusion, it is difficult to maintain that John's Apocalypse has but a Christian "veneer." That Revelation is profoundly Jewish one need not doubt, but with respect to a text from the late-first century that need not signify that Revelation is not also profoundly Christian. John may have been a more conservative Jewish-

---

19. Caird, *Commentary*; Klassen, "Vengeance"; Sweet, *Revelation*; Boring, "Theology"; Harrington, *Revelation*; Bauckham, *Climax* and *Theology*; and Hays, *Moral Vision*.

20. Swartley, *Covenant of Peace*, 324–44.

21. Bredin, *Jesus*, 34.

22. For an opposing view, appealing to the same basic texts, see Crossan, *God and Empire*, 223–27.

23. Edwards, "Christological Perspectives," 139.

24. Whealon, "New Patches."

Christian than Paul,[25] but Jewish-*Christian* he surely was. This shuts the door on efforts to attribute (alleged) divine vengeance in Revelation to a "reversion" to Judaism, historically a common explanation for the vindictive and vengeful tone of the book.[26]

The opening line of Revelation describes the book as a "revelation of Jesus Messiah," which can mean a revelation either *from* or *about* Jesus Messiah, or, more likely, *both* from *and* about Jesus Messiah. If Revelation is no less *about* Jesus Messiah than it purports to be *from* him, this imposes certain interpretive constraints. An interpretation that does not place *at its core* John's peculiar exposition of the identity and significance of Jesus is not a faithful interpretation of Revelation.[27]

John's Christology is remarkably pluriform, as seen from the following descriptions. Revelation 1:5a describes Jesus as "the faithful witness, the firstborn of the dead, and the ruler of the kings of the earth." His atoning significance is signaled in the phrase, "who freed us from our sins by his death" (1:5b), and his eschatological significance is signaled in the affirmation, "He is coming with the clouds, and every eye will see him" (1:7a). At Rev 1:13 and 14:14, John retrieves from Dan 7:13 the image of "one like a person ['son of humanity']" to conceptualize Jesus, who in addressing the angel of the church at Thyatira is also the Son of God (2:18). In Rev 1:17, 2:8, and 22:13, Jesus is the first and the last, while in 1:18 he is the living one who has experienced death and now holds the keys of Death and Hades. He is God's anointed (11:15; 12:10; 20:4, 6), Lord of lords and King of kings (17:14; 19:16), Faithful and True (19:11), and the Word of God (19:13).

An important dimension of John's understanding of Jesus is that what is said of God can also be said of Jesus. If God is the Alpha and Omega (1:8; 21:6), so too is Jesus (22:13); if God is the beginning and the end (21:6), so too is Jesus (22:13; cf. 1:17); if God is enthroned, so too is Jesus (4:2–3; 5:6; 22:1). Praise of God (4:9–11) is paralleled by praise of Jesus (5:9–12), which culminates in Rev 5:13–14 with praise and worship of both God and Jesus. God's wrath (14:10, 19; 15:1) is also

25. Revelation 2:14–15, 20–22 indicate that John had stricter views than Paul about eating food offered to idols.

26. See Klassen, "Vengeance," 302.

27. On the Christology of Revelation, see Johns, *Lamb Christology*; Bauckham, *Theology*, 54–108; Bredin, *Jesus*; Boring, "Narrative Christology"; Slater, *Christ and Community*; and Hoffmann, *Destroyer and Lamb*.

paralleled by the wrath of the Lamb (6:16), although here it might be prudent to say that God's wrath parallels that of Jesus, since the wrath of the Lamb is mentioned first. So, not only is John's Christology pluriform, it is also exalted.

As pluriform and exalted as John's Christology is, on twenty-eight occasions Jesus is referred to as "Lamb," making this John's dominant or "most comprehensive"[28] christological image. Moreover, as Swartley observes, "'Lamb' is used 28 times in Revelation and is the only designation for Christ in the narrative plot other than 'Son of Man' in 14:14; other titles are used in the frames of the drama in chapters 1 and 22."[29] Paradoxically, the Lamb is one who triumphs in battle; however, it is precisely as the slain Lamb that the Lamb triumphs (5:6, 9, 12; 7:14; 12:11; 13:8). This paradox fits the dual emphasis on the Lamb's humiliation and exaltation. As Udo Schnelle explains:

> The foundation of Revelation's Christology is the saving act of God in Christ. This act establishes eschatological salvation and saves from the world's realm of power (cf. e.g., Rev. 1.5b, 6; 5.9–10; 7.15; 12.11). The distinctive christological dignity of Jesus is expressed in the title *arnion* (lamb, used 28x as a title in Rev.), which at one and the same time expresses Jesus' giving himself for his own and his exaltation as Lord (Rev. 5.6). The exaltation of the Lamb is based on his humiliation (cf. Rev. 5.9, 12); the firstborn of the dead (Rev. 1.5) is the slaughtered lamb. Jesus acts as God's authorized agent who in Rev. 5 is explicitly portrayed as being commissioned to accomplish God's plan of eschatological salvation.[30]

Schnelle's concluding observation is crucial. If it is as "slaughtered lamb" that Jesus is God's authorized agent of eschatological salvation, this has a significant bearing on how the realization of the divine will and purpose should be understood. Crucial in this regard is the work of Loren Johns, in which both the *origins* of John's Lamb-Christology and *his own innovative use of it* are explored with a view to ascertaining its ethical force. With Johns and others, I consider John's Lamb-image to be his central and controlling christological motif.[31] Significantly, John's

28. Slater, *Christ and Community*, 200.
29. Swartley, *Covenant of Peace*, 338.
30. Schnelle, *History and Theology*, 535.
31. Johns is primarily concerned with the ethical implications of John's Lamb-

first reference to the Lamb occurs in Rev 5:6, within the heavenly vision recorded in Revelation 4–5.

TRUE VISION IN REVELATION 4–5

Revelation 4:1 marks a decisive transition in the book's structure. Following letters to seven churches in Revelation 2–3, the scene changes from earth to heaven. John is invited to transgress the boundary between heaven and earth, with the promise that he will be shown what is to come. His "translation" into the heavenly sphere is described as a form of Spirit-seizure, without mention of any journey of ascent. Thus the form of what follows is that of vision, perhaps recounting a recollected visionary experience.[32] More important, perhaps, is that the content of the opening scene of John's second vision (cf. Rev 1:10–20) is worship in the throneroom of the Lord God "almighty" (*pantokratōr*).[33] Here John perceives—and describes in symbol and imagery—what is ordinarily hidden from human perception.[34]

The central image in Revelation 4–5 is a throne surrounded by other thrones. The one seated on the central throne cannot be described precisely, but what is clear is that everything centers on this figure, clearly representing God. While John's vision may be of one enthroned in the heavenly court, it is nevertheless a profound challenge to the sovereignty of those who occupy earthly thrones.[35] Not the emperor, but the creator God is sovereign over all; not the emperor, but the creator God is entitled to adoration and worship. Worship serves to focus on primary things. When, in worship, people hymn God with adoration and praise, they acknowledge God as the only one worthy of such adoration and praise. But if God is the *only one worthy* of adoration and praise, other claims on human loyalty are false claims, as is the common assumption that those in power ultimately shape history and human destiny. Worship of

---

Christology, whereas I am *also* concerned with the theological implications of this decisive christological image.

32. See Boxall, *Revelation*, 30–36.

33. This divine designation occurs in Rev 1:8; 4:8; 11:17; 15:3; 16:7, 14; 19:6, 15; 21:22. Boring, "Theology," 259, points out that of the ten occurrences of this term in the New Testament, nine are in Revelation.

34. On what follows in this section, I acknowledge my indebtedness to Yoder, *Politics of Jesus*, 228–47, and "To Serve," 127–40.

35. Cf. Bauckham, *Theology*, 35–39.

God is a reminder that there can be no higher claim on human loyalty, a reminder that the scroll of history and the future is in God's hands, not in the hands of the powerful and the wealthy.

Since Revelation 4–5 is a vision of heavenly, that is, authentic, worship, this implies that the worship described is also a form of vision—a perception of reality shaped by faith in God as creator and redeemer. The vision described in Revelation 4–5 likely reflects features of worship from both the synagogue and the early Christian housechurch. Then, as now, it was difficult to imagine that this world is in God's control; then, as now, it was difficult to acknowledge God as king.

"The central theological question of chapters 4–5 as well as of the whole book [of Revelation] is: Who is the true Lord of this world?"[36] One who answers this question solely on the basis of experience might well say that the powerful, those with wealth and weapons, really govern the world. But that is not John's answer. His heavenly vision enables him to see things on earth differently, to gain an alternative perspective on reality. "John's vision of heaven takes him deeper into reality, rather than removing him from it," as Boxall observes.[37] Precisely this alternative, more profound perspective on reality is crucial for a peace-oriented interpretation of theology and ethics in the Apocalypse.

For the interpreter, Revelation 4–5 is critically significant because the vision it recounts is what Boxall calls the "orienting vision" for the remainder of the narrative.[38] Or, as Johns affirms, "The rhetorical fulcrum of the Apocalypse is the scene in heaven in chapters 4 and 5."[39] Later scenes, signaled in Rev 4:1 as "what must occur after this," must be understood in ways compatible with the perspective of this heavenly vision.

A crucial feature of John's perspective-sharpening vision of worship in the heavenly throneroom is its "bifurcated sense of reality," in which the earthly and heavenly dimensions coexist as competing realities but in such a way that the heavenly sphere is conceived as both more real and ultimately more true and enduring than the earthly sphere.[40] Revelation 4 is recognizable as little different from traditional Jewish

36. Schüssler Fiorenza, *Revelation*, 58.

37. Boxall, *Revelation of Saint John*, 82.

38. Ibid., 79.

39. Johns, *Lamb Christology*, 158.

40. See Howard-Brook and Gwyther, *Unveiling Empire*, 120–35.

Merkavah ("throne-chariot") mysticism influenced by Ezekiel 1,[41] but Revelation 5 introduces into the vision-account a distinctly christocentric dimension, in which the figure of the Lamb is praised alongside and in the same terms as the indescribable figure on the throne.

For John, the Lamb is the key to God's way of working in the world, but that insight requires passing through the refining process of having one's preconceptions and assumptions about the way the world works overturned. It requires, as Christopher Rowland suggests, something akin to a Nietzschean "revaluation of all values," a process of having one's assumptions about what is real and worthwhile challenged and inverted.[42]

John achieves this "revaluation" in a dramatic sequence of images: first, a scroll in the right hand of the enthroned one, clearly containing crucial information yet sealed with seven seals; second, the proclamation (as opposed to a simple query) whether anyone anywhere is worthy to break open the scroll and its mysteries; third, the realization that wherever one might think to look, there is no one worthy even to look upon the scroll, let alone open it, which causes John to weep disconsolately; then, fourth, hope, when John hears one of the twenty-four elders say that since the Lion of the tribe of Judah has "conquered" (*nikaō*),[43] he is worthy to unseal the scroll; but fifth, what John sees *in the place of the enthroned one* is a Lamb-as-slaughtered. Spatially speaking, this sequence of images begins and ends with one on the throne,[44] but in between the reader is taken on a magic-carpet ride through all the dimensions of the known created order only to learn that what needed to be found was not one worthy to unseal the scroll but rather a new perspective that enables one to perceive that the "conquering" normally associated with the image of a lion has *already* been accomplished, albeit in the *manner* of a lamb that submits to slaughter. The scope of John's artful innovation is breathtaking but all too often ignored or overlooked as readers rush forward to learn what is loosed from the unsealed scroll.

41. This is not to suggest that Revelation 4 is incidental or has no distinctively Christian elements. See Hurtado, "Revelation 4–5."

42. Rowland, "Revelation," 605.

43. The term *nikaō* occurs fifteen times in Revelation, seven times in Revelation 2–3 and eight times elsewhere (5:5; 6:2; 11:7; 12:11; 13:7; 15:2; 17:14; 21:7).

44. See Knight, "Enthroned Christ," 43–50.

John's weeping ceases when he *hears* of the Lion of the tribe of Judah, the Root of David (cf. Gen 49:9; Isa 11:1, 10). Scholars quibble over what messianic associations in Jewish tradition best explain these specific images, but it is generally agreed that they evoke the image of a messianic warrior-king. But what John *sees* is a Lamb-as-slaughtered. Various interpretations have been offered of the rapid transfer of images from Lion of the tribe of Judah to Lamb-as-slaughtered.[45] One that is well known because it appears in an influential reference work is that by Adela Yarbro Collins. After posing the question whether the image of Jesus as divine warrior in Revelation 19 is transformed by the image of the Lamb in Revelation 5 or vice versa, she writes:

> The character of the book as a whole, as well as the context of the image of the Lamb in chap. 5, suggests that the latter is the case [the image of the Lamb is transformed by the image of Jesus as divine warrior]. The death of Christ is affirmed ... as the event that freed believers from their sins (1:5b). In chap. 5, the image of the "lamb, standing as if slain" is immediately transformed by the description of the animal as having seven horns (v 6). As is well known, the horn is a biblical and postbiblical image of military might and the horned ram is an image for great military leaders and for a warrior-messiah in the *Dream Visions of Enoch* (*1 Enoch* 85–90). The impression that the older Christian image of the sacrificial Lamb is being reinterpreted in Revelation is supported by the introduction of the figure as the "Lion of the tribe of Judah" (5:5).[46]

Yarbro Collins interprets John's transformation of a nonviolent understanding of Jesus' identity and mission into a militant one as being a response to a threatening situation (or several perceived crises) in the life of the churches for whom Revelation was written. In other words, in response to circumstances in which God's sovereignty seemed undermined by the way things were, John conceived of an alternative vision in which the rule of God and Jesus was reaffirmed, despite appearances to the contrary, and in which the faithful are ultimately rewarded and the unfaithful are condemned to oblivion.

For Yarbro Collins, John reinterpreted the peaceable mission of Jesus into a threatening prospect of eschatological vengeance and retribution

---

45. See Skaggs and Doyle, "Lion/Lamb."

46. Yarbro Collins, "Revelation," 705.

to cope with present circumstances of suffering. The logic of her position is that traditional apocalyptic motifs are wholly determinative of John's meaning.[47] Whether they are determinative, however, or whether they are reworked and thereby provide the means whereby John *reinterpreted* traditional conceptions of divine agency is precisely the point at issue. An important aspect of Yarbro Collins's position is her interpretation of the "seven horns" of Rev 5:6 as signifying military prowess, a view shared by G. K. Beale,[48] among others. There is no reason to deny that the horn is symbolic of power, but again, whether such an image *as used by John* requires that it be understood as power associated with military prowess is open to question. An equally plausible interpretation is to read the "seven horns" *along with* the "seven eyes" as signifying the "seven spirits of God sent out into all the earth," that is, God's irresistible, but not necessarily militant, agency in the world.[49]

One certainly needs to recognize stock apocalyptic motifs employed by John, for example, the so-called "combat myth," but one needs also to attend to ways in which such motifs are subtly reworked to convey new insight. As Johns observes:

> If modern readers have never heard of an ancient combat myth, the Gestalt created by the act of reading the Apocalypse is more likely to emphasize the violence of the images. However, if the violent images are recognized as a standard part of the combat myth tradition, the reader will likely be more alert to the manner in which the combat myth is being reshaped and redefined in John's creative use of them.[50]

The shift of imagery from that of anticipated "Lion of the tribe of Judah," which is first *heard* about so as to evoke certain expectations in the reader's mind, to that of "Lamb-as-slaughtered" unsettles preexisting notions. When we look for the lion, our expectations are turned upside-down by a lamb; in turn, the honor accorded the lamb turns our

---

47. Cf. her critique of Boring, *Revelation*, in both "Eschatology" and "Appreciating," in which at various points her disagreement with Boring's allegedly "allegorical" and less-than-serious interpretation of John's violent imagery takes as given John's retrieval, *but not renovation*, of traditional concepts, e.g., the allusion in Rev 19:11–21 to the Word of God referred to in Wis 18:15.

48. Beale, *Revelation*, 352–55.

49. See Schüssler Fiorenza, *Revelation*, 60; Aune, *Revelation*, 1:353–54.

50. Johns, *Lamb Christology*, 15.

understanding of reality downside-up. One way of expressing the reality behind this clashing pair of images is to say, with Richard Bauckham and Denny Weaver,[51] that the lion symbolizes victory while the lamb symbolizes the means or manner of victory.

In other words, the Messiah of God accomplishes God's purposes for the world not by might but by suffering in solidarity with all that is broken, disfigured, crushed, humiliated, downtrodden. This is the heavenly perspective on the mission of Jesus, which led ultimately to the cross. Yet from the perspective of heaven, the cross was not a defeat but a victory worth celebrating. That God is on a throne does not signify that God's will for the world is best discerned and enacted by those on earthly thrones; indeed, not one on any kind of throne we are used to but one bearing the marks of a cross is deemed worthy.

The strange new song of Rev 5:9–10, in which the same four creatures and twenty-four elders who had earlier praised the Lord of creation now praise the Lamb deemed worthy to open the scroll because it bears the marks of slaughter, signals something profound. It is precisely the scars of suffering that entitle the Lamb to open the sealed scroll in God's right hand. Whatever this scroll symbolizes, whether future judgment, the meaning of history, or something else altogether,[52] what matters most is that one who suffered is deemed worthy to open it. If God the creator is able to bring something meaningful and good out of the Lamb's suffering and death, that same God is able to bring something meaningful and good out of the suffering and woundedness of the world and those in it.

Steve Moyise,[53] in dialogue with James Resseguie,[54] contends that a literary difficulty for this particular interpretation is that elsewhere in Revelation it is usually what John *hears* that interprets or clarifies what he *sees*, rather than vice versa, as in Revelation 5. But the examples he cites (from Resseguie) as establishing the principle that, in Revelation, hearing generally interprets seeing are not compelling instances of what John hears interpreting what he sees. But a lamb's appearance when what

---

51. Bauckham, *Climax*, 179–85; Weaver, *Nonviolent Atonement*, 20.

52. For Bauckham, *Theology*, 80–88, the meaning of the scroll is that the faithful witness of believers, including death, is the means by which the nations of the world will turn to God, thereby establishing the reign of God over the world.

53. Moyise, "Does the Lion," 188–89.

54. Resseguie, *Revelation Unsealed*.

· John hears leads him to anticipate seeing a lion is a clear case of one image *supplanting* and thereby interpreting another.[55] As Johns observes, the juxtaposition of lion and lamb is not sustained throughout John's Apocalypse; the lion, once mentioned, is never actually seen and never actually (re)appears. For Johns, "This suggests that the images of the lion and the lamb were created specifically to address competing visions of how the messiah wields power."[56]

THE RIDER OF REV 19:11–21

The final chapter of Miroslav Volf's *Exclusion and Embrace* addresses the theme of "Violence and Peace."[57] After surveying a series of proposals for countering human violence, especially violence authorized by religion, Volf offers his own Christian proposal for living nonviolently in a violent world. His two main resources for advocating Christian nonviolence are the two christological images of the crucified Messiah and the Rider on a white horse in Revelation 19. There is much wisdom in Volf's discussion, but the disjunction or "clear division of labor" he posits between the crucified Messiah and the Rider on a white horse is disingenuous, especially since he nowhere examines in detail John's vision of the Rider but simply presupposes that the violent imagery of the vision bespeaks divinely authorized vengeance on the part of the Rider. In view of certain key features of the vision, however, this cannot be taken for granted. Yet Volf not only takes this for granted but slams the door shut on any approach that seeks to interpret John's visionary language as signifying anything other than violent vengeance:

> The attempt to exonerate the Revelation from the charge of affirming divine violence by suggesting that the Rider's victory was not "fought with literal weapons," but with the sword "which protrudes from his mouth," which is "the Word of God" . . . is implausible. The violence of the divine word is no less lethal than

55. Ibid., 33–37, the section cited by Moyise, does emphasize that what John hears generally interprets what he sees. In his introduction (pp. 7–10), however, Resseguie notes that what John sees can also interpret what he hears. Cf. Beale, *Revelation*, 353, who contends that a common pattern within Revelation is that "visions are placed directly after heavenly sayings in order to interpret them."

56. Johns, *Lamb Christology*, 191. Moyise, "Does the Lion," 189, 193–94, contends that the lion/lamb juxtaposition requires a two-way dynamic of mutual interpretation, but he accepts that this juxtaposition of images *permits* a nonviolent interpretation.

57. Volf, *Exclusion and Embrace*, 275–306.

the violence of the literal sword. We must either reject the Rider's violence or find ways to make sense of it; we cannot deny it.[58]

Volf's concern is to make sense of the Rider's violence, which he does by arguing that divine vengeance at the *eschaton* is necessary in a twofold way: first, to subjugate whomsoever is so thoroughly habituated by evil as to be no longer reachable by God's grace and love; and second, to enable believers to renounce violence until the time of God's just judgment. Moreover, for Volf, while human violence cannot be condoned, divine vengeance can be affirmed because of the biblically grounded distinction between God and everything else. "Preserving the fundamental difference between God and nonGod," he writes, "the biblical tradition insists that there are things which only God may do. One of them is to use violence."[59]

Volf considers that those who seek a nonviolent interpretation of the violent imagery of Revelation 19 must be naïve or too sheltered from the violence of the world. There is no doubt that the pacifist advocate of nonviolence finds her or his conviction easier to affirm and to practice in situations of relative stability and social order. Even in situations of oppression and violence, however, there are those who refrain from violence because they know that violent retaliation simply breeds further violence. Hence the logic of nonviolence is not necessarily contingent on anticipation of ultimate comeuppance. Moreover, while anticipation of vindication through divine vengeance might enable some to eschew violence here and now, for others the expectation (too easily deemed "knowledge") of vindication through divine vengeance leads inexorably to acting proleptically on God's behalf.

As for the biblical tradition that "looses" for God what is "bound" for humanity, surely Volf would acknowledge that much of what is attributed to divine agency in scripture is but human projection. In the beginning, we are told, people were formed in the divine image, and ever since we have returned the favor. For some, the problem of divine vengeance is precisely the product of the wholesale New Testament affirmation that God's ways, while admittedly not our ways, are precisely the ways of Jesus of Nazareth. On christological grounds, therefore, the disavowal of violence and vengeance is not only a moral imperative

58. Ibid., 296.
59. Ibid., 301.

for human beings but also the consequence of insight into divine reality. That human beings find it difficult to envisage evil being overcome nonviolently is understandable enough, but lack of imagination is no satisfactory basis for affirming either the necessity or the value of eschatological vengeance. At one level, granting God's *entitlement* to execute vengeance is unproblematic, but whether, *in view of the story of Jesus*, God will ultimately resort to violence, either out of necessity or for cathartic purposes, is profoundly problematic.[60]

Is there anything to appeal to in John's vision of the Rider on a white horse in support of a position other than Volf's? Space constraints preclude a full exegetical investigation of Rev 19:11–21, but the following points should be given full weight.[61]

There is broad agreement that this passage is John's visionary account of the *parousia*, even though it differs in a number of respects from other early Christian depictions of the *parousia*. As elsewhere, John innovates to emphasize the ineluctability of divine "conquest" over the forces of evil, but one should not infer from the violent imagery that the mode of conquest is violent. Why not? The first point to make is that insofar as John's vision anticipates a future event, it is beyond the capacity of any human being to know precisely how events will play out. Related to this is the symbolic nature of this pericope. As David Aune notes,

> The literary form of this unit is the *symbolic description*, which focuses on the *description, identity*, and *tasks* of the rider on the white horse.... The indicators of the *symbolic* nature of this description include the mention of the sharp sword that proceeds from his mouth (v 15a) and the metaphorical interpretation of the wine that is pressed as "the fury of the wrath of God the Almighty" (v 15c).[62]

First of all, then, symbolic description within a visionary account should not be pressed literally, which implies that the violent imagery of this passage may signify something altogether nonviolent.

---

60. For more on this debate, see Swartley, *Covenant of Peace*, 377–98.

61. Both Slater, *Christ and Community*, and Hoffmann, *Destroyer and Lamb*, demonstrate that the christological images of the Lamb and the Rider on a white horse, together with the image of "one like a son of man," are integrally interrelated in Revelation, whatever their origins. Revelation 17:14 and 19:16 confirm the identification of the Lamb with the Rider.

62. Aune, *Revelation*, 3:1047.

Aune draws attention to numerous parallels between Rev 19:11–16 and Jewish texts that depict God or God's Messiah as a warrior king.[63] There can be little doubt that such texts form the primary literary and conceptual background to John's visionary description of the Rider on a white horse.[64] But the vital question is what John does with the biblical image of the warrior king. Does he simply take over the imagery of divine warfare against antagonistic nations, or in taking it over does he also innovate?

The following details suggest that John's symbolic description utilizes imagery that signifies divine victory over opposing forces but without violent vengeance. First, the present tense of the verbs *krinō* and *polemeō* ("judges/rules" and "combats") in Rev 19:11c suggests that these functions of the Christ-figure are part and parcel of his characteristic manner of dealing with opposition to God. Aune designates the present tense of these particular verbs "the general or gnomic present, used to express customary actions and general truths."[65]

Moreover, these "customary actions" are done "justly" or "rightly," perhaps even in a "right-setting" way (*en dikaiosynē*). Together, these considerations cut against the view that at the *parousia* the returning Messiah will act in ways contrary to his customary demeanor. For John, there is no "division of labor" (contra Volf) between the crucified Lamb and the Rider. Indeed, the detail that the Rider's garment is *already* blood-stained not only before the birds are called to gather for the feast of flesh but also well before antagonistic armies assemble to wage war against the Rider—not, *nota bene*, the other way around—intimates that it refers to his own death rather than any violent death that he inflicts.[66]

---

63. Ibid., 3:1048–52.

64. For a full-scale investigation of the historical, cultural, and mythical backgrounds to this passage, see Thomas, *Revelation*, 19.

65. Aune, *Revelation*, 3:1053.

66. Cf. Johns, *Lamb Christology*, 184: "The rider approaches the battle dressed in a robe dipped in blood (19:13)—his own blood of witness/martyrdom. In keeping with the pivotal scene in Revelation 5 and the message of the book as a whole . . . the blood here is the blood of martyrdom. This contrasts with Isa 63:1–3, the source of this imagery, where the blood is the blood of the enemies of the divine warrior. John is, in fact, challenging the reader to look more carefully at his language and to reinterpret Isaiah 63 in the light of the Lamb." Carrell, *Jesus*, 199–200, summarizes various explanations of the phrase *bebammenon haimati* ("dipped in blood") and suggests that all are incorporated in this "multivalent image." Not all suggested interpretations are equally compelling, however. Slater, *Christ and Community*, 223–25, considers the most plausible

The means by which the Lamb conquers remain the means by which the Rider defeats all opposed to the purposes of God.

In view of Revelation's reception-history, this point can hardly be overemphasized. Regarding Rev 19:13a, Aune comments:

> The blood mentioned here is not primarily a metaphor for the atoning death of Christ ... but rather a literal reference to the heavenly warrior whose garment is stained with the blood of those he has slain. . . . The imagery of a bloodstained divine warrior coming to destroy his enemies occurs in a number of texts in the OT and early Judaism (Exod 15; Deut 33; Judg 5; Hab 3; Isa 26:16–27:6; 59:15–20; 63:1–6; Zech 14:1–21...), one of the oldest of which is Isa 63:1–3. . . .[67]

Having said this, however, Aune continues by noting: "It was inevitable that this older image of God as the divine warrior with blood-soaked garments transposed into the Messiah as divine warrior would be understood as a reference to the death of Christ by both the author and his readers when placed in a Christian context."[68] Furthermore, in his summary explanation of the passage, Aune concludes: "The single apparent allusion to his [i.e., Jesus Christ's] redeeming death is his robe, which has been dipped in blood (see 1:5; 5:9; 7:14; 12:11), actually a Christian reading of a traditional conception of the divine warrior understood as the Messiah."[69]

In other words, John did not simply take over the motif of the divine warrior but in doing so subtly—*perhaps all too subtly!*—reworked the motif in such a way as to convey that in view of the historic mission of Jesus Messiah, God's victory over antagonistic forces was no longer effected by inflicting violence but by suffering it. The symbolism of Revelation 19 is disturbing, but the reality to which the symbolism points is best interpreted in light of what is affirmed about the Lamb in Revelation 5. No less than the messianic Lion of the tribe of Judah, the messianic Rider on a white horse is to be seen as symbolically affirming

---

interpretation to be that the blood on the Rider's robe is that of his enemies, seemingly because this reading fits a socio-historical context in which Christians are suffering and will be helped to endure by anticipating divine retribution for their oppressors.

67. Aune, *Revelation*, 3:1057.

68. Ibid.

69. Ibid., 3:1069.

the potent efficaciousness of the Lamb's mode of overcoming evil and opposition to God.

One might add that supposed battle scenes in Revelation are not literal battles. As Denny Weaver points out, the battle in heaven in Revelation 12 signifies the cosmic significance of the resurrection and/ or ascension of Jesus, which is that through his death and vindication by God, evil's power is thwarted. As for the imagery of warfare in Rev 19:11–21, Weaver contends that no literal battle is envisaged. He interprets the killing sword as the word of God because it emanates from the Rider's mouth (cf. Eph 6:17; Heb 4:12):

> In the segment of 19:11–21, the beast and the kings and their armies are defeated not by violence and military might. They are undone—defeated—by the Word of God. This passage is another symbolic representation of the victory of the reign of God over the forces of evil that has already occurred with the death and resurrection of Jesus. It is by proclamation of the Word, not by armies and military might, that God's judgment occurs.[70]

Weaver's view is similar to that of Richard Hays:

> We are to understand that the execution of God's judgment occurs through the proclamation of the Word.... Those who read the battle imagery of Revelation with a literalist bent fail to grasp the way in which the symbolic logic of the work as a whole dismantles the symbolism of violence.[71]

It is not simply that John's battle scenes are not to be taken literally. Here there is no battle, symbolic or otherwise. Birds are called to gather for the carrion of everything from kings to slaves, and the beast and kings of the earth muster their armies to combat the Rider and his entourage. But there is no description of battle, only the end result that the beast and false prophet are captured and thrown into the lake of fire while the rest are "slaughtered" by the sword emanating from the Rider's mouth and eaten by birds. The imagery is ghastly but not to be understood literally. As Aune confirms,

70. Weaver, *Nonviolent Atonement*, 33.

71. Hays, *Moral Vision*, 175. Cf. Rowland, "Revelation," 700. Citing Isa 11:4, 4 Ezra 13:9–11, 2 Thess 2:8 and Rev 2:12, 16 alongside Rev 19:15, 21, Rowland remarks: "All of these passages suggest that judgment in the context of an eschatological battle comes by means of the power of the Word of God rather than through force of arms. The effect is devastating, because it functions as a divine illocutionary act."

To be slain by the sword that projected from the mouth of the warrior on the white steed certainly invites metaphorical interpretation; i.e., the "sword" must be the words spoken by the warrior (on the sword as a metaphor for the word of God, see Heb 4:12).... There is reason to suspect that the phrase ..., "the [sword] projecting from his mouth," is a gloss intended to emphasize the metaphorical interpretation of the sword.[72]

Perhaps the best reason to interpret "the sword protruding from his mouth" metaphorically is that in the letter to the angel of the church in Pergamum, the One with the sharp twin-edged sword (Rev 1:16; 2:12) threatens to "combat" the nefarious Nicolaitans with the sword of his mouth unless such pernicious persons are opposed (2:14–16). Apart from Rev 19:11, 2:16 is the only other occurrence of *polemeō* ("makes war") used with John's Christ-figure as subject.[73] Since the "combat" envisaged in Rev 2:16 can hardly be literal, this strengthens the case for interpreting 19:15 metaphorically.

More might be written about this Rider on a white horse,[74] but enough has been said to counter the view that Rev 19:11–21 unequivocally affirms divine vengeance. Not only the form of the pericope but also grammatical and symbolic details within it encourage the interpreter whose perspective is focused on—*and by!*—the image of the Lamb to read this passage as symbolizing God's nonviolent reclamation of the created order.

CHRISTOLOGY, ESCHATOLOGICAL VENGEANCE, AND MORAL VISION

Richard Hays's discussion of Revelation in *The Moral Vision of the New Testament* emphasizes how John's Lamb-Christology and apocalyptic eschatology reinforce a moral vision in which faithful believers emulate the Lamb through nonviolent resistance to injustice and socio-cultural accommodation. His discussion is compelling with respect to the vision of Christian morality portrayed in Revelation, even if he is perhaps too

72. Aune, *Revelation*, 3:1067.

73. Klassen, "Vengeance," 305.

74. Cf. Bredin, *Jesus*, 209–215, on "Trampling the Wine Press," and Carroll et al., *Return of Jesus*, 105, on the reappearance in the New Jerusalem of "kings of the earth" (Rev 21:24), despite their slaughter and consumption in Rev 19:21.

sanguine about "the way in which the symbolic logic of the work as a whole dismantles the symbolism of violence."[75]

Revelation's history of reception suggests that even if this was John's intent, his violent symbolism has more often than not dismantled the symbolic logic of the narrative as a whole. One likely reason for this is that what is often understood to be John's theology overshadows his moral vision, which is to say that people's perception of how Revelation depicts God's ultimate triumph over evil involves more overwhelming violence than the forces of evil can muster. Few dispute that John's explicit ethical exhortations disavow violence and vengeful retaliation. But his depiction of God or God's agents inflicting violence to bring about the divine will has served to sanction *both* nonviolence and violence on the part of believers—nonviolence for those who expect that ultimately God will enact violent retribution (cf. Volf) and violence for those who perceive themselves as acting on God's behalf. Thus, how John's Christology impacts on his readers' conception of God and God's way of working in the world is at least as important as—if not more so than—his explicit ethical exhortations.

In this respect, Hays does not go far enough. He rightly affirms that John's moral vision proscribes human violence, but he indicates that this moral stance is grounded in the divine prerogative to exact vengeance. For example,

> A work that places the Lamb that was slaughtered at the center of its praise and worship can hardly be used to validate violence and coercion. God's ultimate judgment of the wicked is, to be sure, inexorable. Those who destroy the earth will be destroyed (11:18); those who have shed the blood of the saints and prophets will find their own blood poured out on the earth. But these events are in the hands of God; they do not constitute a program for human military action. As a paradigm for the action of the faithful community, Jesus stands as the faithful witness who conquers through suffering.[76]

What this implies is that while human violence cannot further God's will for the world, God's violence can. If so, so be it; perhaps what God wills is good, as opposed to God's willing what is good. But Revelation and other New Testament texts go further than to affirm that Jesus and his way are

75. Hays, *Moral Vision*, 175.
76. Ibid.

to be emulated by Christian believers; rather, Jesus and his way provide a window into the being and character of God, in which case one cannot take for granted that God must ultimately resort to coercion, violence, or vindictive retribution to bring the divine will and purpose to fruition.

If in the fairly consistent New Testament depiction of Jesus and his way of responding to violence and injustice, one catches a glimpse of the very heart of God, that is surely greater warrant for eschewing violence here and now than the anticipation that God will ultimately execute vengeance on those who oppose the divine will. I concur with Hays that "the threat of judgment as a warrant for obedience is implicitly present in Revelation (e.g., 20:11–15),"[77] but without prejudging the form divine judgment will take. After all, we do not and cannot know how God might judge ultimately, but a christologically conditioned religious epistemology suggests that divine judgment is more likely to be restorative than strictly retributive.[78] Speaking of the moral impetus to emulate the Lamb, Hays writes: "Those who follow him [the Lamb] in persecution and death . . . are enacting *the will of God, who has chosen to overcome evil precisely in and through righteous suffering*, not in spite of it."[79] If in the Lamb and in the lives of those who faithfully follow the Lamb, why not ultimately?

CONCLUDING HERMENEUTICAL REFLECTIONS

One can hardly gainsay that the violent imagery that forms the warp and weft of Revelation's narrative fabric has had, and continues to have, a negative history of effects. Even those who consider that Revelation is susceptible of a peace-oriented interpretation are unable to deny the historical reality that Revelation has contributed to a violent God-image and fostered violent and vindictive behavior.

Although contentious, however, it is reasonable to judge that John's vision-inspired narrative is christocentric and cruciform, meaning that the Christ-event, albeit distilled almost to Pauline dimensions (cross, resurrection, and exaltation), is determinative for comprehending God's redemptive activity in the world, including the vanquishment of evil. As

77. Ibid., 180.

78. See Marshall, *Beyond Retribution*, 145–99. Consideration of the restorative or transformative dimension of divine justice and judgment is absent in the otherwise fine study on "Judgment in Revelation" by Bauckham.

79. Hays, *Moral Vision*, 179; emphasis mine.

Patricia McDonald argues, the crucified Christ—depicted as the slain
Lamb—is central to Revelation in much the same way as for Paul and
Mark.[80] As a result, John's christological portrait can rightly be measured against the broad brushstrokes of Jesus' mission and message in
the gospels. When this is done with interpretive care, one finds that the
Christology of Revelation is in step with the peaceable mission of Jesus,
despite John's use of violent imagery. This has theological significance,
meaning that the Apocalypse of John cannot be appealed to in support
of divinely authorized eschatological vengeance. The means by which the
crucified Jesus "conquered" are the means by which God "conquers"—
without remainder.

If, indeed, the Christology of Revelation is in step with the peaceable mission of Jesus as displayed in the gospels, this signifies that all violent associations in John's Apocalypse are susceptible of inner-scriptural
critique. It is, of course, possible to respond to (apparent) eschatological
vengeance in Revelation in a number of ways other than to affirm it. One
might simply turn one's back on the book, or ostracize it on the basis of a
"hermeneutic of suspicion," or deem it sub-Christian (as Dodd was wont
to do), or turn to critical theorists for extrabiblical resources with which
to deconstruct or subvert the image of God it (apparently) fosters. But
only if what Ellen Davis terms an "inner-biblical" hermeneutic[81] is used
to call into question theologically and morally problematic features of
Revelation, while continuing to affirm its canonical status, will readers
with a faith commitment combine charitable respect for John's text with
critical evaluation of its theological and moral difficulties.

Building on the pioneering work of Michael Fishbane, whose
Biblical Interpretation in Ancient Israel demonstrates that biblical tra-
dents often preserved authoritative tradition while at the same time
adapting and reinterpreting it,[82] Davis infers that "faithful transmis-
sion of authoritative tradition must always be something more than
rote repetition."[83] This process she describes as "critical traditioning,"
whereby preservation of tradition goes hand-in-hand with interpretive
innovation. (Indeed, retention of tradition is at times contingent upon
critical reformulation.) If this dynamism is discernible within scripture,

80. McDonald, "Lion," 31–32.

81. Davis, "Critical Traditioning."

82. Fishbane, *Biblical Interpretation.*

83. Davis, "Critical Traditioning," 738.

as it surely is, there is biblical precedent for an analogous hermeneutical strategy, which might be described as a twofold process of retrieval and renovation. Not only is this an "inner-scriptural" dynamic, but the way in which it (purportedly) operates can be measured against the "inner-scriptural" christological criterion of the gospel portrayal of the mission and message of Jesus Messiah, the purported Subject and content of the Revelation to John (1:1a).

The Apocalypse of John both retains and reworks, both adopts and adapts various apocalyptic motifs. Evidence of such "critical traditioning" is sufficient *on its own* to encourage readings of Revelation attuned to possible interpretive innovation that subverts eschatological vengeance traditionally associated with apocalyptic texts. Such readings are further authorized, however, by their coherence with the inner-scriptural christological criterion, which is both fitting and compelling because of John's appeal to the inner dynamic of the Jesus story, namely, divine recovery of the created order by means of the Lamb's willingness to undergo—rather than to inflict—slaughter.

On the basis of John's own "critical traditioning" measured against the inner-biblical christological criterion that the way of Jesus is the way of God, one can *faithfully* read both with and against the grain of the text of Revelation. Reading with the grain of Revelation 4–5 encourages an against-the-grain reading of Rev 19:11–21. In other words, Rev 19:11–21 should be read in light of Revelation 5, not vice versa (*contra* Yarbro Collins). The gruesome details of John's imaginative account of the victory of the Rider on a white horse may serve to warn of the futility of opposition to the will and purpose of God, but they do not reflect on the character of God or signal the means by which God's will and purpose for the created order will be realized.

As noted earlier, the Christian canon of Scripture begins and ends with visions of *shalom*, which witness to the Creator's will and purpose for creation as a whole.[84] The two visions that open and close the bibli-

---

84. This observation is also made by Marshall, "Violence of God," 80–81. See also Sweet, *Revelation*, 13, 47, 51, who makes a similar point with respect to the structure of Revelation, pointing out that "the visions of destruction are bracketed by the overarching vision of God the Creator and Redeemer (4, 5), who makes all things new (21, 22)." Boring's study of "Narrative Christology" argues on the basis of various levels of narrativity within Revelation that the dramatic and often violent events associated with the breaking of the seven seals, the sounding of the seven trumpets and the spilling of the seven bowls must be regarded as a "secondary play-within-a-play," which only makes

cal canon are not empirical, but rather interpretive, realities. They do not describe how any one of the human race has ever experienced life; rather, they express how life *should be* experienced.

Protology and eschatology, first and last things, express the most deeply held convictions about the way things ought to be. That is to say, depictions of first things give expression to what is of *primary* value; what is expressed about what *came first* indicates what *is first* in our perception of reality and system of values. Similarly, depictions of last things also give expression to what is of *primary* value; what is expressed about what *will come last* indicates what we believe and hope *to be lasting*. So, when we read the opening and closing visions of the biblical story, we are as close as ever we can approximate to what is, for Christian believers, the way things should be. Both visions are construed as the result of divine agency, which is to say that these visions of the way the world *should be* are attributed to God's will and purpose for the world and humanity.

But not only so. . . . Beginnings and endings are undoubtedly important for interpreting narratives. In the case of the biblical narrative, however, what is critical from a Christian theological perspective is that the two visions at the beginning and end of the canonical story cohere at the deepest level with the Jesus story in the gospels, which for Christians forms the midpoint *and therefore the fulcrum and norm* of the larger story. There is therefore consonance and resonance between beginning, end, and middle of the canonical story, which attests to divine proneness to *shalom*. This, in turn, coheres with the central Christian affirmation about God, namely, that God *is* love, even deep down into the inner recesses of the mystery called "Trinity."

Beginning, middle, and end of the biblical narrative thus stake out a *determinative canonical trajectory* against which other trajectories and perspectives may be scrutinized and judged. Or, put differently, the canonical trajectory etched by tracing a theologico-moral line from creation through Jesus to the restoration envisioned by John in his image of the New (or renovated) Jerusalem provides a big-picture, inner-scriptural criterion for reading against the grain of specific scriptures that depict

---

proper sense when construed in relation to other, more determinative narrative levels, especially the implicit macro-narrative or narrative world that stretches from creation to the *eschaton* and has the crucifixion of Jesus as its midpoint.

God or God's agency in the world in contradictory terms.[85] Here I am in basic sympathy with J. Clinton McCann's notion of "The Hermeneutics of Grace."[86] Without denying the polyphony of scripture, McCann detects a "single plot" through the Torah, Prophets, and Writings into the New Testament. The notion of a *"single* plot" in Scripture is unsustainable, in my judgment, but the trajectory staked out by the creation story in Gen 1:1—2:3, in which the divine will is initially displayed, the Jesus story, in which the divine will is reaffirmed, and the vision of the New Jerusalem in Revelation 20–21, in which the divine will is ultimately realized, is clearly enough etched to serve as a "rule" of orientation or inner-biblical canon for interpreting texts that speak in another voice.[87] In short, intimations of eschatological vengeance in Revelation (and elsewhere) should be read in accordance with a hermeneutic of *shalom.*

Throughout this study, I have tacitly appealed to an interpretive principle designated by Charles Cosgrove: "the rule of moral-theological adjudication."[88] Analogous to the early church's rule of faith, as articulated by Irenaeus in *Against Heresies* (1.10), and Augustine's interpretive rule of love, as set out in *On Christian Doctrine* (1.84–85, 95–96; 3.54),[89] the rule of moral-theological adjudication proposes that in cases of interpretive ambiguity, "one may view Scripture as properly interpreted only where it is construed according to certain substantive principles, conceived as intrinsic to Scripture itself, taken as a whole."[90] Such an interpretive rule presupposes the authority of Scripture, but without granting that Scripture speaks with one clear voice throughout. In such a situation, the community of faith must inevitably interpret authoritative

85. In certain respects, this proposal combines four of six hermeneutical strategies for dealing with "morally dubious" scriptural passages discussed by Davies, "Morally Dubious Passages," namely, canon-within-a-canon, holistic, paradigmatic, and reader-response approaches.

86. McCann, "Hermeneutics of Grace."

87. This conception has affinities with the proposal of Hays, *Moral Vision*, 304, that metaphorical readings of New Testament texts should be "consonant with the fundamental plot of the biblical story as identified by the focal images of community, cross, and new creation." As far as canonical plotlines are concerned, however, one that stretches from creation to new creation via the cross seems stronger, no matter how important the church's role as interpretive community and constraint might be.

88. Cosgrove, *Appealing to Scripture*, 2–4, 154–80.

89. For a restatement of Augustine's interpretive rule of love, see Tannehill, "Freedom and Responsibility."

90. Cosgrove, *Appealing to Scripture*, 157.

yet ambiguous texts, which implies that responsible interpretive choice is called for—and called forth—by those texts accepted as authoritative by the church.[91]

On broad canonical grounds, similar in certain respects to what Cosgrove identifies as an interpretive "rule of canonical structure,"[92] I submit that a hermeneutic of *shalom* should complement the church's earlier interpretive rules of faith and love. Since the biblical record affirms that *shalom* derives from or is characteristic of divine creativity and therefore precedes human moral judgment, I prefer to speak of theological-moral, rather than moral-theological, interpretive adjudication. Christian moral vision and deliberation occur within the context of, and in response to, what is affirmed to be the divine pattern of relating to humanity and the wider world. For people of Christian faith, that divine pattern is displayed decisively in the life-story of Jesus of Nazareth and confirmed in the stories of creation and restored creation that bookend the canonical metanarrative. *Shalom* has inner-biblical theological warrant and, from the perspective of human flourishing, has more intrinsic moral meaning than violence ever could.

91. Cf. Tannehill, "Freedom and Responsibility," 275–76.
92. Cosgrove, *Appealing to Scripture*, 197.

5

Hastening the Day When the Earth Will Burn?

Global Warming, Revelation, and 2 Peter 3[1]

BARBARA R. ROSSING

FORMER VICE PRESIDENT AL GORE has likened the terrifying prospect of global warming's effects on the world to "taking a nature hike through the book of Revelation."[2] Better still, his nature hike could also include 2 Peter 3, a terrifying chapter that raises troubling questions for those seeking biblical counsel on the environment because it consigns the earth to burning up by fire.

We are well on our way to that burning. Three recent reports from the Intergovernmental Panel on Climate Change (IPCC), released in 2007, read more like the plague sequences of Revelation than like typical scientific reports, with predictions of higher sea levels, more acidic oceans, fiercer storms, deadlier forest fires, more heat-related deaths, longer dry seasons, declining water supplies, catastrophic floods, and increasing infectious diseases around the world. In an ironic coincidence, one of the reports, "Climate Change Impacts, Adaptation and Vulnerability," was released Good Friday, April 6, 2007. Even after the U.S. and other governments watered down the text, the report still predicts the future passion and suffering, even death, of hundreds of millions of the poorest and most vulnerable people of the earth who will be displaced or otherwise affected if temperatures rise only as much as 3.6 degrees Fahrenheit (2 degrees Celsius). This is on top of the suffering of rivers, oceans, coral reefs, and ice sheets, and the consequent extinction

1. Two earlier versions of this essay were published as follows: Rossing, "Hastening," in *The Bible in the Public Square*; Rossing, "Hastening," *Currents*.

2. Gore, *Earth*, 225.

of 20–30 percent of the world's living species. News reports that whole islands and even island nations have already disappeared in the Pacific bear eerie resemblance to the prophetic voice of Revelation 16:20 that "every island fled away."

A few fundamentalist Christians may welcome the prospect of calamitous events as if they were signs of the end-times and Jesus' return. For most Christians, however, the urgent question is whether and how the Bible might provide guidance for addressing our new situation of living at the *end*.

It is becoming clear that we do face the prospect of some kind of an end. At the present rate of emissions growth, atmospheric concentrations of carbon dioxide will rise above 500 parts per million—almost double the preindustrial level—by the middle of the century. America's premier climatologist, James Hansen, of NASA's Goddard Space Institute, says that we can probably survive at those levels but that it would be on a "different planet."[3] If the concentration of carbon dioxide ever were to rise to 666 parts per million—Revelation's number of the beast—we would be toast. Unfortunately, even this number is below the top of the range in the scenarios that may well happen within the lifetime of our children and grandchildren.

Moreover, scientists now think the IPCC projects are too conservative, since they do not take into consideration new data regarding the faster-than-expected melting of both the Greenland and Antarctica ice sheets and mounting evidence since March 2006 of climate changes much more serious than previous models indicated. The reports also do not consider the scenarios of irreversible feedback loops or what scientists call "tipping points." To be sure, the world has so far dodged other planetary perils in the past—most notably the threat of nuclear annihilation. In the past, the *Bulletin of the Atomic Scientists* has moved the hands on its "Doomsday Clock" even closer to midnight than at present.[4] But previous crises did not portend tipping points that would be irreversible, such as the "albedo effect" by which melting Arctic sea ice itself acceler-

3. Hansen, "Why."

4. The *Bulletin of the Atomic Scientists* created its Doomsday Clock to convey how close humanity is to catastrophic planetary destruction—the figurative "midnight." In January 2007 the board of directors of the *Bulletin* decided to move the minute hand from seven to five minutes to midnight, stating that "we stand at the brink of disaster." The last time the hands were closer to midnight was in 1984.

ates further warming (since ice is white and reflects heat back to the sun, whereas sea water is dark in color and absorbs more heat).

Hansen believes that we still have time to avert dangerous sea level rise—but we must reduce carbon emissions significantly in the next ten years, and by 90 percent by the year 2050. Otherwise, it will be too late to save the Greenland ice sheet and avoid other catastrophic tipping points. Even the IPCC report itself says that global carbon emissions must peak and begin declining within the next eight years, by the year 2015, if the world wants to have any chance of limiting the expected temperature rise to 2 degrees Celsius (3.6 degree Fahrenheit) above pre-industrial levels. Scientists, religious leaders, and world political leaders underscore the urgency of acting now to reduce carbon emissions. If not, we risk losing the ten-year window past which we would be unable to avert irreversible, catastrophic, climate change.

So, how can we draw on the Bible publicly to address this crisis, underscoring especially the urgency of that ten-year window?

Since Christian apocalyptic texts address the sense of an *end*, it might seem logical to turn to these texts to speak to our current situation. We must carefully distinguish among various strands of early Christian apocalyptic, however. The New Testament presents a range of perspectives on the end of the world. This chapter will contrast two apocalyptic texts, Revelation and 2 Peter, in terms of how they might help us address global warming. I will argue that whereas the end-of-the-empire perspective of Revelation can be helpful ecologically, 2 Peter's claim that the world is destined to be burned up with fire must be viewed as highly problematic. Building on previous ecologically oriented work on Revelation, this chapter will then explore two elements—Revelation's anti-imperial perspective, including the millennium vision for life beyond empire, and its sense of urgency of the present moment—that may prove helpful in addressing the crisis of global warming.[5]

5. This article builds on previous work in which I have sought to reclaim the apocalyptic book of Revelation as a positive resource for ecological reflection by contrasting the Babylon/Rome vision of imperial justice with the earth-renewing vision of New Jerusalem, and argued for an anti-imperial reading of the plagues of Revelation. See Rossing, "River," "Alas," and "For."

THE SENSE OF AN END: REVELATION VS. 2 PETER

A strong sense of an impending end pervades much of the apocalyptic discourse of the New Testament. Early Christians definitely believed they were living at the end of the age, the end of the world. But the question is: the end of *what* world? What was it that early Christian texts view as coming to an end? With the exception of 2 Peter, the *end* that New Testament texts envision is not primarily the destruction of the earth or the created world. Rather, in proclaiming the dawning of a new age in Christ, they envision an end to the Roman imperial world of oppression, sin, and injustice, an end to the *oikoumene*.[6]

I draw a distinction between several different Greek words for "world." Revelation unveils the end, not of the physical world or earth (the Greek words *kosmos* and *ge*), nor creation (the Greek word *ktisis*), but the end of the imperial world, the *oikoumene*. In my view this distinction can help us navigate the sense of an end today as well.

In Revelation, the earth (*ge*), the world (*kosmos*), and the entire created world (*ktisis*) belong to God. For all its imagery of destruction, Revelation continues the biblical tradition of affirming the fundamental goodness of creation as declared by God in Genesis 1. Commands to "worship the one who made the heaven and the earth, the sea and springs of water" (Rev 14:7)[7] make clear that God created heaven, earth, springs of water, and the sea; they are considered God's creations throughout the entire book. The use of creation-oriented terminology (the Greek root *ktiz-*) in Revelation is overwhelmingly positive: Rev 3:14; 5:14; and especially the emphatic declaration of Rev 10:6 (see also 4:11) that God "created the heaven and what is in it and the earth and what is in it, and the sea." God does not consign the creation to destruction in Revelation.[8]

---

6. Although *oikoumene* is often translated "inhabited world," I have argued that it is more accurately translated "empire" in the New Testament. See Rossing, "(Re) Claiming."

7. Translations of the biblical text are my own.

8. Revelation 21:1: "The first heaven and the first earth had passed away," and 20:11: "Earth and sky fled away," can be read in a number of ways, but certainly not as evidence that God must destroy the first earth before the dawning of the new heavens and the new earth. I have suggested that the "first earth" that passes away is the earth that is captive to Roman imperial power, whereas the new earth of 21:1 is envisioned as the earth free from Roman domination (see Rossing, "Alas," 189). For an argument that Revelation's anti-imperial critique can be a positive resource for ecological reflection see Rossing, "River," and Rossing, "For the Healing."

A key text is Rev 11:18, in which Revelation proclaims not that "the time has come to destroy the earth" but that "the time has come . . . to destroy the *destroyers* of the earth," that is, the Roman Empire.

This is quite different from the perspective of 2 Peter 3, a chapter that I have come to view as the most ecologically problematic chapter in the entire New Testament. I regularly receive emails from Christians asking for help in dealing with 2 Peter's image of planetary conflagration. Second Peter makes extensive references to God's plan for a fiery end to the planet, warning that "the present heavens and earth have been reserved for fire" (3:7) and that when the day of the Lord comes, the "heavens will be set ablaze and dissolved, and the elements will melt with fire" (3:12).

This epistle draws an analogy between the Genesis flood and end-times fire: Just as the world (*kosmos*) that existed at the time of Noah and the flood was deluged by water and destroyed, so too the present heavens and earth (*ge*) are destined for fire and destruction (3:6–7). The King James and Revised Standard Versions include an additional reference to fire at the end of verse 10 that has been modified in the NRSV on the basis of manuscript evidence. The text-critical question is whether the earth and the works that are in it "shall be burned up" (*katakaesetai*, KJV, RSV) or "shall be disclosed" (*heurethesetai*, NRSV).[9] Even without this additional reference to fire in verse 10, there is more than enough burning in 2 Peter 3 to fuel end-time speculations!

Most problematic from an ecological viewpoint is that 2 Peter not only describes the fiery destruction, it actually calls on believers to "hasten" (*speudontas*) the day when the creation will be set ablaze:

> Since all these things are to be dissolved in this way, what sort of persons ought you to be in leading lives of holiness and godliness, waiting for and hastening the coming of the day of God, because of which the heavens will be set ablaze and dissolved, and the elements will melt with fire? (2 Pet 3:11–12)

This call to readers to "hasten" the day makes the burning of the planet not just a far-off future scenario. Rhetorically, it functions to bring the future burning into the present, giving an active role to readers. Today, in the face of nuclear proliferation and global warming, 2 Peter 3:11–12 risks becoming a terrifying, self-fulfilling prophecy.

---

9. See discussion in Metzger, *Textual*, 706.

Throughout Christian history, 2 Peter's scenario of end-times burning has spawned a potent legacy that continues today.[10] When parents in
the Seattle suburb of Federal Way succeeded in blocking the showing of
Al Gore's film *An Inconvenient Truth* in public schools on the grounds
that "The Bible says that in the end times everything will burn up," they
were referring to 2 Peter.[11] Televangelist Jerry Falwell likewise appealed
to fiery imagery to debunk global warming in a February 25, 2007, sermon: "The earth will go up in dissolution from severe heat. The environ-
mentalists will be really shook up, then, because God is going to blow it
all away, and bring down new heavens and new earth."[12] While Falwell
himself did not equate global warming with the end-times fire of 2 Peter,
other Christians draw that equation. A forum on the WorldNetDaily
website called "The Great Global Warming Debate," which discusses
whether or not global warming is human-caused, contained this post:

> God planned for global warming even He created this planet.
> . . . Please consider with me God's words recorded in the third
> chapter of Second Peter in verses 10 and 12: "But the day of the
> Lord will come as a thief in the night; in which the heavens shall
> pass away with a great noise, and the elements shall melt with
> fervent heat, the earth also and the works that are therein shall
> be burnt up."

Similarly, on a website titled GotQuestions.org, an answer to the
question "How should a Christian view global warming?" cites 2 Peter's
fiery vision to claim that "The Bible does in fact mention a form of
'global warming.' 2 Peter 3:7–13, 'By the same word the present heavens
and earth are reserved for fire, being kept for the day of judgment and
destruction of ungodly men. . . . The heavens will disappear with a roar;
the elements will be destroyed by fire.'"[13]

It is not just fundamentalists who have speculated on the fiery
destruction of creation described in 2 Peter 3. A trajectory of interpretation, beginning in the second century, developed from this text and

10. Some fundamentalist preachers applied the "dissolving" and "melting with fire" of 2 Pet 3:10 to the nuclear bombs dropped on Hiroshima and Nagasaki; see Boyer, *When*, 116–20.

11. McClure and Stiffler, "Federal Way."

12. Falwell, "Myth."

13. Got Questions Ministries, "How?"

has continued to influence Christian understandings of the end.[14] One Lutheran professor describes the prevalence of 2 Peter 3 in the church of her childhood: "I often heard missionaries speak of the end times. It was still their urgent mission to hasten the day of the Lord, when, as 2 Peter says, the heavens will be set ablaze and the elements will melt with fire. They looked for it, prayed for it, and worked for it with all their hearts, even on the prairies of North Dakota."[15]

I have pondered the emails and questions from ecologically concerned Christians asking what to do with 2 Peter 3. Many churches' lectionaries assign this text to be read during the season of Advent.[16] We cannot simply ignore 2 Peter 3 and its apocalyptic imagery of a divinely ignited burning planet. But we must also insist that 2 Peter not become the lens through which the rest of New Testament apocalypticism is read.

For preachers and others who grapple with this text, I offer these suggestions: First, we should not attempt to harmonize the New Testament's various apocalyptic cosmologies. The idea of a fiery eschatological conflagration that consumes the entire planet at the end of the world is found only in 2 Peter, an epistle written in the earth second century or possibly the end of the first century by a pseudonymous author.[17] Other biblical texts use the image of a refiner's fire or the fire of purification. But no other New Testament text speaks of a total world-destroying fire, and certainly no other text exhorts believers to hasten the day of burning.[18]

Some scholars claim that 2 Peter 3 draws on a Jewish apocalyptic strand that envisions two destructions—one destruction by water in the past, the Noahic flood, and a future destruction by fire—but this tradi-

14. For example, Apoc. Pet. 5 expands on the fiery imagery of 2 Peter 3, as does 2 Clem. 16:3. See discussion of the origins and development of the cosmic conflagration tradition by Thiede, "Pagan."

15. Grindal, "Hastening," 34.

16. In the Revised Common Lectionary, 2 Pet 3:8–15 is assigned for the Second Sunday of Advent in Year B. I urge preachers to take on this text and preach against the notion of a fiery destruction as being God's will for the earth.

17. Raymond Brown dates 2 Peter to 130 CE, on the basis of its distance from the apostolic generation and its knowledge of an established collection of Paul's letters (*Introduction*, 767); other scholars date it somewhat earlier. See, for example, Elliott, "Second Epistles of Peter," 282–87; Kittredge, "2 Peter."

18. First Enoch 10–11 envisions the fallen Watchers being consumed by fire, but it is the destruction of the *wicked* by fire, not of the *world*. This is the case also for other biblical texts often cited as antecedents for the conflagration imagery of 2 Peter 3.

tion is late.[19] A more probable source of influence is the Greco-Roman philosophical notion of *ekpyrosis* or world-destroying fire, a much-discussed topic in pagan philosophical debates dating back to Plato's *Timaeus*.[20] The author of 2 Peter may have transposed the Jewish notion of the burning of the *wicked* into the more Greek notion of the burning of the *whole created order* as part of his effort to convince a Gentile audience that God is indeed involved in history. The second-century theologian Justin Martyr, for example, makes reference to the well-known Stoic version of conflagration in delineating his own Christian version of end-times fire.[21]

Later in the second century, however, when the idea of an end-times cosmic conflagration became a favorite notion of the Valentinians and other Gnostics who thought of the created world as evil, theologians such as Irenaeus and Origen distanced themselves from this tradition.[22] The important point to note is that already in the second century, Christians realized that there are different trajectories of apocalyptic speculation, and the trajectory of a world-destroying fire ran the risk of being used in a Gnostic, world-denying way. Cosmic conflagration traditions are not shared by Revelation or any other New Testament texts.[23]

Second, we should note that even within the polemics of 2 Peter, cosmic speculation about the burning of creation is secondary to the main point of the letter.[24] While many fundamentalists today fixate on the chronology of end-times burning, that is not at all the intended focus of 2 Peter. Rather, the letter uses such end-times threats as a tool to exhort individual sinners to repentance. The epistle's references to the coming

19. See, for example, Josephus, *Antiquities of the Jews* 1.70–71. In Richard Bauckham's view (*2 Peter*, 300), the author of 2 Peter follows an unknown Jewish apocalyptic source for chapter 3, from which he adopted the imagery. But Bauckham cites no evidence for this "Jewish notion of two universal judgments" (both flood and fire) prior to Josephus and Philo, both of whom may be influenced by Hellenistic tradition.

20. For the thesis that 2 Peter is arguing with Greco-Roman converts who are steeped in the Greek idea of *ekpyrosis*, either through Epicureanism or, simply, Stoicism, see Fornberg, *Early Church*, 67 n. 7; Thiede, "Pagan."

21. Justin Martyr, *First Apology* 1.20, 1.60; *Second Apology* 7: "We say there will be the conflagration, but not as the Stoics, according to their doctrine of all things being changed into one another."

22. Irenaeus, *Adv. Haer.* 1.7.1; Origen, *Contra Celsum*, 4.11.79.

23. David Aune calls it "striking" that "a destruction of the cosmos by fire is not mentioned" in Rev 21:1 or anywhere else in Revelation. Aune, *Revelation 17–22*, 1117.

24. See Russell, "*New Heavens*," 188.

burning of creation address a situation where "scoffers" (2 Pet 3:3–4) have apparently latched onto the continuity of God's care for creation to mean that they can do whatever they want because there is never going to be a judgment day.[25] It is in response to these scoffers that 2 Peter unleashes threats of burning, not out of a desire to see the planet burn per se, but rather in order to assure scoffers that there will be a "day of judgment and destruction of the godless" in the future, just as God sent a destructive flood in the past (2 Pet 3:5–7). God's patience in delaying the day of the Lord should not be used as justification for complacency, but rather as evidence for God's graciousness (2 Pet 3:9).

Most problematic is the exhortation to "hasten" the day of the Lord and the burning of the planet—a verse that must be regarded as a text of terror in our age of nuclear weapons as well as global warming (2 Pet 3:12). This verse should probably not be read in churches' lectionaries as the word of the Lord. To be sure, the notion of hastening the day of the Lord does not counsel a cavalier "bring it on" attitude toward the fiery destruction, even if, in light of our acceleration of global warming today, it could be tempting to take it that way.

Hastening the day of the Lord has rather the sense of "active waiting," as one Latin American liberation scholar has suggested; it is part of the letter's overall strategy of "resistance."[26] Other scholars emphasize that "hastening" is the "corollary" to the assertion in 2 Pet 3:9 that God defers the *parousia* out of a desire for Christians to repent, the idea being that believers' repentance and good works could hasten the Lord's return.[27] Nevertheless, in order for this to become a liberating text, sinners who repent would have to be provided with something analogous to the ark that saved Noah and his family from drowning in the flood. But neither Noah nor the ark is mentioned in this chapter of 2 Peter, only a total end-times burning of the earth, the heavens, and all the elements. As we face the prospect of global warming that will irreversibly endanger the entire planet, perhaps we need to shift our interpretation of the Genesis

25. Jerome Neyrey and others who examine the polemic of 2 Peter in the context of ancient debates between philosophical schools in the Greco-Roman world find that an attack upon those who deny divine judgment closely resembles the apology against Epicurean polemics against providence. See Neyrey, "Form."

26. See Rodriguez, "Wait," 202.

27. See Kelly, *Commentary*, 367; Bauckham, *2 Peter*, 325.

flood story away from 2 Peter, so that we begin to view the renewed earth itself as our ark.

All the fiery rhetoric of 2 Peter leads up to the final promise of the new heavens and new earth: "In accordance with his promise, we wait for new heavens and a new earth, where righteousness is at home" (2 Pet 3:13, NRSV). The "new heavens and new earth" reference has led some scholars to argue that 2 Peter shares with Revelation a notion of the transformation of the planet rather than its total annihilation.[28] In their view, the analogy of the fiery end-times conflagration to the Genesis flood means that 2 Peter does not have in mind the total obliteration of the creation, but only its purification, since the Noahic flood did not completely destroy the plants, sea creatures, and the earth. But this letter does not develop the theme of new heavens and earth in any positive way, except as a reward for the righteous after the wicked have been destroyed. As Ernst Käsemann points out in his critique of the theology of 2 Peter, "This eschatology only presents us with a straightforward doctrine of retribution."[29]

Aside from the reference to "new heavens and a new earth," chapter 3 of 2 Peter has little in common with Revelation, despite apparent similarities. Even the exhortations to repentance function quite differently—perhaps not surprisingly, since 2 Peter was probably written later.[30] While 2 Peter shares with Revelation, and most other apocalyptic texts, the element of exhortation, 2 Peter focuses much more on an individualistic moralism than on the anti-imperial exhortation of Revelation. Only individuals are addressed in 2 Peter's exhortations and references to the Genesis flood.

As Elisabeth Schüssler Fiorenza has pointed out, apocalyptic language can function in two ways, either to control the behavior of individuals or to provide an alternative vision and encouragement of new community structures in the face of oppression.[31] These observations allow us to recognize that 2 Peter definitely represents the moralistic

28. Gale Z. Heide suggests that 2 Peter and 2 Clement might share the notion of a purging fire of judgment rather than an all-consuming fire, since 2 Clem 16:3 says that only *some* of the heavens will melt at the day of judgment ("What is New?" 51n42).

29. Käsemann, "Apologia," 181.

30. Most scholars date Revelation to the mid-90s, although an earlier date may also be possible.

31. Fiorenza, "Phenomena," 313.

use of apocalyptic threats to control individual behavior. By contrast, Revelation targets its primary threats of judgment against the system and structures of empire, especially the economic system (Revelation 18). The New Jerusalem vision (Revelation 21–22) serves to encourage people toward citizenship in God's counter-imperial polis. The book exhorts God's people to "come out" of empire (Rev 18:4) so that they can enter into God's city of blessing and promise.

To summarize: Within the spectrum of early Christian apocalyptic literature, Revelation and 2 Peter represent two very different eschatological perspectives on the *end*. Whereas 2 Peter envisions an end to the earth and the whole created world, Revelation envisions an imminent end to the Roman imperial world.

END OF EMPIRE, NOT THE END OF THE CREATED WORLD

This crucial distinction between the *end of empire* and the *end of the created world* is one that I believe can serve us in these next years. Public theologians and biblical scholars will need to articulate this distinction much more forcefully in order to equip people of faith to address the crises of empire today, manifested in global climate change as well as attendant crises such as "peak oil" (the projected decline of world oil production as supplies become depleted), deforestation, water shortages, and the environmental justice crises being experienced by vulnerable communities throughout the world. What must come to an end today may well be the unsustainable way of life in U.S. culture—a carbon-addicted way of life that could be defined as the most dangerous manifestation of empire today—but not the earth itself. Our task as public scholars will be to lift up New Testament end-of-empire discourses to help people envision life beyond this empire, articulating the Bible's joyful and compelling visions for abundant life in local communities as counter-visions to imperial violence and exploitation.

The New Testament is full of end-of-empire discourses, as Richard Horsley has helped us to see. Horsley is a pioneer among biblical scholars who have emphasized the anti-imperial, political strategies of the Jesus movement.[32] Through their work on the first-century Roman imperial context of Galilee, Judea, and Asia Minor, Horsley and others have demonstrated that the terminology of empire is everywhere in the New

32. Dart, "Up Against Caesar," 20.

Testament. New Testament authors redefine and subvert political terms such as "gospel" (*euangelion*), "savior" (*soter*), and "kingdom" (*basilea*) in deliberately counter-imperial ways.

Another imperial term employed by the New Testament is *oikoumene*. Standard English translations of this term simply as "world" or "inhabited world" mask the aggressively imperial cast this term had taken on by the time of Augustus, as evidenced in imperial propaganda asserting Rome's dominance over the whole *oikoumene* through military, political and economic means.[33] We should translate *oikoumene* as "empire."

Luke Johnson argued already in 1991 that *oikoumene* should be translated as "empire" rather than "world" in birth and temptation narratives in the Gospel of Luke (2:1, the imperial census; 4:5, the "kingdoms of the empire"), as well as in some of the conflict scenes of Acts (11:28; 17:6; 24:5). But Johnson did not extend the translation of *oikoumene* as "empire" into passages about the *oikoumene* falling under judgment or coming to an end.[34]

In my view, the translation of *oikoumene* as "empire" should be applied also to the New Testament end-times discourses. When the Gospel of Luke uses the *oikoumene* in the context of end-times tribulations that will come upon the nations ("There will be distress of nations ... people fainting with fear and foreboding of what is coming upon the *oikoumene*," Luke 21:25–26), this text signals the end of *empire*, not the end of the physical, created world. Similarly, in Revelation, the "hour of trial that is coming upon the whole *oikoumene*" (Rev 3:10) should be read not so much as a general end-times tribulation that God will inflict upon the planet earth to destroy it, as many of today's fundamentalists like to claim, but more pointedly as the time of trial or judgment that God will bring upon the entire Roman Empire and on all those who benefit from Rome's injustice. Two other uses of *oikoumene* in Revelation (Rev 12:9; 16:14) are also anti-imperial, drawing on highly mythological language

33. See Nicolet, *Space*. See also, Rossing, "(Re)Claiming," for first-century Roman imperial texts.

34. Johnson, *Gospel*. Johnson translates *oikoumene* as "empire" in Luke 2:1; 4:5; and Acts 11:28; 17:6; 24:5, but not in Luke 21:26 ("inhabited world"), Acts 17:31 ("world"), or Acts 19:27 ("inhabited world").

of beasts and dragons to counter Rome's own mythological claims of omnipotence.[35]

As we face the global warming crisis, this distinction between the end of empire (*oikoumene*) and end of the created world (*kosmos* and *ge*) will become crucial. Our unsustainable way of life—the empire of a carbon-consuming system that is destroying the earth and endangering its most vulnerable people—must come to an end. But from a biblical perspective, end of empire does not have to mean the end of the physical, created world.

Indeed, Revelation, perhaps more than any other New Testament text, helps us envision this distinction between empire and the created world, with its picture of the millennium in chapter 20, after the destruction of Babylon/Rome in Revelation 17–18. Revelation introduces the millennium as a symbolic thousand-year period of time after Satan has been tied up, that is, after the fall of empire (Rev 20:4). Such an image is not meant to furnish a literal chronology of linear time. The entire book presents us with "vision time," as Steven Friesen describes it, the journey-like experience in which Revelation moves between "different phases of historical time and records them in a disorienting fashion."[36] The millennium of Revelation represents what Friesen calls "vindication time" for the victims of Roman imperial rule, a concrete period of time after the fall of the Roman Empire.[37] Pablo Richard's interpretation of the millennium of Revelation 20 as "not a chronology but a logic" can be helpful.[38] The important point is that Revelation teaches a logic that embraces life on earth beyond empire, that is, after the satanic power of empire has been dethroned.

Other New Testament texts share the conviction of Revelation that the old imperial order was passing away, and the realm of God was already dawning on earth in Jesus Christ. Apocalyptic language of the *end* seems deliberately chosen to counter Rome's imperial and eschatological

35. As a prelude to the exposé of Roman imperial power in chapter 13, Satan is called the "deceiver of the whole *oikoumene*" (Rev 12:9). The fall of Babylon/Rome in Revelation 17–18 is preceded by a description of its own vassals, the "kings of the whole *oikoumene*," assembling for battle (Rev 16:14).

36. Friesen, *Imperial*, 158.

37. Other Jewish apocalypses such as 2 Baruch and 4 Ezra similarly depict a time between the destruction of the Roman Empire and the final judgment of humanity, although "their handling of the theme is much different" (Friesen, *Imperial*, 160).

38. Richard, *Apocalypse*, 157.

claims to eternal hegemony, and to underscore the urgent advent of a new age.[39]

THE URGENCY OF THE PRESENT MOMENT: TIME FOR REPENTANCE AND PUBLIC TESTIMONY

Time is of the essence in Revelation. But interestingly, the book's perspective is not simply of time hurtling towards an inevitable end. Rather, Revelation puts great emphasis on the present moment as a moment for decision and repentance. Shifts from past tense to present and future tenses, along with calls for repentance and use of deliberative rhetoric, all serve to draw the audience into what Harry Maier calls "an abiding sense of the imminent," extending the urgency of the present moment.[40] The entire book of Revelation calls on the audience to "come out" of empire before it is too late (Rev 18:4), in order not to fall prey to the catastrophic judgment and plagues, in order not to share in the collapse of the empire.

Revelation's focus on the urgency of the present moment as a time for repentance and testimony is an aspect of the book that can help us face the crisis of global warming. Scientists tell us that halting carbon emissions at 440 parts per million is possible with existing technology. What is needed is massive public, political commitment that would undertake the actions necessary to reduce carbon emissions by 80–90 percent by the year 2050, with a 50 percent reduction by 2020. How do we mobilize that massive public, political commitment?

Repentance is the first action for which Revelation calls. The writer of Revelation believes that people can still make the changes necessary to "come out" of empire. It is not too late for repentance. To be sure, the book's positive calls for repentance (the imperative of *metanoeson* ["repent"]) are concentrated in the seven opening letters (for example, Rev 2:5, 16; 3:3, 19), whereas later references to repentance are phrased negatively ("they did not repent from . . ." Rev 9:20–21; 16:9, 11). Yet Schüssler Fiorenza has made a persuasive case that even these negative references to repentance in chapter 9 serve as part of the book's rhetori-

---

39. David M. Rhoads offers an important reading of the New Testament "as a manual for facing a possible end to the world," in order to learn from the behavior of early Christians how we might respond to the ecological crisis today. See Rhoads, "Who," 83–85.

40. Maier, *Apocalypse*, 147.

cal appeal to the audience to repent.[41] Moreover, in a departure from the book's extensive use of the exodus story, hearts are never hardened in Revelation. Rather, Revelation 11 lifts up a concrete model of successful repentance, with the "rest" of the people who heeded the testimony of the two witnesses and "gave glory to God" (Rev 11:13).

The book describes plagues that contribute to the call for repentance. They project out into the future the logical consequences of the trajectory that Rome is on, so people can see in advance where the dangerous imperial path is taking them. The terrible calamities of ecological disaster that are described as befalling the earth, rivers, and oceans are not intended as *predictions* of future events that God has preordained *must* happen to the world. The plagues serve rather as warnings, as wake-up calls, like Ebenezer Scrooge's visionary journeys in Charles Dickens's *A Christmas Carol*, where Scrooge is shown horrifying future scenarios not because they must happen, but so that he can alter the course of his life.[42]

We, too, need to alter the course of our life before it is too late.

Even nature itself participates in the warning of the plagues, crying out about the consequences of the deadly actions of imperial oppressors. When waters and springs turn to blood in the third bowl plague, the angel ("messenger") of the waters interprets this through the logic of natural consequences, as a boomerang-like effect: "You are just, O Holy One . . . for you have judged these things. Because they shed the blood of saints and prophets, you have given them blood to drink. It is axiomatic (*axios estin*)" (Rev 16:6). Today, what is axiomatic is that if we continue on our perilous path we will bring about our own demise.

Although the end of the empire is inevitable and axiomatic, the destruction seems to be deliberately delayed in Revelation so that the audience can come out of empire, and so it can have the opportunity to give public testimony. Analyzing what he calls Revelation's "games with time," Maier argues that Revelation makes ingenious use of delay in order to open up the present moment as a time for decision on the part of readers: "Like advertising with its urgent appeal to buy 'while quantities last,'" the Apocalypse "uses the threat of an imminent end to break open

41. Fiorenza, *Revelation*, 72.

42. Rossing, *Rapture*, 85, 91.

an urgent reconfiguration of the present." Revelation offers a kind of never-ending "'not yet' that insists on present action."[43]

Testimony or witness (*martyria*) is the second action to which Revelation calls the community, following the model of the testimony of Jesus the Lamb. "Testimony is not just any word, but a public word," Pablo Richard explains, drawing on his experience of resistance in Latin America. "In Revelation, testimony always has a power to change history, both in heaven and on earth."[44] Revelation places the Christian community in the role of the two witnesses of chapter 11, "calling for a witness of active, nonviolent resistance to Rome's claim of lordship over human history," as Brian Blount argues in *Can I Get a Witness?*[45] Perhaps the analogy today would be the call for a massive witness of active non-violent resistance to the dominating claim of carbon consumption over human history.

"Can I get a witness?" The question that Brian Blount hears at the heart of Revelation is a question we must ask today. We are called to give witness or testimony to the stories of those most affected by climate change—people in the island nations of Kirabati or Tuvalu who have done nothing to cause this crisis, but who will lost their island homes because of our carbon emissions; people in Bhutan in the Himalayas who risk being killed by "glacial lake outburst floods" because of glaciers melting that have never melted before; people in Chicago and other major U.S. urban areas where asthma deaths will rise, aggravated by higher summer temperatures; people in Africa and Central America who will become climate refugees because of severe drought and drinking water shortages. We are called to witness to Revelation's urgent wake-up call, as well as its vision for justice and the healing of the world.

Public testimony must call upon the world, and especially its richest nations, to change our addiction to a carbon-consuming way of life, so that hundreds of millions of people, and creation itself, can live.

It is not yet too late for us to "come out" of this empire. But scientists tell us—and I believe them—that we probably have less than ten years to do so.

43. Maier, *Apocalypse*, 130–31.
44. Richard, *Apocalypse*, 33.
45. Blount, *Can I Get?* 40.

6

Turning the Tables

War, Peace, and the Last Supper

JAMES E. BRENNEMAN

BANQUET OF CONSEQUENCES

ROBERT LOUIS STEVENSON ONCE wrote, "Sooner or later, everybody sits down to a banquet of consequences." For Jesus and his disciples, the Last Supper was one such banquet. The consequences of that meal have stretched across time and into eternity itself. In that ritual meal, Jesus turned the tables on all victory banquets written about and experienced before and since.[1] To the degree that the patterns, protocols, rules, roles, and religious beliefs associated with eating and drinking are windows on the values and norms of our social relationships and society at large, it is not inconsequential that Jesus instituted a ritual of memory and hope while sharing a meal with his followers.[2] The ritual as practiced in almost all settings throughout history has mostly focused on the degree to which the divine presence is present in the communion elements themselves, or the degree to which this meal is important as part of the salvation story (*heilsgeschicthe*) for individual participants, or the degree to which the meal is a communally defining event regulated by catechetical entrance exams, predetermined sanctioned experiences (like baptism) or the degree to which it is open to all.

---

1. Josephine Ford first used the familiar phrase "turn the tables on" to refer to the reversal of the expected table etiquette assumed in Luke's Great Banquet parable in Luke 14. More below.

2. Douglas, "Deciphering," 69–70.

Ironically, participants in the Eucharistic meal have rarely, if ever, connected their liturgical practice to the politics of war, ancient or otherwise. Could it be that as important as other understandings of this sacred meal are in the life of the church, when understood and practiced in its eschatological context, this meal declares its primary and most powerful purpose to be an act of prophetic and political peacemaking?

VICTORY BANQUETS

On May 9, 1945, in the very room in which Germany officially surrendered to the allied forces twenty-four hours earlier, a glorious victory banquet was thrown in honor of the Supreme Allied Commander, General Dwight D. Eisenhower. The banquet was glorious, the cuisine rich, the bread and wine superb, the guest list carefully selected to ensure Russian, American, French, and British officers of notoriety were present. Marshall Gregory Zhukov, the most decorated soldier in Russian and Soviet history and host of the evening's festivities, offered up his second of twenty-four toasts to General Eisenhower. His first toast had naturally gone to his commander and chief, Joseph Stalin.[3] There would be many victory feasts, parades, and joyful celebrations throughout the Allied nations as the news of victory settled in.

Victory banquets, as such, are as old as time. Cato, a second-century BCE Roman philosopher, soldier, and poet, made note of how the rules of war with their elitist hierarchies played themselves out in exclusive society banquets of the time, but even more so in victory banquets. At these great feasts, he opined, "the ancestors would sing and toast the best among them." In the victory banquets, toasts would go up to "the great deeds of manly men."[4]

The Trojan War could trace its cause to a banquet of another sort, the wedding banquet. Peleus and Thetis had failed to invite to their feast, Eris, the goddess of discord. Insulted, Eris crashed the wedding banquet, threw down the gauntlet (a golden apple) onto the table, which unleashed a torrent of reactions leading to war. By turns and times, Hrothgar threw an elaborate victory feast for Beowulf honoring his defeat of the monster Grendel. War and banquets, so it seems, go hand in hand.

3. Gilbert, *Day*, 352.
4. Sciarrino, "Temple," 47.

The victory banquet in Ancient Near Eastern literature was certainly a part of the near universal motif found in other cultures as well.[5] In the *Enuma Elish*, the Babylonian creation story, the god Marduk kills his own mother Tiamat in order to create the world and build Babylon out of her remains. In victory, he throws a great feast for the gods and other elites in the center of Babylon. Jugs of beer, loaves of bread, and fine food are set out for all present to enjoy. Likewise, after the Canaanite god Baal defeats the male god of watery chaos, Yam, Baal then throws a victory party with a very select invitation list: the gods and their earthly counterparts. Food and wine aplenty are brought out that only temporarily satiate the hunger for more war and the appetite for evermore prestige and glory, which, of course, promoting such was the very purpose of such bacchanals. Into this mix of warfare, bloody sacrifice, glorious victory, food, wine, and celebration, it should come as no surprise that the Bible's own narratives, intersect with these same themes in interesting and sometimes surprising ways.

The battle scene of Exodus 14–15 tells the tale of a final show down, a near cosmic battle between Israel's God of War and the mighty god Pharaoh. The Israelites, unable to break through the Egyptian frontier fortresses, had to turn back where they find themselves outflanked and trapped between the sea and Pharaoh's army. One of the great battle scenes of Scripture unfolds with Israel's God throwing Pharaoh's chariots and army into the sea. A "Battle Hymn of the Republic" (Exodus 15) is sung and danced to for generations to come declaring ultimately that "The Lord will reign forever and ever" (15:18). Certainly, the subsequent miraculous provision of quail, manna and water, the right to draft new legislation that shapes the emerging body politic (ten commandments), and the covenant ratifying ceremony thereafter, all speak to the divine right of conquering gods and kings. Often overlooked, but foreshadowing meal scenes to come, Exod 24:9–14 recounts how, with the defeat of Pharaoh behind them, Moses, Aaron and seventy elders of Israel go up the sacred mountain to meet the Lord in person. Using images that later apocalyptic writers' embrace, the Lord meets them on a street paved with pure sapphire stone and there shares a meal with them (v. 11). Soon after, in another divine theophany in the midst of fire, smoke, clouds, and glorious drama (24:15–18) for the next forty days and nights Moses is given the architectural design to the tabernacle, the ark

5. For what follows, see Niditch, *War*, 38–40.

of the Covenant (in which leftover manna is placed) and all the sacred vessels and furniture including a table on which the "bread of Presence" or "holy bread" is placed before God as a perpetual sacrifice (Exodus 25–27). When coupled with the required annual ritual of the Passover Meal celebrating the Lord's victory over Pharaoh, the exodus narrative sets the stage in the rest of Scripture to celebrate Israel's victory over the final defeat of her enemies by perpetual and ritual victory banquets of one kind or another.

LAST SUPPERS

One clear development in Scripture positions Israel's God as greater still than the God of exodus fame, the Conqueror of Egypt. In time, Israel's God would become known as the Lord and Master of all the nations of the world. Indeed, stretching the reader's imagination to its limits, portions of the book of Isaiah (13–35) picture God, Immanuel, as the eschatological, cosmic, universal ruler.[6] Front and center of that eschatological vision, the "Lord of the Armies" throws an amazing, mouth-watering "feast of fatness" and "feast of wine" for "all the peoples" of the world (25:6). Even more exhilarating and worthy of a victory toast, God swallows up forever the last and ruling fate of all humanity, Death itself![7] And then in tenderness wipes every tear from every eye (25:8). The mother of all battles is followed by the mother of all victory banquets at the end of time giving ultimate meaning to the description "the Last Supper."

Elsewhere in biblical literature, the prophet Ezekiel describes a divine victory banquet every bit as gruesome as any war epic depicted in today's movie theatres. Serving as God's eschatological war correspondent, Ezekiel describes in apocalyptic language a cataclysmic battle against God's people living peacefully in the promised land (Ezekiel 38–39). In an account worthy of a Pulitzer Prize, the reader is told of

6. Isaiah 24–27 has been identified in generic terms as "Isaiah's Apocalypse." However, the scholarly consensus has shifted to the term "prophetic eschatology" as a more accurate description of these chapters. Either way, since there is a complete lack of historical allusions in these four chapters, the overall literary thrust is easily projected onto some far off future, some ultimate reality, later associated with the end of time.

7. Possible allusions to the Canaanite high god Baal swallowing up the god of death, *Mot*. Note also, the Aztec cosmic vision in which Death was transformed into a source of cosmic energy in the context of a violent ritual contest in which the winner, in a highly honored act of self-sacrifice, gives his heart over to satiate divine hunger. See, Montoya, *Theology*, 20.

God's annihilation of Gog, the mighty king of Magog, mythic aggressor from some unknown nether region of the North. After the battle, Ezekiel reports that the Lord God assembles the people of Israel to a "great sacrificial feast on the mountains of Israel" to "eat the flesh of the mighty" and "drink the blood of the princes of the earth" (39:17–19). Clearly, the hunger for war, death, sacrifice, blood, and victory combined with eating and drinking to one's satisfaction and joy runs deep in the mythical and eschatological universe of Israel.[8]

Insofar as a future vision helps give shape to current realities, and it does, then an eschatological projection (*telos*) of a "last" victory supper portrayed in Scripture invites us to consider the meaning of any such reenactments in our own lives, including the remembering of the "last supper" of Jesus with his disciples in the Eucharistic meal.[9]

Robert Cahill, in his book *The Gift of the Jews*, argues that the only truly unique and new idea in all the world of ideas is the concept of linear time. For Cahill, this was the great gift of the Jews, beginning with Abraham and Sarah, who broke the never-ending, eternally returning, cyclical worldview by obeying God's call to a future born only by promise.[10] From that point on, throughout the rest of Scripture and history, future visions of possible and promised outcomes are imagined by prophets, priests, kings, teachers, gospel writers and others. It is no great methodological leap then, to argue here for what has popularly been called elsewhere, the "purpose-driven life." Normative claims about Christian practices in general, and the Lord's Supper, in particular, should give special weight to eschatological perspectives in Scripture, since such future oriented accounts provide the purpose (*telos*) or ultimate context for understanding such claims.

It is quite surprising then that few, if any, creeds, confessions, or doctrines associated with explaining the meaning and practice of the Eucharist *begin* with biblical end-of-days texts about heavenly or ulti-

8. See also Jer 46:10; Isa 34:2–8; 51:17–22; Ps 74:13–14; 23:5 as examples of banquet motifs associated with war. In the banquet scene described in Isa 55:1–3 precedent is set for the later overturning of established invitation lists in standard victory banquets. The prophet invites those who thirst and those without money to come.

9. A more practice-based, personal account of understanding Holy Communion as an open, inclusive *missional* practice can be found in Brenneman, "Missional," 158–66. Some of what follows here is found there, though here I reflect on the eschatological, war and peacemaking backdrop to the Eucharist not articulated there.

10. Cahill, *Gift*, 5.

mate table scenes in some future kingdom of God.[11] And yet, these very eschatological meal scenes might well be the normative lens through which one best understands other meal scenes in Scripture, including the Lord's "Last" Supper. At the very least, one must not relegate these eschatological meal scenes to mere footnotes in any discussion of the meaning and practice of Holy Communion.

To add credence to precedent, even a cursory reading of the main Eucharistic and other meal texts of the New Testament underscores their eschatological significance. In every case, whether in the recorded words of Jesus, himself, in other gospel accounts of the Lord's Supper, in parables describing a variety of dining experiences, or in the Apostle Paul's Communion catechism, an eschatological dimension provides the essential horizon.[12] Indeed, the final book of the Bible, the book of Revelation, climaxes in a great wedding feast in which all who overcome are invited and a great toast in the form of a hymn is made to the victorious Lord God Almighty who rules forever and ever.[13] The rabbinical literature of this same period and later also echoes the eschatological nature of a great banquet where God "at the last coming" prepares an endless feast and reclines at table with a resurrected Adam and Eve, the matriarchs and patriarchs, and all the righteous in a renewed Garden of Eden.[14]

TURNING THE TABLES

The book of Luke is structured around common meals that Jesus shared with others.[15] In addition, Josephine Ford has argued convincingly that

11. To cite one example among others, the *Confession of Faith in a Mennonite Perspective*, while citing Luke 14, the Great Banquet scene, in its scriptural references for Article 12 on the Lord's Supper, it does so only as a final cursory point, not as a driving force for understanding the meaning of other meal scenes in Scripture or in how that might influence actual practice. John Howard Yoder argues in his book *Body Politics* that the first and primary meaning of the Lord's Supper—when not read "anachronistically through later creedal formulations"—was a simple, common meal meant to invoke memories of Jesus with his disciples.

12. Matt 24:31//Mark 13:27; Matt 26:29//Mark 14:25; Matt 25:10; Luke 12:37; Luke 13:29–30//Matt 8:11; Luke 14:18–24//Matt 22:2–14; Luke 16:22; Luke 22:29–30; 16–18; 1 Cor 11:26.

13. Rev 19:1–9; cf. Rev. 2:7

14. *Exodus Rabba* 25, 16:4; 2 Esdras 2:38; *Midrash Esther* 1:4; Ethiopian *Enoch* 62:14.

15. Moessner, *Lord*.

one of Luke's primary goals in writing his gospel was to persuade his readers to reject violence and believe in the peacemaking lordship of Christ.[16] It stands to reason that the breaking of bread, symbolically as in life, was for Luke a key to his understanding of making peace. Nowhere is that so clearly indicated than in the table etiquette of Luke's Great Banquet parable (Luke 14:15–24). [17]

The invitation list to the Great Banquet in Luke's account is most unusual by most standards. Rankings at banquets in antiquity, especially those associated with victory in war, are no different really than rankings on the battlefield, itself. Around the table, the elite affirm their positions relative to their social standing in society, not unlike military hierarchies do as standard practice in there own social matrices. The banquets serve as places to toast exploits, affirm social caste, and exclude the unworthy.

However, canonical groundwork had been laid for a more inclusive, upside-down invitation list already in the book of Isaiah. As we saw previously, Isaiah had dreamed of a time when God would spread out a wonderful victory feast for "all people," especially the poor and thirsty (Isa 25:6–7; 55:1–3).

Luke is certainly aware of this biblical precedent. Leading up to the Great Banquet parable in the later part of chapter 14, Luke first describes an incident where Jesus scandalously heals a man with leprosy while eating a meal at the home of one of the leaders of the Pharisees (14:1–6). Jesus then tells a parable whose purpose is meant to warn against claiming the privileged seats around the meal table, but rather in hosting meals one should invite the poor, the crippled, the lame, and blind (14:7–14). The conversation then shifts to the parable of a Great Banquet to be thrown in some future "kingdom of God." Jesus recounts how all the original invitees at the great feast—which we know from victory banquets elsewhere were typically the elite, the chosen, the "elect"—found reasons not to come. So, the host invites the "poor, the crippled, the blind, and the lame" to enjoy the feast at his expense (14:15–24). By all accounts, the great eschatological banquet of Luke turns the standard table hierarchies on their head. But, even more significant, Luke's Great Banquet parable turns out to be a prophetic challenge to the built-in, intrinsic violence associated with most, if not all, victory banquets before and since.

16. Ford, *Enemy*, 22. Also, Wood, *Perspectives*, 123.

17. For what follows, see Sanders, "Ethic," 106–20.

In his study of Luke's Great Banquet parable, James Sanders makes it patently clear that Luke had as his subtext the laws of warfare and conscription in the book of Deuteronomy, chapters 20–21.[18] A conscript in the army of the holy war of God could seek deferment from the battle-front based on four reasons: building a house not yet dedicated, planting a vineyard without benefit of reaping its first harvest, getting married without enjoying the honeymoon, and finally, lacking courage (20:5–8). Later midrashic literature around these holy war deferments indicate the first two excuses allowed for some variance between them, but usually referred to any preoccupation around material goods or commerce that might distract from being a dedicated soldier.[19] Leaving off the fourth excuse (loss of courage), a category Luke doesn't mention, the three excuses used by the invitees to Luke's Victory Banquet sound quite similar to the deferments to holy war listed in Deuteronomy: buying a field not yet inspected, buying oxen not yet examined, and dealing with a recent marriage.

Understood in the sequence of things, Luke's Great Banquet would have been seen by most readers of the time as a victory banquet prepared after the final eschatological holy war had been won. The great irony in Luke's version was that he believed Christ's first coming had moved the eschatological horizon forward and that Christ's messianic reign, the great day of Jubilee, had begun. He imagined that Christ, like a new Moses, had already miraculously fought the decisive battle for all time (cf. Luke 10:18, "I saw Satan fall like lightning from heaven"[20]). In ordinary circumstances, the elite, the chosen, the heroes of war, the elect would have been first in line to the Great Banquet. But instead, they made excuses seeing how they did not want to come to celebrate a war already won without need of them. Who would they toast, if not each other? As suggested by Ford, it's almost as if Jesus was saying to them in this parable, "You found a loophole using the legitimate laws of deferral as excuses for

---

18. Sanders, "Ethic," 110–11. The relation between battles and banquets, guest lists at the banquet, holy war legislation and categories for exemption are all given eschatological import in the literature at Qumran, whether in the *War Scroll* (1QM 10:5–6) or in the messianic banquet scene in the Rule of the Congregation (1 QSa 2:11–22). See also, Pseudipigrapha: 1 Enoch 62:14; 2 Enoch 42: 5; 3 Enoch 48:10a; 2 Esdras 2:38.

19. Sanders, "Ethic," 111 n. 15.

20. Girard, *I See Satan*, shows just how significant and table-turning this declaration of Christ's is, especially so, in that the tools of victory are manifest in the suffering and scandal of the cross.

not participating in God's nonviolent Victory Banquet."[21] Jesus had not invited his would be followers to war, but to an upside-down, inside-out Victory Banquet, a Table of Grace, around which everyone could gather, especially the poor, thirsty, weak, handicapped, unclean, and sinful. The banquet was open for anyone and everyone who responds to the grace full invitation. Here, says Josephine Ford, Luke "turned the tables," using holy war principles to argue for "peaceful kingdom inclusiveness."[22]

THE TABLE OF PEACE

The consequences of the eschatological horizon for the understanding and practice of the Lord's Table cannot be underestimated. From the perspective of God's *telos*, the Lord's Table will be first and foremost one of inclusive invitation in the broadest and most unexpected ways, thereby giving witness to the peaceful reign of God.

Standard orthodoxies tend to cite certain biblical texts as normative for understanding a more exclusive practice of the Lord's table over other texts that clearly suggest a more inclusive, open, invitational, educational approach to this church practice. If one reads the same texts through eschatological lenses, the authoritative weight often given to some texts over others shifts dramatically. Space does not allow for detailing these various shifts apparent in almost any creed or confession that also cites biblical prooftexts (in the best sense of that word) for its understanding.

An eschatological reading stance (hermeneutic) requires a transformation of some of our traditional interpretations of the practice of Holy Communion. Familiarity with traditional doctrinal statements regarding the meaning and practice of Holy Communion across the ecumenical spectrum, will, no doubt, help the reader recognize that a radically inclusive invitation to the Lord's Table departs significantly from some of the standard ways of understanding this church practice.[23] Especially

21. Ford, *Enemy*, 22. Here, I edited Ford's imagined quotation a bit.

22. Ibid. Also, Wood, *Perspectives*, 125. In the messianic banquet scenes in Qumran literature, the poor, crippled, lame, unclean, would have been the very ones excluded (1QM 7:4–6; 1 QSa. 2:6–10).

23. Eleanor Kreider, in *Communion*, provides an excellent survey of the Lord's Supper as understood and practiced across all traditions of modern Christianity from Orthodox to Roman Catholic, Anglican, Protestant, and Believers' Church movements. See also, Article 12 in *Confession*, 50–52.

important is the realization that the hierarchical gatekeepers controlling the rituals of Communion may be more a holdover of the control the social elites and military hierarchies undertook to claim their exclusive sitting arrangement in most victory banquet scenarios.

The eschatologically oriented communion service will be open to anyone who wishes to receive the grace of God's forgiveness and lead in its priestly services. Indeed, the very service of Communion can now be understood as an altar call in its own right led by a lay "priest." Such an egalitarian model allows for the possibility that a person coming to receive the bread of salvation and the cup of forgiveness will not *necessarily* have already committed oneself (in advance) to Christ *before* receiving Communion. The very act of coming to receive the cup of forgiveness may be the recipient's first act of confession before God. No longer will a defensible argument be made that only *our* type of Christian be allowed to participate, as some Christian traditions still practice.

The heavenly banquet scenarios of Scripture serve as warning to all would-be "insiders" defined by whatever orthodox standard or by whatever standard of orthopraxis, that they may be the very ones to lose a place at the Table if traditional hierarchies are insisted upon. One should take seriously the fact that in attendance at the Lord's Last Supper was Judas, the betrayer, and Peter, the denier. Even the other ten, before the night was over, would fall asleep in Christ's final hours or flee the scene completely to avoid the scandal of their association with Jesus. Are any of us that much different than these first disciples when it comes right down to it? In a sixteenth-century Anabaptist Communion liturgy, like so many other Eucharistic liturgies, the participants were very aware of their unworthiness to participate: "God be gracious to us sinners."[24] The Communion Table is a perpetual invitation to all who need God, period.

As a reenactment of the Passover Meal (Exod 12:1–23), which recalls the amazing victory of God over Pharaoh, as the sole warrior on behalf of his people, the Lord's Table bears witness (foreshadows) the ultimate defeat of evil and death by Christus Victor on behalf of all people. The irony of this Victory Banquet is its ultimately nonviolent character, at least as it eschews human participation in the battle. God alone fights.[25] Again, by design and fulfillment, the Lord's Table celebrates the upside-

24. Kreider, *Communion*, 278.

25. Lind, *Yahweh*.

down character of God's kingdom in the symbolism of Christ's body broken and blood shed, the Lord of the Banquet, as ultimate and final scapegoat, victim, and sacrifice. [26] The Table reveals the truth "hidden since the foundation of the world" that the escalating cycle of violence begun in primordial time in humanity's "fall to violence" reached its zenith and denouement in the scapegoating and judicial murder of God in Christ on a Roman cross.

Celebrating the Lord's Table is celebrating the unthinkable, though prophetically imagined, possibility that things might be different after all. As Robert Clouse notes in describing the eschatological features of the Lord's Supper, Christ's coming in the Eucharist is a most hopeful projection in our own temporal reality, a "throwing forward of Christ's final advent into the present."[27] In raising Christ from the dead in history and time, God has turned the tables on the violent assumptions and mechanism under girding all victory banquets before and since. Now the Apostle Paul's admonition that it is possible to "overcome evil with good" (Rom 12:21) in the context of the temptation to avenge oneself makes sense since ultimate evil has been overcome by ultimate good in Christ, thus "throwing forward" the eschatological hope as a real possibility in our own present reality.

An added dimension and beauty of the Passover reenactment is that it too is more expansive than many (most) Christian practices historically allow. Children are also welcome at the Lord's Table as full participants (Luke 22:1–23).[28] During the Last Supper as described by Luke, when Jesus uses the phrase "Do this in *remembrance* of me," the Greek word he uses for remembrance (*anamnesis*) is the same word that we associate with "mnemonic device." By using the bread and wine, Jesus was using mnemonic devices to get us to experience the meaning of his death through all of our senses: taste, touch, hearing, smell, sight.

Long before the days of multimedia, in the times of the Mishna, the Passover Meal or Seder was considered to be an audio-visual re-enactment of the liberation from Egypt *especially for* the children present at the meal. In some communities the father would dress up in white robes, holding a stick with an attached cloth and walk around the table chanting the passage, "We were slaves to pharaoh in Egypt . . ." The whole aim

---

26. Aulen, *Christus*; Girard, *Things Hidden*; see also, Weaver, *Nonviolent*.

27. Clouse, "Eschatology," 129–39.

28. Bieler and Schottroff, *Eucharist*, 54.

was—and continues to be—to stimulate the children to ask questions and get involved in the memory meal. The props—be it the Seder plate, or the cushions for leaning, the search for leavened bread, the search after the meal for the *afikomen*—are all there in order to arouse curiosity in children and to get them asking questions. It is most surprising then that in some Christian traditions, children have been excluded from the Lord's Table as they might have in the elite victory feasts of the ancient mythic accounts.

The rabbis declared, however, that "in each and every generation, a person is obligated to regard himself or herself as though he or she actually left Egypt. . . . As it says in Scripture," they would continue, "you shall tell your son or daughter on that day, 'It is because of this that God took *me* out of Egypt'" (Exod 13:8). The Passover and, later, the Lord's Supper were meant to be and continue to be hands-on interactive learning experiences for children, not just for adults. The Lord's Table can become a place where people of all ages come to experience the truth of God's love for them and come to understand the salvation story as their own. If God fought off Pharaoh on their behalf, will they not now question the temptation to enjoin any future battle in God's place? Perhaps so. Hopefully so.

Perhaps the time has come to include children of the church in the ongoing reenactment of the Passover meal, if indeed, as seems to be the case, one of its primary purposes has always been educational and invitational, a way of incorporating children into the salvation history of the people of God at the level of their understanding.[29] Why not invite children to ask the questions of purpose and meaning as might happen in the traditional Passover service? A child then and there would ask, "Why is this night different from all other nights?" A child here and now

29. Except for the Society of Friends, the Eucharist has not been an issue in which the Believers' churches differed from others as a *confessional* unity. The crises of origins among radical reformers or during the centuries since in the maintenance of distinctive identities was mostly around issues of baptism, not the Eucharist. Some Believers' churches felt "at home" in Zwinglian Communions, some did not. It is my contention that baptism is the primary means of symbolizing one's adult decision to follow Christ, whereas the Communion service is meant to be educational and invitational in its ethos. Even in the case of baptism, however, ecumenical Communions can appreciate the historical differences, but must also recognize the evolution of practice toward each others' perspectives. For example, infant dedications now happen in Believers' baptism traditions and confirmation is viewed as an integral means of appropriating one's faith among pedobaptists. See, Yoder, *Royal*, 282–88.

in a Christian service might ask, "Why is this meal different than other meals we eat?" The adult respondent might then repeat a very short version of the salvation story.

For all listening in, including the little ones, would be invited to imagine themselves as being relationally part of a grand metanarrative in which God alone fights, protects, and saves God's people. They might imagine, "We are the children of slavery set free from Pharaoh. We are feasting at the table with Jesus and the others in the Last Supper. We are children set free from bondage to sin, bondage to violence, and bondage to injustice. We are people of God's peace."

Holy Communion is a meal of memory, a gift passed along of profound identity and blessing to our children preparing them for the time when they will appropriate this belief by a more mature self-conscious decision followed by baptism. Would that the Table of the Lord be that place where we experience alongside our children that God is at table with us! The Lord's table is God's memory meal—a mnemonic device to remind us how Jesus ate and drank with sinners needing liberation, ate and drank with children in need of identity, ate and drank with all in need of love. Before a watching world hungry for table fellowship, starving for authentic relationships, eager to learn about God's saving purposes, an open, inviting, Holy Communion that includes children reminds us all of the process leading to salvation: "Let the little children come to me, and do not hinder them, for the kingdom of God belongs to such as these. I tell you the truth anyone who does not receive the kingdom of God like a little child will never enter it" (Mark 10:14–16).

Scripture also teaches that the nature of the Lord's Supper is one where true community happens when diverse peoples combine their resources and share with one another: "They devoted themselves to the apostles' teaching and *fellowship*, to the breaking of bread and the prayers. . . . All who believed *were together* and *had all things in common*; they would sell their possessions and goods and distribute the proceeds to all, as any had need. Day by day, as *they spent much time together* in the temple, they broke bread at home and ate their food with glad and generous hearts . . ." (Acts 2:42–47, emphases added).

The word "communion" (*koinonia*), translated in the above text as "fellowship," includes in its semantic domain those other expressions in the words "together," "all things in common." Peter seems to be suggesting that the Lord's Supper, as noted earlier in this chapter, wasn't just a special ritual to be celebrated once a month or every week or twice a year in the worship service. The Communion was the daily practice of sharing their meals and possessions with one another, so that no one would go away hungry or without warm clothes or a place to sleep at night.

Later, when the apostle Paul was writing to the Corinthian church about the Lord's Table, he is troubled with how they are celebrating it. He insists that the Communion Table, as in Acts, was meant to be a tangible expression of economic justice for all who participate. He warns the church not to come to the Lord's table "unworthily" (1 Cor 11:22). He criticizes the church by saying, "when the time comes to eat, each of you goes ahead with your own supper and one goes hungry and another drunk"(11:21). In other words, while one is famished another has much to eat and way too much to drink! Paul sarcastically asks: "Do you show contempt for the church of God and humiliate those who have nothing?" (11:22).

Apparently, for both Peter and Paul, the Lord's Supper is not only about bread and wine, but it's also about turning the tables on rank and status![30] The Lord's table is a democratizing meal, a common meal, a meal of justice for all. Nineteen times when the Greek word for "communion" (*koinonia*) is used in the New Testament it is variously translated as "fellowship," "sharing," "contributing to others," "participation with others," having things "in common," "in communion." In a world that still too often divides itself by rank and status, which in turn too easily escalates into mimetic violence, Communion fellowship should be a practice that overturns the age-old perception and reality of the church on most Sunday mornings being the most segregated, economically stratified, and war-infatuated institution in the world.

Indeed, the Table of Peace is a table of nations, peoples, languages, and cultures. The Table of Peace stands for God's future, when a dispersed and exiled humanity, divided against itself, reunites around the uncommon common meal at the messianic banquet once and for all (Matt 8:11; Mark 13:27).[31] Sharing the bread and wine becomes a sacrament only to the degree the actual living body of Christ lives in community as one united people. At the Table of the Lord there is no rank and file: priests are not distinguishable from the laity, the poor and rich eat together, there are no doctors of philosophy above the high school dropout, no

---

30. See Yoder, *Body*, 20–25.

31. Bieler and Schottroff, *Eucharist*, 54–55.

saints who aren't also sinners needing God's grace! In a world structured mostly around social, economic, and other forms of power, such a meal is good news, indeed.

The messianic table of nations as envisioned already in the apocalyptic victory banquet of Isa 25:6 (cf. 2:2–4) must not be underplayed: "On this mountain, the Lord of Hosts will make for all peoples a feast of rich food, a feast of well-aged wines, of rich food filled with marrow, of well-aged wines strained clear." When coupled with the wonderfully provocative vision of Isaiah (2:2–4) of nations gathering on Mt. Zion, voluntarily beating their swords into plowshares, a transformation wrought by God reconciling their differences by means of education, arbitration and persuasion, not through warfare, the eschatological meal takes on its finest ambiance. In Christ, the promised reconciliation has begun that will ensure the very outcome envisioned by Isaiah, anticipated in Luke's Great Banquet feast and still longed for by all who are tired of war and its aftermath.

No wonder that in the end, a fitting understanding of the eschatological meal is also that of an ultimate Thanksgiving meal. Indeed, the familiar expression often used to describe the Lord's Table, the "Eucharist," reflects the Greek New Testament word *eucharistein*, which simply means, "giving thanks." Certainly, today's liturgical practice is meant to be an expression of confident thanksgiving in the spirit of the earliest Eucharistic meals where elaborate thanksgiving prayers were offered over the cup and bread.[32] Perhaps there is no greater way to show appreciation for a good meal—one that embodies the gracious care of its host, one that inspires hope that all wars will cease around a common Table of Peace—than a simple, heartfelt, "Thank you."

32. Eleanor Kreider, *Communion*, 45, suggests that "gratitude to God" was the characteristic feature of early communion liturgies and piety.

7

God, Judgment, and Non-Violence

JOHN E. PHELAN

IT IS NOT UNUSUAL for pastors or teachers to sit across the desk from troubled parishioners or students fresh from reading an account of God's command to destroy the Canaanites down to the last woman and child. It is not unusual for pastors and teachers to face questions in a Sunday School class or Bible study about hell and judgment. "Would a God of love really send a person to hell for all eternity," someone wonders. In recent years the so-called "new atheists" have drawn attention to this particular aspect of the depiction of God in the Bible. "Do you really want to worship a God," they scoff, "who recommends bashing the heads of babies against a wall? Do you really want to recommend a deity who would consign a human being to eternal conscious torment?" These are theological questions and apologetic challenges that cannot be ignored.

Generations of Christians have found it difficult to square a patient and loving God with the fierce God of retribution and judgment found in both the Hebrew Scriptures and the New Testament. Some passages in the Bible seem to depict a vindictive, violent, and even cruel God: a God who calls for the slaughter of innocent children; a God who strikes down hapless Uzzah when he steadies the ark (2 Sam 6:6, 7); a God who throws "all whose names were not found written in the book of life into the lake of fire" (Rev 20:15). The violence of this God has often been used to undergird the violence of human beings. Kings, emperors, and presidents have cited the example of this violent and vengeful God as a justification for war.

Judges have cited this God as they condemned a murderer or traitor or mere thief to death. A violent and retributive God lends credence to a violent and retributive state. A violent and retributive God encourages violent and retributive behavior in his devotees. But is this really the way God exercises judgment?

The difficulty is that this violent God seems inconsistent with the depiction of God elsewhere in the Bible. How could such a God, for example, call on his people to love their enemies? How could such a God call upon his people to forgive? How could such a God denounce the very violence and retribution he practices?

On the other hand, we may wonder: If God is non-retributive and non-violent can he really do anything about injustice? Must God remain deaf to the cries from under the altar, "How long, Sovereign Lord, holy and true, until you judge the inhabitants of the earth, and avenge our blood" (Rev 6:10)? Is God powerless to act? Is this not the God Mary addressed in the Magnificat? Is this not the God who "has scattered those who are proud in their inmost thoughts, ... brought down the rulers from their thrones, ... filled the hungry with good things but ... sent the rich away empty" (Luke 1:51–53)? The comfortable, middle-class Christian can afford to be troubled by the prospect of God's judgment. The oppressed, the martyrs, the hungry, and the lost have little else to look for. For them God's judgment is deliverance! Could God, would God intervene violently on behalf of the oppressed?

How, then, do the love and justice of God cohere? How can the God who wants none to perish oversee the destruction of some? How can the God who promises justice ignore the cries of the oppressed? How can the God who in Jesus Christ endured the suffering of the cross for the sake of the world he loves now inflict suffering on that same world? Are there limits to grace? Can you find the bottom of mercy? And what does it mean for God's people to follow his example? How do we love mercy and do justice? Can Jesus' disciples really "be perfect" as their "heavenly Father is perfect" (Matt 5:48)?

SOURCES AND SOLUTIONS TO HUMAN VIOLENCE

Truth be told, contemporary human beings have little difficulty with violent, retributive justice—if it is not directed toward them. We seem to rather like seeing someone get their "comeuppance." The denigrated and dispossessed frequently turn to violence to restore their "honor." The condemned and executed criminal is said to have "paid his debt to society." The corrupt politician, the philandering celebrity, the addicted athlete are held up by the media as objects of public scorn. These are modern examples of "scapegoating." With the "sacrifice" of the scapegoat, a debt of sorts is settled and societal order affirmed and restored. Many of us find a sort of grim satisfaction in the "sacrifice" of the other. Our media people are particularly adept at judging, condemning, and destroying the scapegoat. They love to pour scorn on the scapegoat of the week. Today we do not use knives to slit the throats of our victims; we use microphones and videotape, blogs posts and editorials. Our high priests are on CNN and Fox. This condemnation of the despised "other" produces unity for a time. But the ritual needs to be repeated over and over again and is perhaps declining in effectiveness.

Over his long and fruitful career René Girard has exposed and explained this deadly process.[1] He has argued that the great human problem is scapegoating violence born out of "mimetic rivalry." Envy, desire, and longing are produced by imitating the desires of others for a limited number of desirable objects. Predictably this rivalry produces intrigue, conflict, and finally violence. Facing the threat of chaos, a society will look for ways to reduce the rivalry and defuse the violence. From the very beginnings of human cultures chaotic communities discovered the value of finding a scapegoat to blame for the violence. With the sacrifice of the scapegoat equilibrium was restored—for a time. According to Girard the Bible uncovers and denounces this mechanism. It demonstrates that the victims are not guilty and that the God and Father of Jesus Christ does not require such sacrifices. In his death Jesus uncovered this mechanism with finality, becoming the scapegoat to end all scapegoats.

Girard argues that the Bible progressively reveals the "scapegoat mechanism." It makes plain what was "hidden from the foundation of the earth."[2] The Hebrew and Christian Scriptures make it plain that the victims of scapegoating violence are not guilty as charged—or at least not as guilty as their treatment suggests. In the Scriptures God shows himself to be on the side of the victim and opposed to all scapegoating violence. Jesus' innocent death as the ultimate scapegoat not only shows the mechanism for what it is, but calls for an end of all such violence. Following Jesus' death and resurrection there is no need to scapegoat and sacrifice the "other." Life in God's kingdom is characterized by peace, not violence; restoration, not condemnation. But a God who seeks ret-

1. Girard, *Things Hidden; Scapegoat; I See Satan.*
2. See Girard, *Things Hidden.*

ribution, who "settles the score" through violence, provides cover for all those who are drawn to such violence. Such a God would find it difficult to challenge the scapegoating violence of his creatures, when he uses it himself! Girard would have us rethink our notions of God as violent and retributive.

This chapter will argue that, on the one hand, God must be free to judge and to act to set the world right. But, on the other hand, God's judgment is not retributive, vindictive, or cruel. God's judgment is not meant to "even the score" or "restore his honor" but to recall and reclaim his creation. God's judgment is God's desperate attempt to demonstrate his love, address human sinfulness, and set the world right. But God's creatures remain free to chose against love and their own best interests. Their choices lead inevitably to their judgment.

GOD AS JUDGE IN THE BIBLE

From the beginning to the end, the Bible depicts the God of Israel as a judge. In Gen 18:25, Abraham challenges God's decision to destroy Sodom with a provocative rhetorical question: "Will not the judge of all the earth do right?" Abraham's question implies not only that God is "judge of all the earth," but a judge obligated to "do right." The judgment of God must not be based on divine whimsy or pique. Similarly when God is ready to destroy recalcitrant Israel and start over, Moses pleads for the people. "In accordance with your great love, forgive the sin of these people, just as you have pardoned them from the time they left Egypt until now" (Num 14:19). Both Abraham and Moses appeal to the character of God. God as a judge is compelled to "do right"; he is "slow to anger, abounding in love and forgiving sin and rebellion" (Num 14:18). God's "vengeance" is not seen as capricious or cruel.

In the end, however, Sodom is destroyed and the rebellious Israelites die in the wilderness. God does not "leave the guilty unpunished" (Num 14:18). Throughout the Hebrew Scriptures prophets and wise men warn kings and princes, priests and merchants of God's judgment. Through Isaiah God declares, "Your rulers are rebels, companions of thieves; they all love bribes and chase after gifts. They do not defend the cause of the fatherless; the widow's case does not come before them" (Isa 1:22). God warns, "I will turn my hand against you; I will thoroughly purge away your dross and remove your impurities" (Isa 1:25). Israel and Judah, Assyria and Babylon, Edom and Moab, all experience the judgment of God. God is full of compassion and grace, but will not overlook the abuses of the powerful.

In the Bible, God's judgment, however, is not simply a way of punishment. It is God's way of setting things right. "I will restore your judges as in the days of old, your rulers as at the beginning. Afterwards you will be called the City of Righteousness, the Faithful City" (Isa 1:26). The goal of God's judgment is God's justice. For this reason God's judgment is not always feared, but often anxiously anticipated. Many psalms express longing for God's judgment. The wicked oppress, the impious scoff, but God's judgment will set the world right: "Let the Lord judge the peoples. Vindicate me, Lord, according to my righteousness. . . . Bring an end to the violence of the wicked and make the righteous secure" (Ps 7:8, 9). God's judgment is exercised in service of the poor, the suffering, and the oppressed. Judgment is not simply a function of outrage, but of love: "I trust in your unfailing love; my heart rejoices in your salvation" (Ps 13:5). God wants to restore, not destroy. God wants to redeem, not condemn. But can God accomplish this without direct actions of violence and retribution?

God is also depicted as a judge in the New Testament. In Matt 12:39–42, for example, Jesus warns the Pharisees of God's judgment. At "the judgment" Jesus declares the Ninevites and the "Queen of the South" will condemn Jesus' contemporaries for their lack of response to his message.[3] Jonah and Solomon had received a better hearing from their contemporaries than Jesus did from his! Many of Jesus' parables allude to a time of judgment, of division, of separation: wheat from weeds, sheep from goats, wise virgins from foolish ones. Jesus as the "Son of Man" is the instrument of judgment: "When the Son of Man comes in his glory, and all the angels with him, he will sit on his glorious throne. All the nations will be gathered before him" (Matt 25:31, 32). Elsewhere in the New Testament Paul declares, "we must all appear before the judgment seat of Christ, that everyone may receive what is due them for the things done while in the body, whether good or bad" (2 Cor 5:10). Finally, in John of Revelation's great vision he "saw a great white throne and him who was seated on it. . . . Everyone was judged according to what they had done" (Rev 20:11, 13). The judgment of God seems inescapable. But does the judgment always need to be violent and retributive? What kind of a judge is God? How does he exercise judgment?

3. Reiser, *Jesus*, 206ff.

In the Bible God is a judge. But God is not always depicted as a judge sitting at a bench handing out punishment. His courtroom is not always given over to criminal trials! God's judgment, that is, is not always retributive. Furthermore, the judgments of the Bible are not always the result of God's direct action.

In the Hebrew Scriptures, according to Stephen Travis, "Obedience to the requirements of the covenant will bring blessing, disobedience will bring ruin (Lev 26; Deut 26–30). But did those who wrote such words regard this judgment of God as retributive? Did they believe that the effects of sin and the blessing which follows obedience were imposed *from outside* and according to some notion of equivalence between the deed and its deserved results?"[4] Are the judgments of God, Travis asks, the result of his direct action or the natural outcomes and consequences of human action? Are sinners being paid in kind for their disobedience? Or are God's judgments a matter of sinners "reaping what they sowed"? Is God a God of direct violence against evildoers? Does God use violence to punish? Or does God permit violence as a natural outcome of sin and oppression? What role does God play in judging wrongdoing?

Travis insists the biblical depiction of God as judge is more complex than it may first appear:

> A key to understanding the tension between inevitable retribution and God's forgiving mercy is the nature of justice in Hebrew thought and its relation to God's covenant with Israel. . . . Christian ideas about justice have often owed more to Greco-Roman philosophical and legal concepts than to biblical thought. In the Old Testament judgment (whether exercised by God or by the king as his agent) is not a matter of dispassionately dispensing justice but of establishing or restoring right relationships.[5]

He goes on to suggest that God in the Hebrew Scriptures is not so much the "judge behind the bench" but "the spouse of the accused one." God's concern in judgment is not merely to punish, but to restore a broken relationship! Hosea famously depicts God as a longsuffering husband wronged by faithless Israel. God is wounded by Israel's unfaithfulness and longs for a restored relationship: "How can I give you up, Ephraim? How can I hand you over, Israel? How can I treat you like Admah? How can I make you like Zeboyim? My heart is changed within

4. Travis, *Christ*, 13.
5. Ibid., 20.

me, all my compassion is aroused. I will not carry out my fierce anger, nor will I devastate Ephraim again. For I am God, and not a human being" (Hos 11:8, 9).

Human beings are prone to punish. Human beings seek revenge. Human beings are violent: "Adah and Zillah, listen to me: wives of Lamech, hear my words. I have killed a man for wounding me, a young man for injuring me. If Cain is avenged seven times, then Lamech seventy-seven times" (Gen 4:23–24). But God is not a human being. God is not bound by retributive violence. God does not need to "get even." God seeks to recover the love of Israel, not destroy her. God's judgments are meant to restore, reclaim, and renew his relationship with his alienated and fearful "spouse."

The "relational" character of God as judge is also clear in the New Testament. According to Jesus his Father loves his enemies, and "causes his sun to rise on the evil and the good, and sends his rain on righteous and the unrighteous" (Matt 5:45). He is the waiting Father eager to receive the Prodigal home safe (Luke 15:11–32). He is a patient God, a forgiving God, a God who "is not slow in keeping his promise as some understand slowness. Instead he is patient with you, not wanting anyone to perish, but everyone to come to repentance" (2 Pet 3:9). Jesus urges his disciples to imitate this God who forgives, watches and waits. Lamech may pay back seventy-seven times, but Jesus' disciples are to forgive seventy-seven times (Matt 18:22). Even the most impossible debts are forgivable (see Matt 18:23–35). This is the God of Jesus Christ who cried out from the cross, "Father forgive them, for they do not know what they are doing" (Luke 23:34).

THE NATURE OF GOD'S JUDGMENT

In fact the nature of God's judgment in the Bible is multifaceted. In his book Travis cites five forms of judgment in the Hebrew Scriptures.[6]

1. *Retributive Judgment.* Although Travis will argue that while this is not the principle form of judgment in the Bible, it is clearly present in both the Hebrew Scriptures and the New Testament. Nevertheless, he largely agrees with Klaus Koch that "even when God is said to be the author of blessing or ruin (e.g. Prov 10:29, 12:2, 15:25) this is not . . . retributive. Mention of [God] simply expresses the conviction that he pays close

6. Ibid., 17, 19, 21.

attention to the connection between actions and destiny, hurries it along and completes it when necessary."[7] Nevertheless, clearly some judgments are viewed as punishment, even as payback.

2. *Disciplinary Judgment.* In Deut 4:25–31 God's intention is not to destroy Israel for their corruption and sinfulness but to produce repentance. "The Lord your God is a merciful God; he will not abandon or destroy you or forget the covenant with your ancestors" (4:31). God hopes they "will return to the Lord *their* God and obey him" (4:30). Travis notes that the Hebrew verb for "discipline" or "chastise" appears frequently in Jeremiah. The coming judgment was disciplinary. It meant to restore Israel to God not destroy them utterly.

3. *Purificatory Judgment.* God's judgment is also seen as a smelting process that removes the impurities. The wicked, unjust practices and people that violate God's law will be removed. "The Lord will wash away the filth of the women of Zion; he will cleanse the bloodstains from Jerusalem by a spirit of judgment and a spirit of fire" (Isa 4:2–6). Similarly, in the New Testament, are the words of John the Baptist: "His winnowing fork is in his hand, and he will clear his threshing floor, gather his wheat into the barn and burn up the chaff with unquenchable fire" (Matt 3:12).

4. *Revelatory Judgment.* Judgment falls sometimes so that people may know that "I am the Lord" (see Ezek 38:22–23). Such judgment reveals God's power and God's displeasure at sin, oppression, and violence.

5. *Judgment as the Presence and Absence of God.* Categories 2, 3, and 4 are notretributive but intended to call God's people back into relationship. Travis' fifth category shows how God's judgment may be effected for the purposes of discipline, purification, and revelation. Perhaps the most important aspect of judgment is God's "hiding his face" from his people. "Divine blessing," Travis argues, "consists not in material prosperity but in knowledge of God; and its converse, the idea that punishment par excellence is the withdrawal of God's presence from a people."[8] This judgment is not retributive "since it is present in the circumstances of seeking or rejecting God, whereas retribution involves a reward or punishment

7. Ibid., 14.
8. Ibid., 21.

imposed *from outside*."⁹ God did not need to punish his people directly. Withdrawing his presence was punishment enough. God's absence opened Israel up to the terrors of life on its own. This is graphically depicted in Ezekiel 10 as "the glory of the Lord" left the temple. The absence of God's glory meant doom and exile for Israel. Or consider Jeremiah's warning, "Cut off your hair and throw it away; take up a lament on the barren heights, for the Lord has rejected and abandoned this generation that is under his wrath" (Jer 7:29). When God withdraws, judgment comes in the form of growing corruption, violence, and threats from enemies (see Ps 81:11–16).

In *Jesus and the Drama of Salvation*, Raymund Schwager argues for a similar concept of judgment in the New Testament. In Romans 1, for example, Paul says three times, God delivered up or "gave them over" to the logical consequences of their actions. "God hands people over to the dynamic and inner logic of those passions and of that depraved thinking which they themselves have awakened by their turning away from God."¹⁰ Commenting on the same passage, Travis writes, "People abandon God; therefore he allows them to experience the consequences of their choices. . . . People are *given up* to a condition which is not a freshly imposed judgment but already exists in the choices they have made."¹¹ God's glory in this case leaves the "temple" of the human body.

God does not need directly to inflict judgment on sinners. They are quite capable of inflicting it on themselves. The Bible insists human beings should not blame their troubles on God: "When tempted," James writes, "no one should say, 'God is tempting me.' For God cannot be tempted by evil, nor does he tempt anyone; but each of you is tempted when you are dragged away by your own evil desires and enticed. Then after desire has conceived it gives birth to sin; and sin, when it is full-grown, gives birth to death" (Jas 1:13–15). Evil desires (mimetic rivalry), sin, and death do not find their origin in God, but in human beings. It does not do, James insists, to blame God for sin and death.

Paul makes a similar point in Romans 7. There is nothing wrong with God's law. It is "holy, righteous and good" (Rom 7:12). The problem is not with God or with God's will. It is with sin that works its will within the individual. God cannot be blamed for human failure. As Paul

9. Ibid., 21.

10. Schwager, *Jesus*, 165.

11. Travis, *Christ*, 61.

said in Romans 5, "sin entered the world through one man, and death through sin, and in this way death came to all people, because all sinned" (Rom 5:12). Sin, judgment, and death are a result of human actions, not of divine action. God's intent is not to condemn us because of our sin, but rescue us from our sin: "For if by the trespass of the one man, death reigned through that one man, how much more will those who receive God's abundant provision of grace and the gift of righteousness reign in life through the one man, Jesus Christ" (Rom 5:17). Sin, Paul insists, pays its own wages, death. But God's eternal life comes not as wage, but as gift (Rom 6:23). God does not wish to judge us, but rescue us from the judgment we have ourselves chosen.

Jesus' announcement of God's kingdom is not an announcement of God's angry intent to judge. It is rather a warning that persistence in disobedience leads to its natural outcome. It is a path we choose—not a path God chooses for us. "Enter through the narrow gate," Jesus warns, "for wide is the gate and broad is the road that leads to destruction" (Matt 7:13). Staying on the road to destruction is foolish, but it is a choice many human beings make. Failing to hear and respond to Jesus' message of the kingdom is as foolish as building on a floodplain.

The message of Jesus is good news precisely because God offers to rescue us from ourselves: "Come to me, all you who are weary and burdened, and I will give you rest. Take my yoke upon you and learn from me, for I am gentle and humble in heart, and you will find rest for your soul. For my yoke is easy and my burden is light" (Matt 11:28–30).

At the end of his blistering critique of the "teachers of the Law and the Pharisees" in Matthew 23, Jesus warns that the blood of the martyrs from Abel to Zechariah was about to fall on them. This does not give him any pleasure. He goes on to express the very anguish of God. He longed to "gather your children together, as a hen gathers her chicks under her wings, but you were not willing." Jesus respects the will of the people and their leaders even if it is leading them to destruction. It was not his will or intention that Israel suffer the destruction of the temple and the loss of lives and hopes before the might of the Roman Empire. In fact, it was a matter of grief and pain. It was something he hoped could be avoided. And it is not God's will that anyone suffer judgment. But our decisions, however foolish, are honored and the outcome of our disobedience is in the end a matter of our own choosing.

Schwager acknowledges this "fundamental tension between the announcement of God's kingdom and the threat of judgment."[12] Nevertheless, he insists that "God is always in himself the kind father who meets sinners with anticipatory love; only if sinners, despite the experience of grace, cling to their own criteria of judgment do they imprison themselves in them. The judgment sayings," he continues, "are not a sign that God has a double face, but they bring out with great seriousness that people possess no power to save themselves and God carries out against them no 'violence to compel love.'"[13] God would set people free from their violence, malice and envy—but they must respond to God's offer.

The Bible makes it clear that this is a morally serious universe. Our choices matter. They matter to us and they matter to God. God honors us by honoring our choices. Jesus asks, Did we bring sufficient oil to wait for the bridegroom? Did we invest our "talents" well? Did we recognize Jesus in the hungry and the thirsty, the stranger and the naked, the sick and the imprisoned? Jesus warns us about such things not because we can earn God's favor by doing them. Rather our failures to account for the suffering and marginalized demonstrate that we do not see the world as God's sees it. They raise questions about our relationship with God and our commitment to his kingdom. When we ignore God's love, forgiveness, and grace, we set ourselves and our world on a path to death. How, then, can we avoid the judgment of God?

According to Schwager Jesus left us his teaching, his example, and his accomplishment so we might not fall under God's judgment:

1. *Jesus' Teaching.* "Jesus in his preaching about judgment did not teach that the goodness of God comes to an end at a particular point and is transformed into its opposite, since he offered only boundless forgiveness as the measure of the new life. However he made clear that all those who do not open themselves to the rule of God remain under the rule of retribution." Jesus longed to help those who "closed themselves up against goodness" and take "the path of self-sufficiency and self-condemnation." Such people in their search for self-security succumb to the "tendency toward lies and violence" and "founder on the goodness of God."[14] How

12. Schwager, *Jesus*, 80.

13. Ibid., 81.

14. Ibid., 108.

can such people be made to understand that lies and violence lead only to death?

2. *Jesus' Example.* Jesus "continued that faith tradition of his people and simultaneously, through small shifts in meaning, drew a new picture of God." But he did more than this. "In his own behavior toward his enemies, Jesus allowed the nonviolence of the servant of God (Isa 50:4–9) to find complete expression in reality." Jesus was willing to offer up his life out of love for his enemies so that the possibilities of God's kingdom might be realized. He modeled nonviolent love and a willingness to endure suffering for God's kingdom purposes. But what did this suffering accomplish?[15]

3. *Jesus' Accomplishment.* "The self-judgment of humankind, in which people shifted their guilt onto Jesus in self-deception, became a judgment on him. But from his viewpoint this was a judgment of a completely different sort. He allowed himself to be drawn into the process of self-judgment of his adversaries in order, through participation in their lot, to open up for them from inside another way out of their diabolical circle and hence a new path of salvation." Jesus bore the judgment of God that was the natural outcome of human sin and disobedience. He bore the evil and turned it into love. "He made himself a gift to those who judged him and burdened him with their guilt."[16] Jesus by his death entered the "dark realm where people judge themselves" so as to "open up this world once more to the father."

This dark realm is a realm of violence, fear, and insecurity. In this realm we seek to secure our safety through scapegoating violence. Jesus entered the violent world of the scapegoat to reveal it for what it was and to banish its self-fulfilling prophecy. He took the judgment upon himself. He refused to permit us to locate the source of envy, desire, and greed in God and God's kingdom. Only by love—the love of God, his way, and his creation—will violence and judgment be overcome. Only by love will God's healing kingdom purposes be realized. In Jesus Christ God dealt with human violence by enduring human violence and revealing it for what it is.

15. Ibid., 108–9.
16. Ibid., 117.

A QUESTION OF READING

The interpretation of the nature of God's judgment outlined above presents the Jewish and Christian readers of the Bible with a crisis of reading. How does this square with the picture of a violent punishing God found both in the Bible and popular imagination? Few, if any, believing readers would countenance the notion that God is either the author of evil or the perpetrator of evil acts. The biblical text itself would deny it. So what is one to make of the commands to slaughter all the inhabitants of Canaan or the bloodthirsty warnings of judgment in Ezek 21:8–15 and Jer 25:32, 33? What is one to make of the irrational outbursts of pique on the part of God (Exod 4:24–36)? Once again you would find few readers of any kind who would not agree that bashing in the heads of babies is an evil act (see Nah 3:1–12).

The explanations for such texts are many and varied. Some simply dismiss them as remnants of a more primitive way of thinking about God. Others understand them in the context of the suffering of Israel.[17] The prophets express rage on behalf of God for the disobedience of the people and injustice of their society. Or they express rage on behalf of Israel's people as a result of the violence of their powerful enemies. Such things may reflect God's "pathos" but not recommend a particular course of action. Other readers simply prefer to ignore them altogether.

The temptation for modern readers of an ancient text is to "modernize" it. Our lectionaries frequently sanitize the text by leaving out the unpleasant parts. When was Ps 137:9 last read in your congregation? Henry Cadbury once wrote a book entitled *The Peril of Modernizing Jesus.*[18] A wag suggested there was an equal danger of "archaizing ourselves." And so there is. We live within this tension. Scripture's authority in the church requires us to take even difficult texts seriously. But for Christians it also requires reading such texts in the light of the life, teaching, death and resurrection of Jesus. The doctrines of the Trinity and of the incarnation require us to view God through the lenses of the man Jesus of Nazareth. We are also to read our times in the light of that same gospel, that same Savior.

Historian Mark Noll argued in a recent work that the Civil War in the United States was more than a political and social crisis—it was a theo-

17. Schwager, *Must There Be*, 53–71.
18. Cadbury, *Peril*.

logical crisis.[19] American Christians had been used to the Bible acting as the supreme religious and cultural authority. But in the years leading up to the war the text seemed to speak with an uncertain voice. Christians in the North were convinced the Bible spoke a word of liberation. Like the children of Israel delivered from the slavery of Egypt, the God of the Bible called for the liberation of slaves in the American South. Southern preachers insisted that, on the contrary, the Bible offered plenty of support for the institution of slavery. God gave the Israelites laws regarding the treatment of slaves. Paul offered instructions to Christians who were slaves. How could this be unless God gave his blessing to slavery? Noll suggests that Christians in the United States are still living in the wake of this crisis. We are still uncertain of the Bible's authority.

Few today would read the laws of Moses or the letters of Paul as a recommendation for the reinstitution of slavery. The slavery of the ancient and Greco-Roman world was quite different from the chattel slavery of the American South. But it still involved the ownership of one human being by another. Today most Christian readers recognize that whatever the cultural patterns of ancient Israel or the Greco-Roman world, the gospel is a message of liberation. Paul's words in Gal 3:28 may suggest that however reticent he may have been to draw out the implications, the apostle recognized the egalitarian line of the gospel: "In Christ you are all children of God through faith. . . . There is neither Jew nor Greek, neither slave nor free, neither male nor female, for you are all one in Christ Jesus." The Bible itself offers direction, nuance, and correction to texts that can only be applied with difficulty to the God and Father of our Lord Jesus Christ. This is not mere cultural accommodation. The Bible itself forces us to draw such conclusions.

It is impossible to deny that the Bible occasionally depicts God as vengeful and violent. But this is not the end of the story. The text itself calls this side of God into question in alternative depictions in both the Hebrew Scriptures and the New Testament. And Jesus calls the depiction into question through his own life and teachings. The New Testament writers also engage in "genre bending" when they use the language of retributive judgment, but reshape the concepts entirely. John's great revelatory experience is a case in point.

19. Noll, *Civil War*. See also, Phelan, "Bible."

UNEXPECTED TEXTS, UNEXPECTED READINGS

Revelation is known for its depictions of conflict with the "empire" and the threat of judgment. It is not a book one would expect to go to in search of the God of peace! In an article entitled "Revelation, Empire and the Violence of God," I pointed out that John's great vision is characterized by irony and parody. This is seen especially in Revelation 4–5:

> Revelation 4 ushers the reader into the divine throne room which itself parodies the Roman imperial court and its ceremonies. All the exclamations of praise and luxury of the throne room belongs to the drama and ritual of the Roman court....[E]mperors from Julius Caesar onward wrapped themselves in Jupiter's clothing to reinforce the claims of their dynasty to divine sonship and inevitable apotheosis.

The throne room scene would be familiar, but what follows . . . is sharply disjunctive.

> John sees the "Lamb . . . standing as though it had been slain, with seven horns and seven eyes" (5:6). The vision of the Lamb, standing in profound tension with the immediately preceding image of the conquering "lion of the tribe of Judah" marks an outcome that contradicts, if not mocks the high-sounding course language that precedes it.[20]

Roman military might and political power are overthrown not by a great army, but by a lamb, the weakest of creatures—and a slaughtered lamb at that! Jesus, victory is won not by military power, but by the self-giving love of his death. According to John, "the Lamb won the victory through death and witness. His final victory over the forces of evil will be won by a 'sharp sword' coming out of his mouth (Rev 19:15). Messiah here wins the victory by his word."[21] And so do his people. As Richard Bauckham puts it, "The martyrs conquer not only by their suffering and death as such, but by their faithful witness to the point of death (cf. 12:11). Their witness to the truth prevails over the lies and deceit of the devil and the beast. For those who reject this witness, it becomes legal testimony against them securing their condemnation. But it entails also a positive possibility: that people may be won from the illusion to the truth."[22]

20. Phelan, "Revelation," 77. Drawing on Maier, *Apocalypse*, 174.

21. Phelan, "Revelation," 78.

22. Bauckham, *Climax*, 237.

Ironically, then, Revelation bears witness to a nonviolent Lamb and a non-violent community standing in opposition to the most powerful empire ever known. Their victory is their witness in words and in blood. Their witness may be ignored—but with disastrous consequences. The fierce judgments depicted in the prophecy are, in the words of René Girard, "no more and no less than a rational anticipation of what men are likely to do to each other and to their environment, if they go on disregarding the *Gospel's* warnings against revenge in a desacralized and sacrificially unprotected world."[23] Human beings' current course will lead them, like the Israel of the prophets, to destruction. It is difficult, for example, to read Revelation 8 without thinking of the ruination of the earth. Our greed, short-sightedness, and foolishness risk the destruction of the very sources of our lives. I can very well imagine "a third of the earth burned up, a third of the trees burned up, and all the green grass burned up" (8:7). Nor is it difficult to imagine "a third of the waters turned bitter" (8:10). Judgment will come upon us not because of God's anger, but human foolishness and sin.

Christian witness, then, warns not so much about what God will do to us, but rather what we in our ignorance and folly are doing to ourselves. Famine, violence, and war are no strangers to us. We know them quite well. Our capacity to produce wreck and ruin are unprecedented. We know the terrors of roadside bombs in Iraq and of nuclear weapons in the hands of the deranged. We know the bitter fruit of racism, the scourge of poverty, and wounds of violence in our streets and homes. But we also must reckon with Iowa's topsoil washing downriver, the savaging of West Virginia's mountaintops, toxic floodwaters engulfing one of our great cities, erosion on clear-cut Western mountainsides, and the emptying of aquifers and oil fields. Are these ills judgments of God? Perhaps so. But they are the actions of foolish and sinful human beings first.

According to John the road of Christian witness is not an easy one. In Revelation 11 John describes two prophetic witnesses. They are described with allusions to a pastiche of Old Testament texts. They are Zechariah's "two olive trees and the two lampstands," and they "stand before the Lord of the earth" (Rev 11:4). Like Elijah they "have the power to shut up the sky so that it will not rain during the time they are prophesying." Like Moses they can turn water in to blood and strike the earth with plagues. Their preaching produces a sacrificial crisis. The "beast

---

23. Girard, quoted in Bailie, *Violence*, 16.

that comes up from the Abyss" kills them. Their bodies lie unburied in the street. "The inhabitants of the earth will gloat over them and will celebrate by sending each other gifts because these two prophets had tormented those who live on the earth" (11:10).

This is quite obviously an example of scapegoating. The whole world conspires against the witnesses that tormented them and throw a party when they are dead. Temporarily they find unity in their hatred of the witnesses and their joy in their public humiliation. Moses, Elijah, and Zerubbabel all dealt with hostile imperial powers. In spite of great weakness and vulnerability they spoke on behalf of the God of Israel. Moses and Elijah were forced to flee for their lives. Zurubbabel's fate is unknown, but some speculate he was removed from office or even executed because of the messianic speculation surrounding him. By alluding to Moses, Elijah, and Zerubbabel, John warns the Christians of Asia Minor that the Roman Empire is hostile to alternative versions of reality. Like all empires it will react with violence if its unity and power are threatened. Witnesses to the "slaughtered lamb" will fare no better that these great heroes of the Hebrew Scriptures.

And yet, John insists, the church is called to bear witness regardless of the threats of imperial violence. The witnesses of chapter 11 will be resurrected. The woman and child threatened by the great dragon in chapter 12 will be protected by God. The great dragon will be hurled out of heaven. He will make war against the woman, her child, and "the rest of her offspring—those who keep God's commands and hold fast their testimony about Jesus" (12:17). But he will not prevail. In chapter 17 John sees a woman dressed in scarlet and seated on a great beast. She is drunk with the blood of God's people, "the blood of those who bore testimony to Jesus" (17:6). The great beast will "make war against the Lamb, but the Lamb will triumph over them because he is Lord of Lords and King of kings—and with him will be his called, chosen and faithful followers" (17:14). The followers of Jesus are called upon to bear witness in the face of scapegoating violence—and it will not be easy.

The great task of the church, according to John, is faithfully and nonviolently to bear witness to Jesus. The church bears witness by offering the world an alternative to the violent, greedy, materialistic, individualistic, and sexually obsessed empire. It offers the kingdom of God. It lives in anticipation of the new heavens and the new earth. It offers life, not death; hope, not despair; salvation, not judgment; reconciliation, not estrangement. The seven letters at the beginning of the book are sent to churches that had lost confidence in their own message. They had lost the love they had at first (2:4). They were poor and persecuted (2:9). They were drawn to appealing and false teachings (2:14–16). They were engaged in sexual immorality and idolatry (2:20, 21). They had a reputation for being alive, but were dead (3:1). They were "wretched, pitiful, poor, blind and naked" (3:17). They were, in other words, very much like the compromised church of North America.

According to Harry Maier, "at the end of Christendom the Christian church exists to insist on the troubling story of the cross and to form this-worldly believers who contribute to and enrich pluralistic society through lives of spiritual public witness to the God incarnate in Jesus of Nazareth, who reveals a way of being human on terms other than the insatiable desire for more, military domination and national security."[24]

The church can only offer this alternative if it is confident in its gospel, sure of its Christ, and committed to its common life. It will not be afraid to warn of judgment—not the judgment of an angry and vindictive God, but the judgment the world is bringing upon itself. It will warn the world that the old sacrificial methods, the old victimizations, are losing their effectiveness. A crisis is coming where a convenient victim will be lacking. With René Girard, "in future, all violence will reveal what Christ's Passion revealed, the foolish Genesis of bloodstained idols and the false gods of religion, politics and ideologies. The murderers remain convinced of the worthiness of their sacrifice. They too know not what they do and we must forgive them. The time has come for us to forgive one another. If we wait any longer there will not be time enough."[25]

Judgment is looming. Only witness to Jesus will enable us to avoid it. The church is the world's "truth and reconciliation commission." Only by speaking the truth about violence and bloodshed and acknowledging our part in it will we be able to bring about the reconciliation so desperately needed. When we hold up the judgment of Jesus on the cross, we expose the world at its worst and the love of God at its best. Only by this love will our world evade the crushing judgment it has prepared for itself.

24. Maier, *Apocalypse*, 58.
25. Girard, *Scapegoat*, 212.

8

The Dragon Lives Still

J. DENNY WEAVER

O FFICIALLY, THAT IS, BY the constitution of the United States, the country is formally a secular nation with no established religion. Unofficially, but incontestably present, religion plays a shaping and material role in the society of the United States. More specifically it is the Judeo-Christian religion that plays this role, with emphasis falling on the Christian side of the hyphen. No serious candidate for national office could succeed without a public profession of faith in God. And although it is never stated in plain language, candidates who express faith in terms of the God or gods of Islam or Hinduism or Buddhism need not apply. All coins and currency of the United States bear the phrase, "In God we trust." In 1954 President Dwight Eisenhower signed a law that added the words "under God" to the well-known "Pledge of Allegiance" that is recited daily in many classrooms across the country. Coming in the midst of the Cold War, the move was meant to signal the difference between the professedly "Christian" United States and the communist and officially atheist Soviet Union. Some recent legal challenges to the presence of this phrase have provoked significant public outcry. One can only imagine the size of the outcry if the phrase were successfully challenged on coins and currency.

Seldom confronted by the many supporters of God on money and in the Pledge and in the beliefs of candidates is the question, "What is the character of the God in this national profession in the beliefs of candidates and in the Pledge and on money?" A cartoon in my collection hints at an answer. The cartoon features two high-ranking military brass standing in front of a phalanx of rockets. One of the officers holds a coin and reads the inscription, "In God we trust." One could read the cartoon as a straightforward image of the belief that God supports the United States against other nations, including most specifically supporting the nation's military endeavors. In this case, God has a violent character. However, it is a cartoon. The more likely intent of the cartoon is to point to the irony of claiming to trust God while actually placing faith in a humongous military establishment. This essay speaks directly to that irony.

By using the images of the dragon and two beasts from Revelation 12 and 13, the essay provides clear answers to the question about the view of God in these national symbols, and what it means theologically to proclaim faith in God while supporting a gigantic military apparatus. In the process of developing that theological explanation, the essay will also constitute a short introduction on how to understand the book of Revelation.

TWO PROBLEMS IN READING REVELATION

Interpreting Revelation requires confronting two widespread assumptions about the book. One is that it predicts the future and lays out a calendar of end-time events. The other is that the book features much violence and a God who wreaks great violence on the wicked. In common perception, these assumptions are almost as widespread as the fervent belief that the nation depends on or stands under God. Even people who have some awareness of Revelation's content but do not accept it as true or as scripture often assume that it claims to be a book of predictions.

Those who hold to the predictive view believe that a book written some 2,000 years ago made predictions about the distant future that are beginning to come true in our time. The fulfillment of the predictions then supposedly indicates that Jesus' second coming and the end of the world are near. The predictions concern contemporary politics and natural disasters.[1] In recent history, for example, as the United States invasion of Iraq approached in March 2003, prophecy websites hummed with the suggestion that the invasion was related to events predicted in Revelation and could signal the start of the end-time countdown. However, as the war and occupation dragged on with no end in sight, such claims soon disappeared from these websites. Their owners may now speculate on

1. See Boyer, *When Time*.

whether the tsunami that ravaged Southeast Asia the day after Christmas in 2004 or hurricane Katrina that devastated New Orleans in August of 2005 or the January 12, 2010 earthquake that wasted so much of Haiti are predicated calamities that signal the start of the end-times.

Failed website predictions soon disappear, but those in print hang around to display failure. One of the higher profile failed predictions was made by Hal Lindsey, whose *Late Great Planet Earth* sold millions and made Lindsey a very wealthy man in the 1970s. Lindsey wrote that if the calculations of his end-times scenario were correct, "then within forty years of so of 1948, all these things could take place."[2]

Along that same line of argument, Edgar Whisenutt attracted great publicity when he famously wrote *Eighty-Eight Reasons the Rapture Will be in 1988*.[3] An example of the shifting nature of failed predictions, selected at random, is provided by the ongoing efforts of Ron Reese. I have a four-page mimeographed article by Reese, in which he suggests that there is strong evidence for the rapture to occur between September 6 and 8, 1994. He was obviously wrong. Reese has now posted an article on the Internet with a different kind of speculation about fulfilled predictions. At the time of this writing, he is currently pushing the conjecture that Barack Obama may have revealed himself as the Antichrist in Ghana on July 11, 2009. Such speculation will likely continue until the time that Obama leaves the president's office. The Left Behind series, written by Tim LaHaye and Jerry B. Jenkins and still popular as I write, bills itself as a fictional portrayal of end-time events. However, it contributes specifically to the view of Revelation as a book of predictions on the verge of fulfillment.

The second common assumption about the book of Revelation is that it pictures a violent God and a violent Jesus who together unleash enormous righteous violence on the wicked before consigning them to eternal torment in a fiery hell. Along with its predictive orientation, the Left Behind series illustrates this second popular assumption as well. As David Kirkpatrick wrote in a review in *The New York Times*, in depicting the return of Jesus "few have portrayed him wreaking more carnage on the unbelieving world than Tim LaHaye and Jerry B. Jenkins. . . . With all the gruesome detail of a Hollywood horror movie, Jesus eviscerates the flesh of millions of unbelievers merely by speaking." And Kirkpatrick

2. Lindsey, *Late Great*, 54.

3. Whisenant, *88 Reasons*.

quotes from one of the volumes: "Men and women soldiers and horses seemed to explode where they stood.... It was as if the very words of the Lord had superheated their blood, causing it to burst through their veins and skin.... Even as they struggled, their own flesh dissolved, their eyes melted and their tongues disintegrated."[4] It goes without saying that this image of a violent God is compatible with the God who supports the United States military.

READING REVELATION

A common-sense approach to Revelation renders the predictive approach completely invalid. It is claimed by all serious readers of the Bible that it has a message accessible and comprehensible to its readers. The first readers of Revelation were the seven churches of Ephesus, Smyrna, Pergamum, Thyatira, Sardis, Philadelphia, and Laodicea, that are addressed in chapters 2 and 3. If these readers were to understand a letter addressed to them, then the symbols of the book must refer to people and events accessible to them in their time or earlier.

On the other hand, if Revelation predicts events coming true only now at the beginning of the third millennium, then its symbols refer to things and events such as the following: computers, the World Wide Web, the international banking system linked by computers, credit cards, space travel, nation-states, European and Middle Eastern political alliances, and the United Nations located on a continent unknown to the first century, along with such basic entities of modern everyday life such as electricity, telephones, automobiles, television, airplanes, and more. None of these things would be comprehensible to first-century readers; they would have no frame of reference for understanding predictions of such things. A Revelation dealing with such things would be revealing nothing to first-century readers but confusion and apparent nonsense syllables.

To state the obvious in terms of a question: From the standpoint of the first-century readers to whom the book was addressed, does it make more sense to claim that the symbols of Revelation refer to events at the beginning of the twenty-first century and reported in *The New York Times* or on air in CNN, or to see that these symbols certainly refer to first-century events accessible to the first readers in Asia Minor?

4. Kirkpatrick, "Return."

It seems obvious that Revelation would be directed to and accessible to first-century readers, and our first task of interpretation is to understand the message that first-century readers would have grasped. And it follows that the reason predictions based on Revelation always fail is quite simple. These predictions always fail *because Revelation is not a book of predictions; it is not making predictions about the future.* Reading Revelation as a book of predictions for the future makes as much sense as reading an account of the first World Series of baseball in 1903 as a prediction for the winner of the World Series in 2103. Reading Revelation as a book of predictions would be like reading Jonathan Swift's *Gulliver's Travels* or Mark Twain's *Connecticut Yankee in King Arthur's Court* as coded predictions of events to unfold in 3011.

Although Revelation is not a book of predictions and its message was directed to first-century readers, it nonetheless has an important message relevant for Christians at the beginning of the twenty-first century. Grasping that message begins with understanding the message that Revelation conveyed to its first-century readers. And understanding that message then deals with the second problem of interpretation, namely that of violence and the image of God in Revelation. The following discussion provides brief sketches of these answers as well.[5]

THE UNHOLY TROIKA

Revelation 12 and 13 feature three ugly creatures—a dragon and two beasts. These are curious brutes. All have characteristics that identify them as symbolic depictions. The dragon is red in color, and has seven heads, seven diadems or crowns, and ten horns (Rev 12:3). The first beast—hereafter Beast I—arose from the sea. It received its power, throne and authority from the dragon. Like the dragon, Beast I had a number of heads, likely seven, and ten crowns on its horns (13:1). It had recovered from an apparently mortal wound to one of its heads, and people thus marveled at Beast I. They became followers of Beast I and worshipped the dragon who had given the beast its power. The people also worshipped Beast I and were awed by it, saying, "Who is like the Beast, and who can fight against it?" (13:2–4). Beast I blasphemed God,

---

5. Important resources for the interpretation that follows include Bauckham, *Theology*; Boring, *Revelation*; Collins, *Crisis*; Eller, *Revealing*; Grimsrud, *Triumph*; Howard-Brook and Gwyther, *Unveiling*; Johns, *Lamb*; Reddish, *Revelation*; and Rossing, *Rapture*.

using the name of God in vain (13:6) and also received authority to rule for forty-two months. During this time it made war on God's people—the saints—and even conquered them, and had "authority over every tribe and people and language and nation" and all people whose name is not written "in the book of the life of the Lamb" (13:7–8). Frightful indeed was Beast I.

The second beast—hereafter Beast II—rose up out of the earth. It had two horns that gave it the appearance of a lamb, but when it spoke it had the voice of the dragon. Beast II exhibited all the evil characteristics of Beast I, since it exercised all the authority of Beast I and led people to worship it (13:11–12). Further, it caused fire to descend from heaven and performed signs on behalf of Beast I. Such acts deceived the people into building an image of Beast I that was made alive by Beast II, and anyone who did not worship the image of Beast I was killed. Further, Beast II caused people to be marked with either the name or the number of Beast I as a requirement for participation in the commerce of the time.

The dragon and two beasts are parodies. The dragon, called Satan in Rev 12:9, is the parody of God the Creator. Among several classical references, the appearance of Beast I from the sea and Beast II from the land are adaptations of Jewish tradition in which God created the mythical creatures of Leviathan, a sea monster, and Behemoth, a land monster. In that Beast I receives authority from the dragon and that Beast II causes people to worship Beast I and the dragon, alert readers will recognize these images as a satirical depiction of a blasphemous and unholy threesome or counterfeit trinity, a distorted reflection of biblical counterparts. I will call this unholy threesome a troika, with the dragon parallel to God the Father, Beast I as a counterpart to Jesus Christ, and Beast II positioned over against the Holy Spirit. We should see the dragon and two beasts as caricatures or exaggerated cartoon figures, perhaps even humorous ones. Today they might appear in an animated feature film as creatures with slithering, scaly bodies and snarling heads, all so ugly as to make the viewing audience laugh.

But more important than recognizing that it is an unholy troika is to understand who or what the imagery of this threesome represents. In Rev 12:9, the dragon is identified as "the Devil and Satan." Further, the dragon's seven heads, ten horns, and seven crowns all identify the dragon with the Roman Empire at the time of the writing of Revelation at the end of the first century. The seven heads recall the legend of the city's construction on seven hills. Seven emperors wore the imperial crown between the time of Jesus' crucifixion and the writing of Revelation—Tiberius (14–37 CE), Caligula (37–40 CE), Claudius (41–54 CE), Nero (54–68 CE), Vespasian (69–79 CE), Titus (79–81 CE), and Domitian (81–96 CE). Between Nero and Vespasian was an eighteen-month gap, during which Galbo, Otho, and Vitellius each claimed the crown but did not survive long enough to consolidate a hold on the office. I suggest that the seven crowns on the heads of the dragon correspond to the crowned emperors, while these seven plus the three short-lived claimants together account for the ten horns. It thus becomes clear that the dragon actually has its feet firmly planted on earth and is a human entity. It is the Roman Empire that is identified as a representative of the devil or Satan.

With the dragon identified as the Roman Empire, then Beast I, which receives power and authority from the dragon, becomes visible as a caricature of the emperor—any emperor. As the troika's counterpart to Jesus Christ, this beast is the opposite of Christ or antichrist. Beast II exercises the authority of Beast I and leads the people of the earth to worship it. This unholy troika exercises a distorted reflection of their biblical counterparts. Mimicking the way Jesus Christ exercised the authority of God on earth while the Holy Spirit is of God and testifies to Christ, Beast I displays the emperor as representative of the empire, the earthy embodiment of Satan, and supported by the evil spirit of Beast II. And since the Holy Spirit or the Spirit of God can witness to and represent Jesus Christ, Beast II also constitutes a parody of Christ with its "two horns like a lamb" but speaking with the voice of the dragon.

But the distorted parallels go farther. Alongside the resurrection of Jesus, affirms his deity, Beast I also has a parody of resurrection and deity. That is the meaning of the statement in Rev 13:3 that one of the beast's heads "seemed to have received a death blow, but its mortal wound had been healed." The idea of surviving a death blow most likely refers to the legend of emperor Nero, who was so evil that it was said that after his death he would come back from the underworld to plague earth again. Thus a following evil emperor could be called *Nero redivivus* or "Nero resurrected" or "Nero reborn."

Further, as Beast II exercises the authority of Beast I, great signs are performed in the name of Beast II. It caused an image to be made of Beast I, and then it even gives life to this image. This description appears to mirror claims for the Holy Spirit in whose name or power the apostles preached and healed as described in the book of Acts. In addition, the symbols depict claims of loyalty, when it is said that those who do not worship the image of the beast will be killed (13:15), and that only those with the so-called "mark of the beast" can engage in commerce. These symbolic utterances depict the loyalty demanded by empire and emperors—participation in the yearly loyalty oaths required of Roman citizens as the basis for full involvement in Roman society. This image of a mark is a symbolic depiction of the temptation for Christians to give loyalty to empire that belongs to God and the risen Lord, Jesus Christ.

Observing that Beast I represents the Roman emperors as a caricature of Jesus Christ, and that the "mark of the beast" is a symbolic depiction of loyalty to empire, coupled with the knowledge that Revelation is not a book of predictions or a calendar to end-time events, should eliminate any idea that Beast I of Revelation 12 and 13 is a prediction of an evil ruler, an "antichrist," who will arise in the end-times as the ruler of the entire world or head of a one-world government. Antichrist is not an evil ruler who could appear at any moment in our present time in early twenty-first century. These images depict the ultimate claims of loyalty made by empire and emperor on the one side, and the church with Christ as its head on the other. Far from being a prediction, the so-called antichrist, our counterfeit Christ, is a satirical and perhaps humorous image of first-century Roman emperors—the opposite of Christ—who made claims of deity and demanded ultimate loyalty over against Jesus Christ, the head of the church, whose followers gave their ultimate loyalty to him.

Revelation 12:8–11 pictures an important and decisive point. Here the reader learns that the dragon, that is, Rome, has been defeated by the resurrection of Jesus. Following the image of the cosmic battle between the dragon-Satan and the archangel Michael and his angels—actually the historical confrontation between Roman Empire and the Jesus movement, in which the Romans crucify Jesus—the victory is signaled by the heavenly voice that proclaims, "*Now* have come the salvation and the power and the kingdom of our God and the authority of his Messiah, for the accuser of our comrades has been thrown down, who accuses them day and night before our God" (12:10; emphasis mine). Two factors contribute to the victory for the forces of God—the "blood of the Lamb" and the testimony of the martyrs. These witnesses proclaim that loyalty to the reign of God is more important that human life, while

God's resurrection of Jesus puts on full display the ultimate weakness of the powers of evil in the face of the God who can restore life where there is no life. This is a God who overcomes the worst that the evil powers can do, namely to annihilate life, not by using greater violence but by doing the opposite, namely restoring life.

Numerous other parts of the imagery of chapters 12 and 13 also point to the ultimate victory of the reign of God. The voice in the heavenly victory song declares that although the devil, that is Rome, can still harass Christians, "his time is short" (12:12). In other words, as powerful as the empire appears to be, when observed from the perspective of the ultimate reign of God, it has already been rendered powerless. That limitation is also pictured in the last image of chapter 12, namely the defeated dragon's pursuit of the beautiful woman, who represents the church. Here the earth swallowed the river flowing from the dragon's mouth, thus saving the woman—an image of the inability of the dragon-empire to do ultimate harm to the church.

Further, limitations and defeat of the dragon-empire are signaled in the limits placed on the authority of Beast I—forty-two months or 1,260 days or three-and-a-half years. That figure stands in sharp in contrast to the "one thousand years" of God's time—the famed, supposed millennium in Revelation 20. This reference to a thousand years is no more a prediction of a future epoch in our history than is Beast I or the antichrist a prediction of a future antichrist as world ruler. In biblical imagery, one thousand is a metaphorical way to say "a very large number," the way a busy person today might say that she has "a million things to do." The binding of Satan in chapter 20 is the same thing that secured the victory of Michael's forces over the dragon's forces in chapter 12, namely the resurrection of Jesus. The limitation and defeat of the dragon-empire is then signaled by assigning the empire a minimal "forty-two months." This limited time contrasts sharply with the infinite expanse of God's time, namely the extremely large number of one thousand years in Revelation 20.

That victory via resurrection displays Revelation's view of time and sets up the meaning of Revelation for the past, present, and the future. The past meaning is obvious since the symbols refer to first-century elements. The resurrection, an event of the past, reveals that the definitive defeat of the forces of evil has already occurred and thus it makes plain to eyes of faith the identity of the ultimate power in the universe. Stated from another perspective, the resurrection of Jesus is the future reign of God breaking into the world now. Thus the resurrection is the beginning of the culmination of the reign of God, which means that Revelation also speaks a definitive world about the future.

The resurrection assures us that the future belongs to God and that history will culminate in the reign of God. This victory for the reign of God, manifested in the resurrection of Jesus, attracts and demands the loyalty of Christians. This is a theological statement about the direction and meaning of the future and an affirmation that the future belongs to God. In no way is it a prediction of when or how that future unfolds, nor does Revelation provide any predictions of events that indicate the nearness of that culmination. Revelation does not lay out a calendar of events at the end or culmination of history.

Understanding the resurrection of Jesus as a past event that also reveals the future culmination of history shines light on an obvious point that bears stating explicitly: the Roman Empire, pictured as dragon, and the church, pictured in various images, exist at the same time. Although defeated by the resurrection of Jesus, the forces of evil embodied by the empire are still around. This simultaneous existence of empire and church is the reason that the faithful can expect harassment and persecution even though the reign of God is already victorious.

The ultimate fulfillment of the divine will in spite of human violence and disobedience will occur at the final consummation with the return of Jesus. In the meantime, although evil has been defeated by the resurrection, it is still thrashing around and able to inflict suffering. It is as though we are playing late in the fourth quarter of a football game, in which the outcome of the game was settled at the end of the first half when the winning team—our team—capitalized on opponents' errors and scored three touchdowns to put the game out of reach. That scoring spree is like the resurrection. The game continues, we may be injured, perhaps even intentionally, but the outcome is determined. The reign of God is victorious, even as suffering and evil are still present.

The church of the first century is still in existence. We are part of its current manifestation. The forces of evil that were embodied in the Roman Empire still exist as well. In other words, the dragon and beasts still live! The possibility of confrontation, harassment and persecution remain with us, and thus the temptation to be deceived by a benevolent appearing "empire" also exists. To receive Revelation's message for our time, we ask what structures constitute the current manifestation of the dragon and the two beasts. What entities challenge the reign of God for ultimate authority, like the dragon-Rome did in the first century, and who or what is it that uses the name of God in vain or has the look of the lamb-Christ but speaks and acts like the dragon-Rome?

WHERE IS THE DRAGON TODAY?

In actuality, many structures claim ultimate allegiance as rivals to the reign of God. Howard-Brook and Gwyther declare that empire exists "wherever sociopolitical power coalesces into an entity that stands against the worship of YHWH alone."[6] Here I note only examples in which we are complicit in the United States.

Currently the United States claims to be and claims the right to be the world's leader. National leaders of the U.S. are quick to claim God's blessing on the nation and that God is on "our" side. George W. Bush, the former president of the United States, made much of his profession of Christian faith. He even famously called Jesus "his favorite political philosopher."

But this president who professed faith in Jesus waged a preemptive war in Iraq. Many people now believe that this president justified the invasion on the basis of manipulated if not outright fabricated evidence. And then as the first claimed reason for the invasion—the much anticipated weapons of mass destruction—proved false, he proposed other reasons for the war while simultaneously denying that he had ever changed the justification for the war. Such actions by one who claims the name of Jesus Christ certainly sounds like the one who looks like the Lamb, that is, "had two horns like a lamb" but "spoke like a dragon" (13:11).

However, the president who manipulated evidence to justify invading Iraq is in no way unique. The Vietnam War cost the lives of more than fifty-eight thousand American soldiers and perhaps two million Vietnamese, both soldiers and civilians. There is now significant evidence that the Gulf of Tonkin Resolution, the congressional act that gave President Lyndon Johnson the authority to make war in Vietnam, was based on manipulated data.

6. Howard-Brook and Gwyther, *Unveiling*, 158.

Barack Obama, the United States president in office at the time of this writing, seems intent on pursuing the policies of the previous administration regarding wars Iraq and Afghanistan. President Obama has stated a tentative timetable for withdrawal of "combat troops" from Iraq, meaning that occupation forces will remain, and he has escalated—euphemistically called a "surge"—the number of United States soldiers in Afghanistan. These actions come from a man who describes his return to Christian faith via an African-American church in Chicago. These actions of past and current presidents also reflect the image that looks like a lamb but speaks with the voice of the dragon.

Nothing in the New Testament story of Jesus indicates that he would declare a pre-emptive war and then lie about the reasons for it. Nothing in the New Testament indicates that Jesus would continue that war, costing thousands more lives and billions of dollars, in order to "finish the job" or to show that those who have already died did not die in vain. Nothing in the New Testament story of Jesus indicates that Jesus or the God of Jesus Christ would favor the United States over other nations, or sanction one political party as God's party over the others. Sometimes I wear a t-shirt that asks, "Who would Jesus bomb?" From the perspective of the church of Jesus Christ, which follows the nonviolent Jesus, the nation in which we live and its leadership sound much like the dragon-empire that claims ultimate authority over against God, and the two beasts who use the name of God in vain and look like the lamb-Jesus but speak and act like the dragon-Rome.

The political system of the United States is certainly not the only modern parallel to Rome. A different suggestion comes from Wes Howard-Brook and Anthony Gwyther, the authors of *Unveiling Empire*. These authors note that although the United States would never admit to being an empire, the review of its history reveals the "imperial earmarks that accompanied the growth of the nation: slave labor; demonization, genocide, and displacement of indigenous people; colonization of distant lands (e.g., Hawaii, Alaska, the Philippines, Guam); cultural arrogance; and global military power." But they suggest that the United States is no longer the dominant imperial force. Howard-Brook and Gwyther's suggestion for the largest, current manifestation of empire is "global capital." They accept a definition of "imperialism" as "a mechanism for transferring income from the middle to the upper classes." This transfer of wealth at the service of global capital has functioned in recent decades under the idea of "free trade."[7]

The notions of free market and free trade are treated as ultimate and intrinsically true values. It is claimed that they benefit everyone. However, in fact, these ideas serve the interests of the wealthy and powerful to the detriment of the poorer countries, labeled "underdeveloped." Through controls operating under the International Monetary Fund (IMF) and the World Bank (WB) to produce free trade, the wealthy nations pursued policies that produced enormous, unpayable debt among the poorer countries. In response, the IMF and WB forced "restructuring" on the local economies, which eliminated any preference for locally produced goods. This process of "free trade" allowed cheap, imported goods from North America and Europe to flow into the local economy. Sale of these goods under the banner of "free trade" benefited the wealthy countries, while putting thousands of local workers and farmers out of business.

James Harder noted the destructive capacity of free trade in the case of Mexico. The North American Free Trade Act (NAFTA) of 1994 opened Mexico to the sale of agricultural products grown in the United States. The local Mexican farmers could not compete with the megafarms and agribusiness from their northern neighbor. As a result, thousands of Mexican farm families were devastated. Many moved to the already overcrowded Mexico City, where they join the swelling ranks of poor people hoping desperately to survive as day laborers.[8]

It bears pointing out specifically that these applications in our present time of the images from Revelation 12 and 13 are not predictions. Revelation's images of dragon and two beasts present a warning to first-century readers, a warning not to become complacent and become deceived by a benevolent-appearing empire. They are a warning not to succumb to the temptation to express symbolic loyalty to the emperor when their loyalty belongs to Christ the Lord. However, although directed to the church of the first century, that warning applies equally well to the church in the twenty-first century. We also have national and international structures that claim loyalty but that also oppress.

The warning of Revelation to first century readers applies to twenty-first-century readers as well. Do not be deceived by leaders who use the name of Jesus but practice the opposite of his teaching.

7. Howard-Brook and Gwyther, *Unveiling*, 238ff.
8. Harder, "Violence."

Do not be deceived by the rhetoric of the international market system and the free trade slogan that promise riches to all, but actually benefit only a few to the detriment of many. It is just as true in the twenty-first century as in the first century—the dragon and the beasts still live, and they surround us.

REVELATION'S MESSAGE FOR PEACEMAKERS

What does this scenario mean for adherents of the peace church? It means recognizing that our ultimate home is in the reign of God. The church is the earthly structure that gives visibility to the reign of God, and we live in it as exiles in a foreign land. From the perspective of our nation, we are citizens of this foreign land. We carry identity papers it issues and we are subject to its laws. And we can involve ourselves in its activities, such as participating in the vote, hoping to choose the candidate who seems the least likely to lie and manipulate data. But with such participation comes the warning—remember our ultimate identity. Participating in, working with or in the national structures is not working with God or God's party or selecting God's earthly leaders. The warning of Revelation is to remember that however benevolent it may appear at the current time, however publicly its leaders speak the name of Jesus Christ, this government too is like the dragon. Its "two horns" may give it the appearance of being Christian, but its voice and its actions are those of the dragon.

A different kind of involvement is also appropriate, perhaps more appropriate than trying to become involved in the government of the "dragon." This is the involvement of witness. When the church carries on its affairs—its internal governance, conflict resolution, economic sharing, rejection of violence, recognizing and using the gifts of men and women equally, acceptance of same-sex preference, and more—this is a demonstration of the character of the reign of God in contrast to the character of the dragon. This demonstration of life in the reign of God is a public display of what the world is called under the rule of God.

This witness is also inevitably a critique of the social order—after all, the church that gives this witness follows Jesus Christ while the nation does not. At times, the result will be tension between the church and the social order. In fact, as the history of martyrs makes clear, it may be dangerous to bear this witness to the injustice of the social order. Revelation is not speaking idly with its warning that the structures of the social order are the dragon. If we are truly the peace church, our ultimate loyalty resides with God, who loves all peoples and nations equally. May the peace church truly live that way.

THE NEW JERUSALEM

However, Revelation goes beyond the warning about the true character of the powers that rule the social order. The book concludes with a testimony to how glorious it is to heed that warning and to be the church that witnesses to the presence of the reign of God. This testimony comes in the image of the New Jerusalem in Revelation 21.

This image is frequently interpreted as a view of a future heaven. However, I accept a different interpretation of New Jerusalem. It is an image of the church in our world as it faces the "dragon." Consistent with the fact that the church and dragon-empire exist simultaneously, Howard-Brook and Gwyther argue that Babylon in Revelation 19, an image of a fallen world, exists simultaneously with the New Jerusalem in chapter 21, an image of the church that lives in the midst of Babylon.[9]

That New Jerusalem is the church in time, and not a vision of a future heaven, is more than a theological conjecture. It appears in the text. In Rev 21:3 a voice from the heavenly states, "See, the home of God is among mortals, He will dwell with them as their God; they will be his peoples, and God himself will be with them." This declaration is true if the following description of New Jerusalem refers to the church in the world. A bit later, as the lead in to the description of the city, the angelic guide says, "Come, I will show you the bride, the wife of the Lamb" (Rev 21:9). Bride of Christ is a New Testament name for the church.

Time clues appear throughout the description. Revelation 21:8 pictures judgment still to come. Then in 21:25–27 one reads that the gates of the city are never shut during the day while there is no night, "But nothing unclean will enter it, nor anyone who practices abomination or falsehood, but only those who are written in the Lamb's book of life." The clear implication is that the righteous and the wicked exist together, which could not be the case if this were an image of a future heaven. This same juxtaposition of the righteous and the wicked occurs in 22:10, 14–15.

---

9. Howard-Brook and Gwyther, *Unveiling*.

With the idea in mind that the wicked and the righteous exist simultaneously, it is evident that the statements about those who do and do not enter the city are not statements about physical displacement but about identity and belonging and loyalty. As Howard-Brook and Gwyther state, "Babylon exists wherever human society becomes empire, asserting its power over creation and usurping the privileges of God. Similarly, New Jerusalem is found wherever human community resists the ways of empire and places God at the center of its shared life."[10] The imagery of the New Jerusalem portrays the church as a glorious entity. It is a cube—"its length and width and height are equal" (Rev 21:16). The equal sides represent perfection, a contrast to the topsy-turvy development of ancient cities.

The New Revised Standard Version gives the length of each edge as "fifteen hundred miles" (Rev 21:16). That describes a huge cube, with the area of each side approximately that of the United States east of the Mississippi River. A footnote explains that the fifteen hundred miles is "twelve thousand stadia," making one stadion the approximate length of two modern football fields. However, the significant number is the twelve. The number of 12,000 stadia comes from an equation: 12 x 1000. Recall that as a figure, one thousand should not be taken literally or as an exact number. The 12,000 stadia is thus a way to use the number twelve in picturing an enormous city.

But the image features many more twelves. The walls of this city are 144 cubits thick (about two hundred feet). The important point to notice is that 144 cubits is the product of an equation, 12 x 12. Other descriptors also include twelves—twelve gates (three on each wall) with names of the twelve tribes of Israel, twelve foundations of the city and each foundation having the name of one of the twelve apostles.

The number twelve symbolizes God's people. The description of New Jerusalem should not be understood literally; it does not describe an actual city either present or future. It is a highly symbolic depiction whose symbols all indicate that the city represents God's people, the church.

The city is built of gold, and the twelve foundations are twelve different precious stones—jasper, sapphire, agate, emerald, onyx, carnelian, chrysolite, beryl, topaz, chrysoprase, jacinth, amethyst—and the twelve gates are each fashioned from a single giant pearl. Further the city needs

10. Howard-Brook and Gwyther, *Unveiling*, 158.

no sun or moon for light because the glory of God is its light and its lamp is the Lamb. The city is gloriously arrayed, but the description also indicates that when compared with the glory of God, the most valuable of human materials are still merely building materials.

Revelation was written as a warning to these Christians not to be deceived by a seemingly benevolent empire. In actuality, Revelation says, Rome is a beast—the dragon—that opposes the rule of God. This beast, the seven-headed dragon that is Rome built on seven hills, is laying in wait to deceive and destroy the followers of Jesus Christ. Christians should resist the dragon (i.e., resist Rome) because Rome and all the evil that it represents have *already* been conquered by the resurrection of Jesus. Even if Rome ends up killing Christians, which remains a possibility, loyalty to the reign of God is still worthwhile because in the resurrection of Jesus, Rome and all the evil it represents has been conquered.

Chapter 21 pictures the church—the New Jerusalem—from the perspective of the reign of God that has triumphed over all evil in the resurrection of Jesus. This huge, fantastic cube, the New Jerusalem, is an image of the flesh and blood church living in Asia Minor in the midst of the Roman Empire at the end of the first century. The imagery proclaims how glorious it is to live in the reign of God, even in the face of the momentarily benevolent Roman beast. Living in the midst of the Roman Empire, the gates of the church are open but wickedness remains without as long as people live in the rule of God.

Recall the earlier discussion of the so-called "millennium" in Revelation 20. The images of one thousand years, the binding and then the loosing of Satan in chapter 20 should now be clearly visible as additional images that depict the simultaneous existence of evil empire-dragon and church, of Babylon and Jerusalem. Satan is indeed bound or defeated by the resurrection for the unlimited expanse of God's time— one thousand years as "a very large number of years"—in contrast to the finite time of human history—symbolized by the very brief three-and-a-half years—that evil can wreck havoc before the final consummation.

Seeing this view of New Jerusalem in particular and Revelation in general makes clear that the book of Revelation is a statement about the meaning of Jesus' life, death and resurrection. It is another way to convey the gospel's story that in Jesus' life and teaching, the reign of God was confronting the evils and injustice of the world. These evils killed him, but with the resurrection the reign of God triumphed over those evil powers. It should be more than obvious that God does not triumph through greater violence than Satan can command. On the contrary, God triumphs not through the taking of life but through restoration of life. It is a gross misreading of Revelation to see its images as predictions of events coming true in our time and/or as images of God and of Jesus Christ waiting until the end of time in order to unleash overwhelming violence and destruction on an evil world. Not only is the God revealed in nonviolent Jesus not that kind of God. But if the final defeat of evil awaits a great, future battle, then the resurrection of Jesus was not the ultimately decisive event pictured in Revelation.

Revelation called first-century Christians in Asia Minor to believe in the resurrection strongly enough to live in the story of Jesus in the face of imperial Rome. Do we in the twenty-first century believe in the resurrection enough to live in the story of Jesus in the face of today's empire? Living in the story of Jesus today, I suggest, invites us to reject our nation's call us to trust in guns and bombs for security and to resist the allure of leaders who claim the name of Jesus but pursue war and distort truth. Loyalty to the reign of God invites us to resist the idolatrous patriotism that currently shapes the national ethos. And it calls us to seek out ways to resist the consumer mentality, which teaches that happiness comes through acquisition of material goods, that measures success by acquisition of money and ever more possessions, and that turns a blind eye to the suffering in the world caused by the violence of the system of global capital that enables this wealthy nation to continue to enrich itself to the detriment of many other nations. The dragon does indeed still live.

PART TWO

Toward Compassionate Eschatology

9

Is the Apocalypse Inevitable?

Native American Prophecy and the Mimetic Theory

MICHAEL HARDIN

IN THE FALL OF 2009, Michigan State University Press released the latest book in René Girard's distinguished career, *Battling to the End: Conversations with Benoît Chantre*. The focus of these "conversations" is the thought of the nineteenth-century Prussian military theoretician, Carl von Clausewitz.

Now that *Battling to the End*[1] is out and being read by eager Girardians everywhere, a distinct rift in the Girardian community is taking place. On the one hand there are those who cannot help but feel that Girard's Clausewitz book is an aberration from the theory of mimesis and sacred violence they learned from the master. The sheer cultural pessimism, the lack of hope in humanity's essential goodness, and for some the problems of theodicy it creates relegate *Battling* to the musings of a depressed octogenarian or to a wrong and twisted turn in the road of mimetic theory. There are, on the other hand, some who would argue that Girard is being realistic in *Battling* when he speaks rather morbidly about the direction the human species is taking in relation to sacrificial violence. For still others, the apocalyptic overtones of *Battling* smack of Christian *apologia*.

Jozef Niewiadomski points to the way apocalypse has been, at times perversely, longed for in the church through its history but disdained in the theological academy.[2] Does René Girard belong in either

1. Girard, *Battling*.
2. Niewiadomski, "Denial."

of these two categories? I will suggest he does not. Girard neither denies apocalypse nor seeks it. He simply *unveils* it. Mimetic theory *apocalypses* apocalypse.

This bifurcation into camps can be seen in the theme of the Girardian study group, the Colloquium on Violence and Religion, at its annual meeting in Riverside, CA, in 2008: Convergence or Catastrophe.[3] This conference included a celebration of the French edition of *Battling* (*Achever Clausewitz*). It is the case that *Battling* raises in spectral fashion the ominous situation in which we find ourselves as we open the twenty-first century. It is not difficult to multiply examples of the dire straits in which we humans find ourselves, from proliferation of weapons of mass destruction, population estimates, resource shortages to global warming and environmental degradation, genocides and wars, more wars and rumors of wars.

IS MIMETIC THEORY PESSIMISTIC?

My essay will focus on the question, "Is mimetic theory inherently pessimistic?" by juxtaposing the apocalyptic element in mimetic theory and Native American prophetic traditions.[4] It may be the case that the "genre" of apocalyptic came to the Native Americans' storytelling by hearing the Christian story about Jesus. If that is the case, then Girard's anthropological reading of biblical apocalyptic has support as a hermeneutic. This anthropological reading of "the signs of the times" is completely differentiated from that of most Western Christian readings of apocalyptic. The cause of the apocalypse had everything to with humanity and not God. "But God who is rich in mercy" sees it through with us to the very end and into a gracious beyond. The real question is not whether the apocalypse is inevitable. The real question becomes one of God's location in relation to apocalypse. This is where Girard and certain Native American prophetic traditions converge.

3. This essay was originally presented at that conference, June 18–22, 2008. I thank James Alison and Jonathan Sauder for their comments on this revision.

4. I am cognizant of and in harmony with George E. Tinker's concern that Euro-Americans use Native traditions and philosophy without understanding the context in which they arise. Tinker, *Spirit,* is an important warning about the grave possibility of misunderstanding, misappropriating and misrepresenting Native cultures. I will do my best to heed that warning.

Still we might ask the question: Is *the* apocalypse inevitable? Such a question might seem utterly pessimistic and without hope. René Girard has been accused of such pessimism. But is it pessimism to suggest that there is a convergence of negative and detrimental existential *realia* that require us as a species to either change or face the consequences of our behavior?

Robert Doran, in a series of enlightening interviews with Rene in 2007, asked about the importance of turning points in human history, in particular, how Rene understood the events of September 11, 2001:

> RD: You yourself see 9/11 as a kind of rupture, a seminal event?

> RG: Yes, I see it as a seminal event, and it is fundamentally wrong to minimize it today. The normal desire to be optimistic, to not see the uniqueness of our time from the point of view of violence, is the desire to grab any straw to make our time appear as the mere continuation of the violence of the twentieth century. I personally think that it represents a new dimension, a new world dimension. What communism was trying to do, to have a truly global war, has happened, and it is real now. To minimize 9/11 is to try to avoid thinking the way I do about the importance of this new dimension.

What makes 9/11 such a profound event is that it is a religious event. According to Girard:

> 9/11 is the beginning of this [new dimension], for in this attack technology was used not for humanistic ends but for radical, metaphysico-religious ends, which are not Christian. That is why it is such an amazing thing for me, because I'm used to considering religious forces and humanistic forces together, not as if one were true and the other false; and then suddenly archaic religion is coming back in an incredibly forceful way with Islam. Islam has many aspects of the Biblical religions minus the revelation of violence as bad, as not divine but human; it makes violence totally divine. This is why the opposition is more significant than with communism, which is a humanism. It is a bogus humanism, the last and most incredibly foolish form, which results in terror. But it is still humanism. And suddenly we're back in religion, in archaic religion—but with modern weapons. What the world is waiting for is the moment when the Muslim radicals will somehow be able to use nuclear weapons.[5]

5. Doran, "Apocalyptic," 21.

It is this turn back to archaic religious responses that Girard sees as fore-shadowing apocalypse.

> RD: Then could one say that you are pessimistic in an a priori sense?
>
> RG: I am pessimistic in the sense that everybody understands the word pessimism. But I'm optimistic in the sense that if one looks at the present world, it already verifies all the predictions. You can see the shape of the apocalypse increasing every day: the power capable of destroying the world, ever more lethal weapons, and the other threats that are multiplying under our eyes. We still believe that all of these problems are manageable by man, but if you take them all together you can see that this is not the case. They acquire a kind of supernatural value. Like the fundamentalists, many readers of the Gospels are reminded of the world situation when they read these apocalyptic chapters.[6]

Now I for one am not a Christian fundamentalist. I do not believe in the triumphalist stance of so-called Christian America, nor do I think there is some fire-escape rapture scenario awaiting all true believers. But rejecting the apocalyptic projections of certain forms of the Christian tradition does not mean turning a blind eye to the realities that we face today, hoping in some old-fashioned liberal naiveté, that things will get better in the by and by.

Already in 1978 (*Things Hidden from the Foundation of the World*) Girard saw the importance of apocalyptic as a tradition of warning to humans bent on violence and destruction. Two decades prior to the Jesus Seminar questioning whether or not Jesus was an apocalyptist, Girard bluntly observed that

> We now have in our hands all the threads of the logic that transforms the announcement of the Kingdom into an announcement of the Apocalypse. If humans turn down the peace Jesus offers them—a peace not derived from violence, which by virtue of this fact, *passes understanding*—the effect of the gospel revelation will be made manifest through violence, through a sacrificial and cultural crisis whose radical effect must be unprecedented since there is no longer any sacralized victim to stand in the way of its consequences.[7]

6. Ibid., 27.
7. Girard, *Things*, 203.

HARDIN—*Is the Apocalypse Inevitable?*   159

In 1982, Girard put it a bit more pointedly, concluding his book on *The Scapegoat* by saying that "the time has come for us to forgive one another. If we wait any longer there will not be time enough."[8]

What is troublesome for some is that it is precisely the proclamation of the demise of the "Generative Mimetic Scapegoating Mechanism" (to use Robert Hamerton-Kelly's designation) that is facilitating the breakthrough of this apocalypse. Girard's *Things Hidden* points in this direction; his chapter on the Paraclete in *The Scapegoat* confirms it; and in 1999, his *I See Satan Fall as Lightning* cements this kerygmatic influence to our current crisis:

> The knowledge we have acquired about our violence, thanks to our religious tradition, does not put an end to scapegoating but weakens it enough to reduce its effectiveness more and more. This is the true reason why apocalyptic destruction threatens us, and this threat is not irrational at all.[9]

Contradicting all forms of liberal theology and indeed even liberation theology, Girard, in 2006 interviews with Pierpaolo Antonello and Joao Cezar de Castro Rocha, says, "The gospel does not provide a happy ending to our history."[10] Coupled with the Doran interview cited at the beginning of this essay it would appear that *the mimetic theory itself facilitates our current apocalyptic crisis in that it incorporates the unmasking of the victimage mechanism in the preaching of the passion of Jesus Christ.*

The most significant advance that mimetic theory makes to our definition of apocalypse, however, is that the consequences we face are not divine or transcendent in character but are absolutely anthropological. This is why Girard understands our current crisis as religious but not "theological" in character; that is, the crisis we face is created by human/religious constructs not by the character or will of God. This insight vitiates all of the speculations that Christian apocalyptists proclaim grounded in their triumphalist Constantinian worldviews.

There is an intellectual imperative regarding this perspective. As Girard notes,

---

8. Girard, *Scapegoat*, 212. On the "kairos" moment we are in and the need to forgive rather than retaliate, see also Girard, *Evolution*, 225, 262.

9. Girard, *I See*, 184.

10. Girard, *Evolution*, 237.

This is the reason why one has to see this process from the mimetic perspective and in Christian apocalyptic terms, in the sense that the more there is an opening in the world where ritual is dead, the more dangerous this world becomes. It has both positive aspects, in the sense there is less sacrifice, and negative aspects, in that there is an unleashing of mimetic rivalry.[11]

NATIVE AMERICAN PROPHETIC TRADITIONS

It is in the anthropological rendering of apocalypse that we can find certain similarities with Native American prophetic traditions. In these apocalyptic prophecies, the consequences that humanity faces are not to be seen as coordinated with an eschatological deity of wrath, but rather are recognized as the inevitable results of human self-destructive tendencies.

Before citing a few examples from the American Southwest, it should be pointed out that Native prophecies are divided in two categories, those permitted to be revealed to the non-Native and those that are kept within the various tribes themselves, as they pertain only to the survival of the tribe.

Native prophecies are oral in character, not written down. Hence, unlike Jewish or Christian prophetic traditions, one has to rely on testimony from an elder. Also unlike Jewish-Christian prophecy replete with successions of events and timelines, Native "prophecy reasserts the powers of Indian mythology and cosmology over mere chronology."[12]

Willard Johnson observes that there are discernable periods to Native prophecy. Prior to the coming of white Europeans to American shores, there is no evidence of Native prophetic traditions. It is only after the encounter with Euro-American people that Native prophecy, as we know it, emerges.[13]

The significant historical markers for Native prophecy are 1745-1890 when Natives were involved in a "religiously charged struggle for unity" and prophets "led nativistic resistance movements that drew upon indigenous religious traditions and ritual forms to create intertribal movement . . . [opposing] parties who wished to accommodate the

---

11. Ibid., 254.

12. Nabakov, Native, 469.

13. Johnson, "Contemporary."

invaders."[14] After the suppression of Native traditions, the demolition of tribal structures and affiliations at the end of the nineteenth century, Native prophecy went underground and did not emerge until the 1970s during the dawning of the New Age movement. Johnson cites a Juaneno prophet, Ka'chi, who avers that "when a prophecy's time comes and if its message refers to all humanity, it can be made public." This is because "some will heed and believe" and "some from every race and nation will begin to retrace their footsteps and find the sacred path again."[15]

A problem arises in that most of the post-1970s native prophecies have been influenced (not always beneficially) by New Age speculations. So, there are very few prophecies that are authentically (uncorrupted) Native that have gone outside Native circles.[16] I will use three examples from the American Southwest: Hopi, Zuni, and Apache.

These Native prophecies stress four elements:

1. Ecological degradation and consequences

2. The problem of human violence

3. A time of turning

4. Hope for the coming age.

One of the best-known prophecies is that of Hopi Thomas Banyacya, one of the few Hopis allowed to translate Native prophecies into English, who in 1976 addressed the United Nations-sponsored Habitat Conference in Vancouver, British Columbia. He offers this interpretation of Hopi prophecy:

> What have you, as individuals, as nations and as the world body been doing to take care of this Earth? In the Earth today, humans poison their own food, water and air with pollution. Many of us, including children, are left to starve. Many wars are still being fought. Greed and concern for material things is a common disease. In this western hemisphere, our homeland, many original native people are landless, homeless, starving and have no medical help.
>
> The Hopi knew humans would develop many powerful technologies that would be abused. In this century, we have seen the First World War and the Second World War in which the predicted

14. Ibid., 577.

15. Ibid. 579.

16. In addition to Johnson, see also Page, *In the Hands*, 404ff.

gourd of ashes, which you call the atomic bomb, fell from the sky with great destruction. Many thousands of people were destroyed in Hiroshima and Nagasaki.

For many years there has been great fear and danger of World War Three. The Hopi believe the Persian Gulf War was the beginning of World War Three but it was stopped and the worst weapons of destruction were not used. This is now a time to weigh the choices for our future. We do have a choice. If you, the nations of this Earth, create another great war, the Hopi believe we humans will burn ourselves to death with ashes. That's why the spiritual Elders stress strongly that the United Nations fully open the door for native spiritual leaders as soon as possible.[17]

Frank Waters recorded the Hopi prophecy,

World War III will be started by those peoples who received the light [the divine wisdom or intelligence] in the other old countries [India, China, Egypt, Palestine, Africa]. The United States will be destroyed, land and people by atomic bombs and radioactivity. Those who take no part in the making of world division by ideology are ready to resume life in another world . . . the War will be a spiritual conflict with material matters. The emergence of the Fifth world has begun. It is being made by the humble people of little nations, tribes and racial minorities[18]

A tradition from the Zuni tribe of New Mexico describes the mimetic character of the future crisis:

Cities will progress and then decay to the ways of the lowest beings. Drinkers of dark liquids will come upon the land, speaking nonsense and filth. Then the end shall be nearer. Population will increase until the land can hold no more. The tribes of men will mix. The dark liquids they drink will cause the people to fight amongst themselves. Families will break up: father against children and the children against one another . . . our possessions will turn into beasts and devour us whole. If not, there will be an odor from gases, which will fill the air we breathe and the end for us shall come. But the people themselves will bring upon themselves what they receive. From what has resulted, time alone will tell us what the future holds for us.[19]

17. This text can be found in many places and is easily referenced by a Google search.

18. Waters, *Book*, 334.

19. Nabakov, *Native*, 470, quoting from Zuni, *Zunis*.

My third example comes from a most unusual source, an Apache scout/shaman who lived from about 1880–1970. Stalking Wolf was trained in an elite medicine society and had virtually no contact with the "Wasichus" (the Sioux term for white Euro-Americans) until after 1930. His apocalyptic vision stems from before this time, most likely between 1925 and 1930. Tom Brown Jr. recorded them in 1962.[20]

In this vision Stalking Wolf saw a series of signs that would precede the changing of the ages. The first sign is that of famine.

> The world will one day look upon all of this with horror and will blame the famine on the weather and the Earth. This will be the first warning to the world that man cannot live beyond the laws of Creation, nor can he fight Nature. If the world sees that it is to blame for this famine, this senseless starvation, then a great lesson will be learned. But I am afraid that the world will not blame itself but that the blame will be placed on Nature. There will come starvation before and after this starvation, but none will capture the attention of the world with such impact as does this one.

According to Stalking Wolf's interpreter, Tom Brown Jr., the first sign was "fulfilled" by the great famine in Africa in the 1970s. A second sign occurs

> During the years of the famine, the first sign, that man will be plagued by a disease, a disease that will sweep the land and terrorize the masses. The doctors (white coats) will have no answers for the people and a great cry will arise across the land. The disease will be born of monkeys, drugs, and sex. It will destroy man from inside, making common sickness a killing disease.

It is not difficult to see a possible reference to HIV/AIDS here. A third sign:

> Looking skyward, the sun seemed to be larger and more intense; no birds or clouds could be seen; and the air seemed thicker still. It was then that the sky seemed to surge and huge holes began to appear. The holes tore with a resounding, thunderous sound, and the very Earth, rocks, and soil shook.

20. All citations of Stalking Wolf's prophecies are taken from Brown, *Quest*. For more information on Stalking Wolf and my relation to his tradition, I refer the reader to Hardin, "Ecospirituality." I note in that essay that there are currently no Euro-American Christian theologians seeking to integrate the Native and Christian traditions. Dr. Terry LeBlanc (Micmaq) in a June 11, 2008, conversation at Princeton University confirmed this suspicion.

> The skin of the sky seemed to be torn open like a series of gaping wounds, and through these wounds seeped a liquid that seemed like the oozing of an infection, a great sea of floating garbage, oil, and dead fish. It was through one of these wounds that Grandfather [Stalking Wolf] saw the floating bodies of dolphins, accompanied by tremendous upheavals of the Earth and of violent storms.

This seems to be a reference to the destruction of Earth's atmosphere and the ozone layer accompanied by the destruction of Earth's seas.

The fourth sign of the impending apocalypse is cosmological in character. Possible interpretations might include extraordinary volcanic eruption or fallout from a nuclear war.

> The night of the bleeding stars . . . will become known throughout the world, for the sky in all lands will be red with the blood of the sky, day and night. It is then, with this sign of the third probable future, that there is no longer hope. Life on the Earth as humans have lived it will come to an end, and there can be no turning back, physically or spiritually. It is then, if things are not changed, that humanity will surely know the destruction of the Earth is at hand.

NO VIOLENT GOD

What is most intriguing about these Native prophecies is that in spite of the Christian influence on Native prophetic traditions since 1745, there is no trace of a violent god such as one sees in contemporary Christian fundamentalist interpretation of biblical prophecy. In every case that I have investigated, apocalyptic consequences are strictly anthropological. This, I think is of signal importance. It suggests that the Girardian reading of Christian apocalypse as an anthropological datum or religious phenomenon is not isolated.

Biblical and theological studies also reflect this shift in the numerous books on "empire" that have come out in recent years.[21] These studies read the New Testament, particularly apocalyptic references, in the context of and opposing the phenomenon of empire, that is, the so-

---

21. A seminal, prescient work is a commentary on the Apocalypse of John by Stringfellow, *Ethic*. Three contemporary examples of exegesis would include Richard, *Apocalypse*; Grimsrud, *Triumph*; and Horsley, *Paul*. Theological titles would include Rieger, *Christ*; Schüssler Fiorenza, *Power*; Jewett, *Mission*.

cial-religious world structured on violence, dominion, and oppression. Walter Wink has drawn our attention to the way mimetic theory can be used to illumine "the powers and the principalities."[22] Empire has both physical (social) and spiritual (religious/sacrificial) dimensions. New Testament writers, primarily Paul, use language that reflects both sides of this phenomenon.

What Scripture calls "the principalities and powers" comes under the rubrics "greed, jealousy, or evil inclinations/spirits" in Native prophecy. In either case, both traditions refer to the "bent" ways we humans structure our relationships, to the Creator, the creation, and one another. Far from creating a colonial Christian culture (as Christian missionaries to the Native Americans sought to do by "killing the Indian in the child"), the gospel of peace deconstructs the "bent" ways of all culture, including the civil religion of the United States, so-called "American Christianity."

In the Doran interview Girard says,

> Those who say that Christianity is anarchistic are somewhat right. The Christians are destroying the powers of this world, in the sense that they are destroying the legitimacy of all violence. From the point of view of the State, Christianity is a force of anarchy. Anytime it recaptures its old spiritual strength, this reappears in a way.[23]

Interestingly, post-1970 Native prophecies contain the same list of problems identified by Girard in the Doran interview and *Evolution and Conversion*. Many of these are reflected in (or from?) the gospel apocalypses (Mark 13, Luke 21, Matthew 24–25). Common apocalyptic features include:

- Ecological degradation and it's potential effects
- Conflict/war around the world
- Destructive weapon technologies
- Overpopulation
- Diminishing resources (gas, water, air)
- Unstable economies
- Religious conflicts (internal and external)

---

22. Wink, *Naming*; *Unmasking*; *Engaging*; *Cracking*; and *Powers*. See also an engagement of this series in Gingerich and Grimsrud, eds., *Transforming*.

23. Doran, "Apocalyptic," 25.

So we might, with Girard, ask the question, are we to understand the Jewish-Christian apocalyptic tradition as depicting a linear, chronological sequence of events or a conflict within religious/spiritual traditions?[24] Both Girard and Native prophetic traditions argue for the latter. This suggests that a reading of apocalypse as a transcendent otherworldly reality is not the best or most sufficient reading. It is our collective response to these crises that will determine just how close we get to apocalypse *by the way we read and understand apocalypse*. It is our hermeneutic or our perspective that is the key to our future.

When we respond with the hermeneutic oriented to sacred violence we end up reversing the human moral and intellectual development brought about by the gospel. Girard observes, "Not too long ago people would have had a Christian reaction to 9/11. Now they have an archaic reaction, which does not bode well for the future."[25]

It may well be that Native prophetic traditions from 1745 to the present reflect the influence of the biblical prophetic tradition. It has been argued that Girard and Native American prophetic traditions conceive their "apocalyptic" scenarios under biblical influence. If so, it shows that the reading of New Testament apocalyptic from a mimetic anthropological perspective is a viable alternative to transcendental violent readings.

Osage Native Robert Allen Warrior contrasts the neo-colonial perspective of reading the Bible from a position of power with a Native reading "from below." He argues that, "as long as people believe in the Yahweh of deliverance, the world will not be safe from Yahweh the conqueror."[26] The importance of this cannot be gainsaid. We can apply Warrior's rejection of a triumphalist rendering of the Exodus to the modern dispensationalist transcendent violent rendering of apocalyptic texts. Any

24. My friend Jonathan Sauder asks, "Can we say that the crisis is between divergent hermeneutics *within* each religious tradition?" I think this is more to the point. Our current crisis then is not between Islam and Christianity as much as it is between "the violent deities" of jihadist Islam and Christendom (as a social-ecclesial matrix).

25. Doran, "Apocalyptic," 25.

26. Warrior, "Native," 284. I am indebted to Gingerich, "Was," for bringing this essay to my attention. From a Christian perspective Gingerich goes on to add, "Unless Yahweh is perceived and worshiped as the nonviolent deliverer, even as is Jesus." Warrior, following narrative hermeneutics (Childs, Lindbeck, Hauerwas), notes that while the history behind the text may be different than the biblical narrative, popular reading of the Bible only knows the narrative. From the perspective of mimetic theory, this is a "mythic" reading of the text.

reading of a text from a position of power is *ipso facto* colonialist (or, if Christian, Constantinian). In other words, to read apocalyptic texts as transcendent is to read them from the perspective of archaic religion.

Native Americans were employing a "reading from below" from the perspective of the persecuted and scapegoated long before it was fashionable to do so. The difference is that Native cosmology sees the relation of history to apocalypse within the framework of a spiraling-forward cycle, thus according to some traditions we are at the end of one age (the Fourth) and the dawning of the next age (the Fifth) of humanity. For Girard, as a Roman Catholic Christian, apocalyptic mimetic crises have come and gone (were transitioned through), but there remains the possibility of an extinction of humanity because of our technological ability (as Jacques Ellul warned us sixty years ago). But Girard is not without hope, hope that we can recognize our enchantment by violence and reject its spell in favor of a new orientation of non-retribution grounded in the coming kingdom of God, even as Jesus did.

ORIENTED TO HOPE

Both Native prophetic traditions and the "eschatology" of the mimetic theory as deployed by Girard thus are oriented in the final analysis to hope. It is the hope that the Creator will make all things new and in right relationship, all creation including the human species. For the Native this call to conversion has two aspects, a deep commitment to be a good steward of Earth and the desire to relate to a loving Creator. Girard would also affirm these two desires but adds a third, the renunciation of violence.

The renunciation of violence is grounded not simply in Jesus (or some generalized form of his ethic), but also in the anti-sacrificial project of Jesus' Scriptures.[27] Like the Hopi, Girardian eschatology is not "pie in the sky by and by" but is grounded in real history, actual human interactions, in other words, the entire earthly warp and woof of life.

Now if mimetic theory only asserts that mimesis and violence lead to apocalypse when unchecked and that the preaching of the gospel leads to the breakdown of the mechanism, one could assert that it is inherently pessimistic and that apocalypse is inevitable. Thankfully there is a "*but*." That "but" is the call to conversion or repentance.

27. See Hardin, *Jesus.*

The call to conversion is for every religious tradition to find within itself the constructive tools to deconstruct itself in the light of the possibility that God, the Great Mystery, the Creator of all things, is loving and forgiving, reconciling and peacemaking, giver of Life; rather than bringer of both Life and death, existing in a perpetual Janus faced state. The warning part of the tradition is frightening but the belief in the continuation of life grounded in a God of Life gives courage and elicits gratitude. I think, ultimately, both René Girard and most Natives could affirm this. A mimetic reading of the apocalyptic scenario, bears witness to what my wife Lorri calls "compassionate eschatology." It understands the Creator to be ever drawing us toward life-giving behaviors. George Tinker puts it this way,

> While acknowledging that our spirituality is enormously complex in this regard, it must suffice in this context to say that we are pressed *by God* to understand the *Basileia Theou* as the space that encompasses the entirety of the universe(s), hence, creation. Thus, no one and nothing can be left out of the *basileia*. In the spirit of the prayer "*mitakune ouyasin*," we all belong.[28]

Neither Natives nor Girard are without hope. How then might we understand our current crisis? It is time for us to be realistic about what we are seeing. In the current popular Christian interpretation of our situation what we see is a modern turn back to the past, in fact, way back to the dim mists of our prehistory. The sacrificial response and the call to arms by many persons of many faiths in the United States after 9/11 is a cultural recidivism. We have regressed as a species, at the very least, in our hermeneutics.

What ultimately happens depends on how we respond. The call to conversion is not from one religion to another, for religion is the problem not the solution. Like Saul on the road to Damascus,[29] all of us, particularly those of us whose background is in one of the major monotheistic religions, must answer the question "Why are you persecuting me?" We are called to convert from violence to peacemaking and forgiveness. To be realistic about our current predicament ought to be motivation for those of us who use the mimetic theory to preach and teach with even more vigor and passion.

28. Tinker, *Spirit*, 112.
29. Acts 9:1–19.

I will conclude this essay with lyrics to a song I composed in June 1993. It asks the question about apocalypse and the angry God in modern America (with a bit of sarcasm). As long as Christians believe in a vengeful God and an avenging Jesus there is little hope for the world, and good news, gospel, God's Story, is impossible from the pulpit. May it be given to us to learn to hear the life-giving hope of the Way of Peace and so be children of Earth, children of the Creator.

WHY IS JESUS ALWAYS COMING BACK PISSED?

Got on an air-conditioned bus this morning
Read every sign that passed along those city streets
Lady Poverty was in the streets a-borning
But folks still found the time to smile at those they'd meet.

Ahead of me and to my right there rose a steeple
In a world of hate and violence amiss
A symbol of love with a simple sign that read
"Jesus is coming back and boy is He pissed!" Tell me,

(Chorus:)
Why is Jesus always coming back pissed
In a never-ending rhetoric of apocalypse?
It's fire and brimstone that we always kiss
In a story whose love we miss.
Tell me, why is Jesus always coming back pissed?

I was reading yesterday's bad news in the *Post*
But reflected that the world still held firm
Though I'm aware of our poison and evil
I don't believe that we were meant to burn

You find you're born, you eat, you sleep, you live, you drink, you die
And wonder if you're worth anything at all
Sure life can suck and then you find it's over
But who's to say we didn't have a ball?

(Chorus)

At least in the Sixties we had the Jesus movement
We danced and spoke of love and peace and light
Now all that we're left with are the dregs of believers
And God forbid, the Christian Right

"Jesus is Just Alright," said the Doobies
And that's more credible than most of the shit
You can hear on any given Sunday morning
From the thousands of angry pulpits, Oh tell me,

(Chorus)

10

Redeeming the Entire Universe

The Spirit of Institutions

WALTER WINK

ALL OF US DEAL with the Powers That Be.[1] They staff our hospitals, run city hall, sit around tables in corporate boardrooms, collect our taxes, and head our families. But the Powers That Be are more than just the people who run things. They are the systems themselves, the institutions and structures that weave society into an intricate fabric of power and relationships. These Powers surround us on every side. They are necessary. They are useful. We could do nothing without them. Who wants to do without timely mail delivery or well-maintained roads? But the Powers are also the source of unmitigated evils.

A corporation routinely dumps known carcinogens into a river that is the source of drinking water for towns downstream. Another industry attempts to hook children into addiction to cigarettes despite evidence that a third of them will die prematurely from smoking related illnesses. A dictator wages war against his own citizens in order to maintain his grasp on power. A contractor pays off a building inspector so he can violate code and put up a shoddy and perhaps unsafe structure. A power plant exposes its employees to radioactive poisoning; the employee who attempts to document these safety infractions is forced off the road by another car and dies. All her documents are missing. Welcome to the world of the Powers.

---

1. This essay was first published in Cobble and Elliott, *Hidden*. It has been revised for this publication. My thanks to Michael Hardin who suggested its revision and republication.

But the Powers aren't always that brutal. Some people enjoy their jobs. Some businesses make genuine contributions to society. Some products are life-enhancing, even life-saving. The Powers don't simply do evil. They also do good. Often they do both good and evil at the same time. They form a complex web that we cannot ignore or escape.

One legacy of the rampant individualism in our society is the tendency to react personally to the pain caused by organizations. People blame themselves when they get laid off. Or they blame the executive officers for their insensitivity. But to a high degree, corporate decisions are dictated by larger economic forces—invisible forces that determine the choices of those who set policy and fire workers, dictate corporate decisions.

So the Powers That Be are not merely the people in power or the institutions they staff. Those people are, in fact, more or less interchangeable. Most people in their position would tend to make the same sort of moves. Their decisions for a large part are being made for them by the logic of the market, the pressures of competition, and the cost of workers. Executives can be more humane. But a company owner who decides to raise salaries and benefits will soon face challenges from competitors who pay less. Greater forces are at work—unseen Powers—that shape the present and dictate the future.

TRACKING THE POWERS

For over forty years now I have been tracking these Powers. I was interested in their systematic qualities, to be sure, but it was their invisible dimension that most fascinated me. Religious tradition has often treated the Powers as angelic or demonic beings fluttering about in the sky. Behind the gross literalism of that way of thinking, however, is the clear perception that spiritual forces impinge on and determine our lives. There is more to what goes on in the world than what newspapers or newscasters report. I was prepared to wager that our ancestors were in touch with reality when they spoke about the Powers, and that they might even know something our society had lost, spiritually blinded as it is by a materialism that believes only in what it can hear, taste, see, smell or touch.

My first real breakthrough in understanding these invisible Powers came when I stumbled over the angels of the churches in the New Testament book of Revelation. Why, I wondered, is each of the seven letters in Revelation chapters 2 and 3 addressed, not to the congregation, as in Paul's letters, but to its *angel*? Clearly the congregation was being addressed through the angel. The angel seemed to be the corporate personality of the church, its ethos or spirit or essence. Looking back over my own experience of churches, I realized that each did indeed have a unique personality. Furthermore, that personality was real. It wasn't what we call a "personification," like Uncle Sam or the Quaker on the box of oats. But it didn't seem to be a distinct spiritual entity with an independent existence either.

The angel of a church was apparently the spirituality of a particular church. You can "sense" the angel when you worship at a church. But you also encounter the angel in its committee meetings and even in its architecture. People self-select into a certain congregation because they feel that its angel is compatible with their values. Hence the spirit of a church can remain fairly constant over decades, even centuries, though all of the original members have long since departed.

I searched for data that might shed light on these corporate angels. Daniel 10 extended my understanding to encompass the angels of entire nations, who represented their nation in the heavenly "court." Cities too, had angels, as did individuals. As I explored ancient Jewish and Christian sources, I discovered ancient sages who believed that everything in creation has its own angel. That meant, I concluded, that everything has both a physical and a spiritual aspect. The Powers That Be are not, then, simply people and their institutions, as I had first thought; they also include the spirituality at the core of the institutions and structures. If we want to change those systems, we will have to address, not only their outer forms, but also their inner spirit as well.

I found the implications of that ancient view staggering. It means that every business, corporation, school, denomination, bureaucracy, sports team, indeed, social reality in all its forms, is a combination of both visible and invisible, outer and inner, physical and spiritual. Right at the heart of the most materialistic institutions in society we find spirit. IBM and General Motors each have a unique spirituality, as does a league for the spread of atheism. Materialistic scientists belong to universities or research labs that have their own corporate personalities or pecking orders. Like the new physics, which went right through materialism and out the other side into a world of spirit-matter, so too we are now capable of seeing the entire social enterprise of the human species under the dual aspects of spirit and matter. We are on the brink of rediscovering soul at the heart of every created thing. There is nothing, from DNA to the United Nations, which does not have spirit at its core. Everything is connected to spirit. Everything is answerable to the divine.

As I have already suggested, however, the spirituality that we encounter in institutions is not always benign. It is just as likely to be pathological. And this is where the biblical understanding of the Powers surpasses in profundity the best of modern sociology. For the angel of an institution is not just the sum total of all that an institution is (which sociology is competent to describe); it is also the bearer of that institution's divine vocation (which sociology is not able to discern). Corporations and governments are "creatures" whose sole purpose is to serve the general welfare; when they refuse to do so, they become "demonic."

I had never been able to take demons seriously. The idea that fallen angels possessed people seemed superstitious. But if the demonic is the spirituality produced when the angel of an institution turns its back on its divine vocation, then I could not only believe in the demonic, I could point to its presence in everyday life. If the demonic arises when an angel deviates from its calling, then social change does not depend on casting out the demon, but recalling its angel to its divine task.

It is merely a habit of thought that makes people think of the Powers as personal beings. In fact, many of the spiritual powers and gods of the ancient world were not conceived of as personal at all. I prefer to think of the Powers as impersonal entities, though I know of no sure way to settle the question. Humans naturally tend to personalize anything that seems to act intentionally. But we are now discovering from computer viruses that certain systemic processes are self-replicating and "contagious," behaving almost willfully even though they are quite impersonal. Anyone who has lost computer files to a virus knows how "personal" this can seem. For the present, I have set aside the question of the actual status of these Powers, and instead have attempted to describe what it was that people in ancient times were experiencing when they spoke of "Satan," "demon," "powers," "angels," and the like.

Think, for example, of a riot at a championship soccer game. For a few frenzied minutes, people who in their ordinary lives behave on the whole quite decently, suddenly find themselves bludgeoning and even killing opponents whose only sin was rooting for the other team. Afterwards people often act bewildered and wonder what could have possessed them. Was it a "Riot Demon" that leapt upon them from the sky, or was it something intrinsic to the social situation: a "spirituality" that crystallized suddenly, caused by a conjunction of an outer permissiveness, heavy drinking, a violent ethos, a triggering incident, and the inner violence of the fans or what René Girard would call "mimetic rivalry"? When the riot subsides, does the "Riot Demon" rocket back to heaven, or does the spirituality of the rioters simply dissipate as they are scattered, subdued, or arrested?

THE SPIRITUAL DIMENSION OF CORPORATE ENTITIES

There is a growing recognition, even among secular thinkers, of the spiritual dimension of corporate entities. Terrence Deal and Allan Kennedy, for example, have written a text for business entitled *Corporate Cultures*[2] while other analysts have discerned the importance of a business's symbolic system and mission as clues to enhancing its efficiency. The corporate spirits of Microsoft and Google are palpably real and strikingly different, as are the national spirits of the United States and Canada. What distinguishes the notion of an angel of an institution is the Bible's emphasis on vocation. The angel of a corporate entity is not simply the sum total of all it is, but it also bears the message of what it ought to be.

In the past, the demonic spirits that people sensed at the heart of institutions, systems, and structures were projected out upon the screen of the universe and treated as metaphysical beings. Today we are able to withdraw those projections and recognize that the real spiritual force we are experiencing emanates from actual institutions. I hasten to add that the demons projected onto the screen of the cosmos are really demonic, and play havoc with humanity. Only, they are not *up there* but *over there*, in the social-spiritual structures that make up the one and only real world. They exist in factories, medical centers, agribusiness, universities, and airlines, to be sure, but also in smaller systems, such as families, churches, the Boy Scouts, and Medicare. The New Testament insists that demons can have no impact on us unless they are able to embody themselves in people, or in pigs, or political systems.[3]

Students and faculty often complain that universities operate for the convenience of administrators, or sacrifice pedagogy for prestige,

2. Deal and Kennedy, *Corporate.*
3. Mark 1:21–28, 5:1–20; Matt 12:43–45; Luke 11:24–26; Rev 12–13.

or quantify education like a product at the cost of the faculty-student relationship. Universities, even many with denominational connections, basically function to propagate the ideology of materialism. Far from being the unifying force that their name implies, universities have fragmented knowledge into specialties and lost a sense of the whole. They have embraced reductionism and have lost a sense of the soul. They are a massive force for indoctrination in our society, but they have lost a sense of vocation. Their spirit is real, but that spirit denies the existence of spirit. To call these and other institutions back to their divine vocation will require more than self-examination; it demands a critique of materialism itself, and the development of a new worldview that permits discourse about the inner spirits of things, including the institutions in which we live and move, and lose our beings.[4]

In biblical terms, the Powers are good, they are fallen, and they can be redeemed.[5] They are good because they are part of the good creation of God. They are absolutely indispensible as ways to organize human life optimally. They are fallen because they invariably put their own self-interest ahead of the long-term interests of the whole. They place profit or success above service to the general welfare, which Adam Smith insisted is the only legitimate end or goal of an institution. And finally, the Powers can be redeemed and called back to their higher vocations. A truly *compassionate eschatology* redeems the entire universe, physical and spiritual. I cannot stress this enough.

The relevance of the Powers for an understanding of evil should by now be clear. Evil is not just personal but structural and spiritual. It is not simply the result of human actions, but the consequence of huge systems over which no individual has full control. Any attempt to transform a social system without addressing both its spirituality and its outer forms is doomed to failure. Only by confronting the spirituality of an institution *and* its physical manifestation can the total structure be transformed.

4. See Wink, "New Worldview."
5. See Wink, *Engaging.*

11

From Ontology to Iconochrony

A Positively Anthropological Second Coming

ANTHONY W. BARTLETT

PROLEGOMENON

To BEGIN LET US think about ontology by means of its radical Christian alternative, eschatology. The practical lived content of Christian eschatology is a relationship to the object freed from death and sorrow. We know this prophetically from the great biblical texts: "I saw a new heavens and a new earth" (Rev 21:1). All that we see, touch, feel, the universe of things, all these are separated from any element of death and destruction. But "relationship to the object" is of course not simply objective. It must contain a critical human or anthropological element. It's not a matter of God waving a magic wand and saying, "There, all pain is gone!" It means that the power of the human to make a world has been freed from its inner content of death. This is surely what is also meant by descriptions of the agents of death, the beast and the false prophet, thrown in the lake of fire (Rev 20:10, 14). These are forms of cultural existence that are finally rejected. Thus the objective material nature of the universe is changed, but hand in hand the relational human character that goes with it and constructs it according to death and violence, this too is changed. And that must happen first.

The philosophical science that deals most fundamentally with the relationship to the object is ontology. Ontology thinks the ultimate character or status of our relationship to the object, the *being* or "what is" of our world. But as Parmenides famously observed, "thought and being are the same," placing being in the strictest relationship with thought—the classic mode of relationship for the Greeks. However, if we say with Heraclitus, "all things happen because of strife and necessity" (fragment 80) and "conflict is the father of all" (fragment 53) then "what is" gains a strong relational quality of violence, including and especially in philosophical thought. Whatever Heraclitus might have meant we can safely say he did not exclude a relationship of violence from being. So we can quickly see that eschatology and ontology converge on the same general ground, but from opposite directions. They both have a relationship to the object, but one is very possibly violent, and the other brings peace. Eschatology may very well then be a matter of a changed ontology. The question of how this might come about gives us our starting point, one by which to develop a grounded statement of "compassionate eschatology."

I will do this by examining the thought of René Girard through the lens of Heidegger, a creative fusion that, I believe, releases a transformative sense of human existence. The path we will follow is divided in three parts of unequal length: first, the longest, will merge the thought of Girard and Heidegger via Karl Rahner, showing that an ontology reconfigured as love suits Girardian anthropology much more than classic onto-theology; second, in this framework the form of Christ in the world can be understood as an iconochrony, a time of human transformation produced by the cross; finally, examples from political and popular culture provide data of the actual transformative effects of the cross in contemporary existence.

PART I: GIRARD AND HEIDEGGER, UNWILLING BEDFELLOWS

René Girard has provided us with probably the most powerful set of hermeneutical tools in contemporary thought. He has given biblical studies a rocket-boost, equivalent in creative power, if not so far in extent, to Heidegger's impact via Bultmann. He offers an interpretative approach that is not simply historical-critical, but a powerful reason for historical criticism in the first place. He enables students of the Bible to understand how and why we should think about, for example, the raw pre-monarchical material in Judges, or the folklore of the primeval and patriarchal narratives, or the enormous textual weight of the gospel passion accounts. These are all narratives replete with violence, and by means of Girard's hypothesis of the revelation of the scapegoat we can evaluate the biblical tradition on a continuum of sensitivity and response to violence and its victims.

In the case of the story of the first parents in Genesis 2–3, for example, we are led to see how it is an astute commentary on desire, including desire for knowledge or wisdom. Putting this together with standard historical and literary criticism, we can approach closer to the revelatory process itself: thus the Garden of Eden text was likely produced in an exilic or early Second Temple setting as a polemic on the role of grasping desire, including the desire for self-serving, instrumental wisdom.[1] It makes clear that alienation from God is the result of this desire, something immediately mirrored at the intra-human level by the conflictive desire and rivalry between Cain and Abel. Thus the text evinces its own counter-wisdom—or anthropology—that becomes a key part of the revelatory process. In other words it is easy to put historical criticism and Girardian anthropology together to show that the Bible is continuously worrying the problem of violence.

So we begin to discern across the whole face of the Bible an evolutionary trajectory leading to the complete forfeiture of violence, first in the Suffering Servant and finally in Jesus. Girard's method sets the Bible in motion and the present human world with it. In effect, his thought is both evolutionary and kinetic—not only does it show a progressive human change, in an exemplary biblical way, but it mobilizes our own existence. It sets the world moving under our feet, like a train stalled at a station suddenly lurches into motion. The rolling stock of the human world is set free from the frozen switches of eternal truth, from a paralyzed history understood as simply a punched ticket for a "spiritual" afterlife.

But the way I have just presented the kinetic effect of Girard's work does beg an important authorial question about the nature of the movement he himself suggests. His recent book *Evolution and Conversion* noticeably displays Darwin and the Darwinian hypothesis of evolution as a scientific backdrop for his own anthropology.[2] This suggests a forward movement, but the book also concludes with an apocalyptic view of his-

---

1. According to George Mendenhall the story of the garden of Eden was produced in the context of exile, or soon after, as a *mashal* (parable) against the ideology of power and wealth which used practical wisdom to justify itself, even as it filled the "master's house with violence and fraud" (Zeph 1:9). It was this violent wisdom that led ultimately to destruction and exile. See "Shady Side of Wisdom," especially 329–31.

2. Girard, *Evolution*.

tory presented in stark terms: ". . . the Gospel does not provide a happy ending to our history. It simply shows us two options (which is exactly what ideologies never provide, freedom of choice): either we imitate Christ, giving up all our mimetic violence, or we run the risk of self-destruction." Or, "Any great Christian experience is apocalyptic because what one realizes is that after the decomposition of the sacrificial order there is nothing standing between ourselves and our possible destruction. How this will materialize, I don't really know."[3]

While these statements are realistic in one sense, they lack at an equivalent structural level the transformative motif of the gospel. In particular, they lack the positive organic sense that the gospels present in the great parables of the kingdom, viz. the immense fruitful harvest, the great tree growing from the seed of the Word, the leaven through the huge batch of dough, etc., etc.

But rather than trade scriptures I want to approach the matter on a more analytic level. It is not possible to assert a scientific viewpoint with such absolute outcomes, and what's more to do so out of biblical revelation, and not address questions of an ultimate philosophical nature. What I am referring to is precisely the ontological dimension of Girard's thought, something that remains the great "unsaid" of Girardian anthropology. The confluence of science and revelation gives mimetic anthropology a huge claim to "reality," to "what is," but this has not been examined ontologically. While many scholars have explored the scriptural and doctrinal implications of Girardian anthropology, very few have undertaken a serious inquiry into its ontological character or consequences.[4] Here is not the place to do this in any thoroughgoing way, but a number of observations can be made. And these observations in turn will be of immense help in the articulation of a consistent eschatology developing from Girard's work.

3. Ibid., 237 and 235. Girard's more recent *Battling to the End* presents an even more pessimistic assessment, a textual and historical dialectic that casts serious doubt on humanity's ability to pull out of its ever more deadly spiral of violence.

4. Gianni Vattimo has put Girard in the context of his thought of "weakness of being" and the end of metaphysics. See his *Belief*. This certainly has a validity, which Girard to some degree accepts (*Evolution*, 253). Vattimo, however, also describes a purely "textual" role of Christianity in secular culture, something that Girard rejects because "there is no grounding, no point of departure in this long chain of good imitation" (ibid., 255). Girard thus implies in some way a *strong* ontological meaning.

In the *Girard Reader* interview, conducted by James Williams, Girard makes a brief remark on being. He suggests that Heideggerean being is "the wrong being" and that there is a traditional concept, going back to Augustine and Aquinas, "of God as a source of peace and being" (and so, by implication, the "right" being).[5] The issue is left open whether Augustine and Aquinas got it right because their ontological framework was correct as metaphysics, or because they were representative in fact of the revelatory peace of the New Testament.

In other words, is the question about classic philosophical truth or the overcoming of violence through Christ? It's difficult to escape the feeling that it's a bit of both. But in this case we have to ask whether the received sense of scholastic metaphysics, of a static philosophical universe, is more appropriate to Girard's project than Heidegger's much more dynamic historical sense of being. Was Girard talking about *ipsum esse subsistens*, God conceived as being eternally present to itself and present to us in the concept (onto-theology), or was he talking about the work of transformation set in motion by Christ? In the latter case the changed style of thought that Heidegger represents and of which, I believe, Girard himself is part would seem a much more apposite ontology.

Heidegger has had the impact he has for a reason, and not least among Christian theologians. There is his well-known influence on Karl Rahner who was a student at Freiburg and registered in Heidegger's classes over four semesters from 1934 to 1936. Rahner's doctoral dissertation was refused at Freiberg in part because it was over-influenced by Heidegger. And lest we should say, well, that's just Rahner, there is also a fundamental impact of Heidegger on Hans Urs von Balthasar, Rahner's rival theological star, today in some ascendance.[6]

If we turn more closely to Rahner's work we see he declared, "Dogmatic theology today has to be theological anthropology," adding that, "Such an anthropology must, of course, be a transcendental anthropology."[7] By this he means that the human is the place where mystery is inscribed in the world and by paying attention to the human we can discover the divine. Now this turn to anthropology in order to do theology is remarkably similar in essential method to Girard. Girard is

---

5. Girard, *Girard Reader*, 283.

6. See *Cambridge Companion to Balthasar*, 137, 229–37.

7. Rahner, "Theology and Anthropology," 1–2.

more concrete and intra-human in his perspective, but we may indeed say that Girard employs a type of transcendental method, deriving the original conditions of possibility for culture not from direct observation but from a general human structure. But most importantly, standing behind Rahner is Heidegger, from whom the theologian learnt so much of this approach, and stepping back there we are confronted with an anthropology and ontology that are viscerally closer to Girard. Perhaps too close for comfort.

While very prepared to recruit Heidegger's turn to the pre-Socratics and their more primal (i.e., sacrificial) language as a great thinker's intuition of the genetic role of violence, Girard is unwilling to follow him more constitutively.[8] I would like to rectify that reserve to some degree, by showing the harmonic wavelengths between the two, and in the process point up some ontological implications. Consequent on this will be an emerging perspective on eschatology.

Heidegger's historical human being or self is called existence or *Dasein*, and it stands much closer to the acutely mimetic identity of the Giaradian self than classical notions of a soul or intellect somehow separate from the world. Heidegger's human is not a substance or an ego but a relentless movement beyond itself: in Thomas Sheehan's pregnant phrase it is "a kinesis appropriated by its ever receding and unreachable term."[9] The name that Heidegger later gave to this whole phenomenon was *Ereignis*, which can simply be translated as "event," but Heidegger discovered in it a much richer semantic possibility, along the lines of "appropriation" or "owning": it is the primordial movement of Being itself (*das Sein*) by which everything comes into "its own". Entities come to presence, man belongs to his mortality, and at the same time being conceals itself or withdraws into absence. Thus *Ereignis* as appropriation is also expropriation: "Expropriation belongs to Appropriation [*Ereignis*] as such."[10]

In this light we can also easily get to a level of sympathy, a certain similarity of frequency, between Heidegger's *Ereignis* and Girard's mi-

8. Girard, *Things Hidden*, 267–70, and an unpublished paper presented at the Boston COV&R meeting, 2000. Note *Things Hidden*, 267: "Heidegger becomes crystal clear when we read him, not in a philosophical light but in the light . . . of the 'meta-anthropology' we have been sketching out."

9. Sheehan, *Rahner*, 108.

10. Heidegger, *On Time and Being*, 23.

metic desire. In Girardian anthropology, rather than ontological expropriation there is expropriation by the condition of human desire, but in both frames there is a loss of being. They converge therefore at what may be seen as their respective metaphysical levels: in the former because Being removes being, in the latter because it is the human that removes being. I hasten to add that I am not making a reductionist identification—because that would lose the specific power of each thinker's thought, a muddying of the waters that gets us nowhere. However, it is not at all illegitimate to see what is standing in front of us: that for Heidegger the things of the world are revealed by a recessive or expropriative movement of being, and for Girard the things of the world are revealed by the competitive desire arising between hominids, i.e., precisely in the object's recessive or expropriative manifestation.[11]

Can we suggest, therefore, that at a deep existential and phenomenological level there is an overlap? What for Girard is experienced as inter-human or interdividual is experienced by Heidegger as an event of being. And what for Heidegger is the mystery of being's self-concealment is in Girard the withdrawal of the object in the mutual crisis of desire. And once we see this mutuality we can propose another, mutually reflexive account: that Heideggerean ontology is in fact the nature of being arising in a mimetic universe, and, on the other side, a mimetic anthropology will automatically have a kinetic ontology as its horizon. In other words, in Girardian anthropology what other kind of ontology could possibly arise? The only way around this would be for Girard to posit an entirely extrinsic intellectual truth, which his whole anthropological method makes implausible. This has profound implications for Girardian thinking.

However, it is when we come to the other key term in Heidegger's *Being and Time* that things really line up between these two thinkers. The term is of course time or temporality. Temporality is *Dasein's* own most basic structure, i.e., time is at the core of human meaning. It is the movement by which human existence exceeds itself and in that movement—toward its future and thus opening up both the past and

---

11. See *Evolution*, 107–11. A developed symbolic system is produced by the original crisis of mimetic desire "contained" first in formal ritual and then in the manifold of language. What is there at the genesis of meaning remains within its full symbolic flowering. If we take the "presence" of the god out of the symbolic world—as Heidegger does—everything reverts to its original sense of violence and alienation.

the present—it makes beings meaningfully present. As we know *Being and Time* as planned by Heidegger had two parts, but only the first was completed, the analysis of existence and temporality. The second part was to include the elaboration of the time-determined structure of all modes of being. The very last line of the book is: "Does *time* itself reveal itself as the horizon of *being*?"[12] In other words does time show itself as the final meaning of being?

In a short preface to the seventh German edition Heidegger stated the designation "first half" had been dropped, noting that "after a quarter of a century, the second half could no longer be added without the first being presented anew."[13] The strong hint is that the starting point of human existence was no longer desirable for the elucidation of this deeper, mysterious sense of time, but the fact is Heidegger never made the revision. Heidegger was never able completely to free himself from the circularity of human temporality and the disclosure of a primordial meaning of being. *Being and Time* remains the foundation and triumph of his philosophical enterprise, and it is its human or anthropological starting point that gives it its compelling strength.

It is a question, therefore, why Girard does not find a greater affinity with Heidegger in view of this shared starting point, and above all when we compare the temporal structure that emerges in both. There is an enormously powerful temporal quality to Girard's thought, which is of course why we are discussing it in terms of eschatology. And indeed Heidegger shares precisely this eschatological dimension, one in fact *borrowed* from Christianity.

John Caputo says in respect of Heidegger's own lecture course, teaching Christian temporality in his early Freiberg professorship, that this New Testament sense of time was then "recast in terms of a relationship to one's own death, and this analysis became a centerpiece of *Being and Time*."[14] Caputo is by no means the only one to make the point of Heidegger's dependence on Christian revelation, and his general statement can stand for the opinion of many: *Being and Time* amounted to the "Hellenizing and secularizing [of] a fundamentally biblical conception of the history of salvation—a ruse both compounded and betrayed

---

12. Heidegger, *Being*, 398.

13. Ibid., xvii.

14. Caputo, *Prayers*, 140. The Freiburg course was 1920–21, "Einleitung in die Phänomenologie der Religion."

by the radicality with which he tries to exclude the biblical provenance of these operations."[15] This biblical pedigree is surely part of the explanation for the book's kinetic effect, for the way it can mobilize human existence for the reader.

But if it is the movement that counts in Heidegger's ontology, setting us free from formal hierarchies of being, and this movement is in fact historically in the world because of the impact of the cross, then how is this different from Girard? As he says it in one of many places: "In the long run [the cross] ... is quite capable of undermining and overturning the whole cultural order."[16] Heidegger's kinetic ontology or even his ontochrony, as it can be called (being *as* time),[17] is already a movement produced by the cross. It must be therefore—and this is a conclusion toward which I have been working—that his general ontological framework of movement is a much more favorable philosophical medium for Girard's crucial insights than any formal scholastic universe. There is a kinetic ontological character that Girard has in common with Heidegger and it cannot be stressed enough.

But here precisely is the probable reason why Girard does not countenance Heidegger's ontology. There is a radically different goal to the released movement in the two thinkers, and even more so after Heidegger's "turn" in the period following *Being and Time*. As Rahner himself describes it, Heidegger's digging deeper than logos as reason or metaphysics, down to something more original, was an effort "to resurrect ... gigantomachy."[18] The barely concealed violence of Heidegger's intellectual spirit in this respect, and especially in the 1930s, has acted as a kind of anti-Heideggerean vaccine in Girard's thinking. He and Heidegger tread the same path, but going in opposite directions, and Girard does not overcome the crisis of this doubling. But Heidegger's philosophical yes to primordial or original violence should not blind us to the revelatory kinesis of his work, to its original anthropological basis borrowed from the New Testament. Ultimately the frame of his thought sits so much closer to a biblical sense of humanity set in motion toward God than the static framework of medieval Christianity.

15. Caputo, *Demythologizing*, 181.

16. Girard, *Things Hidden*, 209.

17. This is a term used by Rahner that he took from Heidegger; see Rahner, "Concept," 135; quoted in Sheehan, *Rahner*, 127.

18. Rahner, "Concept," 130, quoted in Sheehan, *Rahner*, 119.

RAHNER TO THE RESCUE

And so it is that we turn to Rahner for a correct appreciation of the revelatory impetus of Heidegger's thought, to understand that at a profound
level Heidegger is already an eruption of Christian theology. Rahner is
indebted to Heidegger especially for the sense of an absolute term which
disposes us toward itself. In Heidegger's case this is Being, in Rahner's
terminology it is "Holy Mystery." This absolute mystery is not given ob-
jectively to cognition but transcendentally, as the necessary condition
of subjectivity, yet at the same time it is a real self-communication that
opens the human toward itself in love, even as in so many ways it remains
silent and hidden. Thus it conditions history in a universal way. "This
ever present and supernatural existential . . . has a history individually
and collectively."[19] In this universal context the particular biblical history
of revelation is the instance where the universal history achieves self-
consciousness, and in Christ becomes definitive and irrevocable. The
main point at the moment is the way Rahner's theology sets the world
in motion toward its goal. I quote here directly from Rahner in his own
re-envisioning and re-enactment of the Heideggerean movement.

> To jar man loose from the pure idea and to cast him into his
> own existence and into history, as Heidegger is doing, would be
> to prepare him, to make him attentive in advance to the existen-
> tial, historical fact of a divine revelation. It would be to open him
> to "the God of Abraham, Isaac, and Jacob," to the "Word of Life,
> seen, heard, touched" by human hands, "Jesus of Nazareth" . . .[20]

This is so akin to the effect of Girardian anthropology, which in fact
works at a more radical level still: the casting of humanity into a history
shaped by the historical fact of revelation. What of course is missing in

19. Rahner, *Foundations*, 141.

20. Rahner, "Concept," 137, quoted in Sheehan, *Rahner*, 127–28. I have to remark
here for the Barthians who might dismiss a supernatural existential out of hand that,
from a Girardian perspective, there remains an absolute intervention in biblical revelation in the emergence of the innocent and forgiving victim while, at the same time, this
remains an anthropological possibility because it is in fact an anthropological emergence. What is attractive in Girard from a Barthian perspective is that this emergence
is inconceivable without a supervening divine project, and yet at the same time it is an
anthropological possibility waiting to happen at the deepest level of existence. Thus
we can say that Girard can satisfy both Barth and Rahner: the breakthrough of the
Crucified and Risen Word could not happen without the sovereign act of God, but it
was always an abyssal truth of the world yearning to be born.

Rahner is the generative role of violence that presumably would have some distorting or misconstructing effect on the transcendental relationship with the Holy Mystery. This question would have to be pursued in more detail as regards Rahner—and paradoxically Girard would seem closer here to the later Heideggerean anthropology, in respect of its sense of violent transcendence. But in Christian theological terms—and here is the point insisted on—Rahner must have the final argument and last word: "grace is the reason for creation."[21]

What is named Mystery in Rahner is also Holy because it is a transcendence that moves toward us in freedom and love and invites our reciprocating freedom and love. The end of the cosmos is therefore also its beginning.[22] Now, if this originality of love is true universally it is even more so in the particular, categorical history of salvation, the history of Jesus. Through Jesus it is possible to understand that at the heart of the mysterious distance of the divine there is the depth of love, love as a constituent of the universe so utterly different from the way we in fact construct our universe that it can easily appear itself as a recessive term, or, in Rahner's words, as a "dark abyss."[23] It is only when the Crucified assumes the abyss in willing conformity that it becomes transformed into intelligible, accessible address, into what we so glibly, and yet also truthfully, call love.

But here is the crucial point where Girard parts company with Rahner, in a fashion that can only be called apocalyptic and in a negative sense. Although Girard certainly names a God of grace and nonviolence, the structure of his anthropology of revelation lacks a clear and primary account of love. What we get is the steady process of a disclosure but not the absolute primacy of love that mobilizes it. We get the power of a text and a history that vindicate the victim but not the primordial anthropology of love that underpins that text and history. We get the undeniable kinesis of a world jarred free by the cross, but not the aboriginal quality of love that gives motive and goal to the movement. Consequently he appears to end with a dire and dubious choice for humanity, between destruction and an improbable moral or external imitation of Christ in the renunciation of violence.

21. Rahner, *Foundations*, 445.
22. Ibid., 191.
23. Ibid., 2.

But if we place the template of Heidegger over Girard, or rather the Rahnerian Christian retrieval of Heidegger, we see at once that there is an ontology of love at work in the revelation of the victim. Because this ontology shapes anthropology at a transcendental point, and then at the categorical level of revelation the anthropology definitively reveals the ontology, this love becomes more and more real, historical, and effective. It provides a structure of itself in the cosmos that is kinetically more powerful than the structuring effects of violence. This is so in Rahner.[24] But also, in terms internal to Girard's thought, the anthropological disclosure of the victim could only happen if the trace of love first made the disclosure possible: it is only the thematic indifference of love to violence—providing thereby the absolute difference—that can break the closed circle of collusion in generative violence. Therefore both in Rahnerian terms and the inner logic of Girard's own reflection love is the nerve of the disclosive process, the onto-anthropological source of the disclosure.

In a world still controlled by violence this love only makes itself known obliquely, abyssally, mysteriously, but it *is* revealed: like the dark of night by which the stars are seen, the infinite sable depths around them. Rahner has placed that love theologically in the foreground, as of course a Christian theologian should do, but he does so kinetically, in a way that displays the depths and their mysterious gravity. Girard shares fully in those depths and derives the power of his work from their kinetic effect. In consequence, therefore, a Girardian onto-anthropological perspective is obliged to say: *there is the emergence of a transformative cultural phenomena opposite to and ultimately greater than cultural chaos.*

Girard seems almost completely to lack this mysterious structuring anthropology of love and so gives an obsessive sense to human violence.[25] Surely that obsessive sense represents the time we are in, but

24. See *Foundations*, Rahner's comments on the "absolute savior," 192–95. "[T]he success, the victory and the irreversibility of this process [of God's self-communication to the world] has become manifest in and in spite of [the] ongoing dialogue of freedom. It is precisely this beginning of the irreversible and successful history of salvation which we are calling the absolute savior, and hence in this sense this beginning is the fullness of time . . ." (194).

25. It is fascinating that Girard's intuition at the base of his anthropology came from what he called "novelistic conversion," a crucial change of approach observed in certain key writers (see Girard, *Deceit*). He understood this as essentially Christian conversion but it happened in a secular context—the writing of novels. Christian conversion is always a turn to self-giving love so how is it possible not to recognize the anthropology of love at work in the world? In novels and everywhere else?

it does not represent the time of love, the ontochrony of the cross. It does not represent the transformative movement of the gospel that is more powerful than the generativity of violence. This movement may be oblique and indeed contradicted by violence but its ontological and anthropological primacy cannot be gainsaid. By supplying this other abyssal element in mimetic anthropology we will in fact arrive at a fully biblical and contemporary eschatology. We will see in fact that the mimetic world is permeated with compassion, and carries within itself the possibility of the thematization of compassion. It contains the possibility of a progressive rising to the surface of love, as an evolutionary human form and choice.

PART II: A TIME OF HUMAN TRANSFORMATION

Let me briefly lay out now some elements of a contemporary anthropology of transformation that can be seen to arise from and within a Girardian disclosure of the victim. The biblical pathway culminating in the cross is in fact a restructuring agency that dissolves the cultural foundations of violence precisely not by virtue of violence but love. It does this by injecting into the human system an alternative possibility that reaches its climax in the figure of the Crucified.

Thinking about this figure I would like to make brief reference to the theological aesthetics of Urs von Balthasar. Balthasar adopts a very different method from Rahner and this is not the place to discuss the difference in detail. But in broad terms we can say that while Rahner makes a turn to the human to construct his theology, Balthasar reverts to traditional metaphysics. Yet he does so in an aesthetically grounded way, which in a subtle fashion repeats Rahner's gesture. There is therefore more overlap than might at first be assumed and much of it may indeed be attributed to a common debt to Heidegger.[26]

The core of Balthasar's thought is the use of form (*Gestalt*) as the starting point of theological truth, form that communicates and is the deep structure of beauty. As one of the transcendentals, beauty coincides

---

26. For Balthasar Heidegger's philosophy of being is "permeated with Christian theological motifs in changed form," *Glory of the Lord*, vol. IV, 429, quoted by Fergus Kerr in *Cambridge Companion to Balthasar*, 235. In the same place Kerr notes that according to Balthasar " For Christian theology, and particularly for the theology of God's glory. . . . Heidegger's project is by far the most fertile in modern philosophy."

with truth and being, and thus is an essential pathway to knowledge.[27] At
the same time theological form releases in the human "a movement of the
entire person, leading away from himself through the vision to the invisible God . . ."[28] We are, therefore, once more in the realm of the kinetic, of
the human movement toward God. But what is crucial here is that this
movement is founded in the person of Christ. "[T]he Jesus of history
is, precisely, not a mere sign, but a form, and, indeed, the definitive and
determinant form of God in the world . . . from a Christian standpoint,
there is no possibility of distinguishing between God's act of revelation
and the content of this revelation, for this revelation is inseparably both
the interior life of God and the form of Jesus Christ."[29] The deep beauty
of God is the beauty of Christ and it has become a mobilizing force in
human existence.

Balthasar had previously contrasted the experience of Being in
Heidegger with the disclosure that comes in Christ. While the former is
a threat to human existence, because it places existence within a ground-
less abyss, in Christ the abyss is transformed into love. "In his incarnation
God has taken this threat on himself. The finite spirit's giving of itself
into the abyss of this love, because it lives from this same love, is indeed
a renunciation of all finite securities—even spiritual ones—but it occurs
within that handing over of self which is free from anxiety regarding its
destiny in God."[30]

Thus the form of Christ transforms Heideggerean being, even as it
opened it up to view in the first place. But the point here is by no means
purely speculative. I am arguing that the form of Christ is a historical
agency that focuses being as love, and so now precisely from the point of
view of form or image we have a transformative function in the world.
There cannot, as I say, be a disclosive function (of violence) unless there
is first a form (Gestalt) of love. It is the positive function of the cross,
parallel to its negative disclosive function, and as a true aesthetic form it
cannot help but work in historical terms.

27. "The form as it appears to us is beautiful only because the delight that it arouses
in us is founded upon the fact that, in it, the truth and goodness of the depths of reality
itself are manifested and bestowed . . ." *Glory of the Lord*, vol. I, 118.

28. Balthasar, *Glory of the Lord*, vol. I, 121.

29. Ibid., 182.

30. Ibid., 159.

And, again, even if this form is oblique to normal human view because of the way it contradicts the world—because of the way love is self-effacing as opposed to the unavoidability of violence—it nevertheless operates in the human sphere as the transcendence at root of all contemporary movement. It is the transcendence that discloses the victim (Girard) and the very same transcendence that opens the abyss as the place of truth (Heidegger). Love must be seen therefore as slowly making itself known within the decay of all forms of violence around it (which, even though more intensely violent as they decay, must as decaying leave space to love as the one remaining possibility of being.)

In effect, therefore, the cross is a transformative iconology shaping the human to itself, and because of this, because of the movement it produces, it is also more and more an iconchrony, the production of human time and meaning by reason of the cross. This is the form and its time that gave release to Heidegger's thought of being, but it is also a form and time at work in popular culture. And here the evidence gathers day by day.

PART III: CULTURAL DATA

I want now to demonstrate my argument with three summary examples, taken from the different realms of politics, literature, and cinema. These examples could be multiplied almost indefinitely because of the pervasive effect of the form and time of the cross in our contemporary world. It is simply a matter of looking out for them, of seeing the slow but unending eruption of the compassion of the cross in our world.

First, the official ban on images of military personnel killed during the Iraq war. In March 2003, the Pentagon issued a directive saying, "There will not be arrival ceremonies of, or media coverage of, deceased military personnel returning to or departing from air bases."[31] In July 2008, a news photographer by the name of Zoriah Miller photographed the bodies of three Marines killed by a suicide attack in Al Anbar province. Ninety-six hours after they died, Zoriah posted photographs of the attack on his Internet site. Several of the photographs depicted the bodies of the slain Marines. The army demanded that he take the photos

---

31. *New York Times*, August 11, 2008.

down. When he refused his clearance as an embedded journalist was removed and he was flown out of the area.[32]

Why is the army so keen on blocking images of fallen soldiers? In the past soldiers were not brought home from war. If found their bodies were buried or cremated and their memory preserved at cenotaphs and memorials. The subsequent ceremonial occasions were charged with intense polarized violence. (Think of the wrath of Achilles as he builds the pyre under the corpse of his slain comrade, Patroclus.) Why is the returning or photographed corpse of a soldier not guaranteed to fill the native populace with the same terrible resolve for action, rather than inspire fear of exactly the opposite reaction? You would think the flag-draped coffin of a soldier would work as perfect propaganda piece, but there seems in fact a subversive compassion taking control.

Compassion is always a human possibility, but its development into a historical theme with significant political power can only have one anthropological explanation: the revelation of the victim by the cross is rooted in and now continually enhances an infinite letting go of violence. The form or image of the Crucified pulls into its outline the figure of all the wounded and murdered in war and so produces its own progressively more effective history, the iconochrony of the cross. For that anthropological reason, and that reason only, the military cannot allow these images to be seen.

My second example is from a contemporary novel, *Enduring Love*.[33] The book paints a typical postmodern landscape, of secular sufficiency and the absence of God packaged by febrile relationships, suspicion, fear, desire, and violence. It's written by Ian McEwan, the author of *Atonement*, recently made into a motion picture. The plot of *Enduring Love* is set in motion on its first pages by a remarkable scene: the protagonists converge by chance around a hot-air balloon that has landed but is out of control.

In the attached basket is a young boy, and a helpless adult on the ground is fighting to anchor it against the successive tugs of a strong wind. Five men race from different points where they have witnessed the drama; arriving at the scene they grab trailing ropes, attempting to secure the craft. A freak gust, exceptionally powerful, carries all five into the air, blowing the balloon toward some power lines. As the basket

32. Online: http://uwire.typepad.com/iraqinfocus/2008/07/war-photographe.htm.
33. McEwan, *Enduring Love*.

quickly rises first one and then all the would-be saviors let go, fearing for their lives. All, that is, except one. A solitary individual hangs on, a man by the name of John Logan, a medical doctor. Drifting and rising until he is three hundred feet in the air, he slips little by little down his single rope, until he falls to a shattered death in the field below.

This event serves in a strange but necessary way to prompt a series of crises of desire in the lives of the main characters and those related to them. God is absent from the individuals' lives; rather there is a constant antiphon of Darwinian determinism from the narrator. Nevertheless, it is John Logan's extraordinary act of selflessness, his being singled out from and by the crowd, his hanging and falling in an attempt to save the boy, which subtly brings resolution to the crises, giving meaning to the world essentially through forgiveness.

If the actual name "Jesus" is mentioned in the story it happens dismissively. Nevertheless, the core structuring role of the solitary exception, whose self-giving death both destabilizes and remakes the world, is unmistakable. Take that away and the book doesn't work. In other words, at a formative level the novel is set in motion by the work of the gospel, and my suspicion is that the novelist was himself aware of this dependence. At one point the central character, whose life has been completely disrupted by circumstances arising from the incident of the balloon, returns to the scene to retrace his steps. He says: "These were my stations of the cross."[34] Thus once again the form of the cross serves to draw culture toward itself, providing the single difference of compassion and forgiveness. Only these effects of the Crucified are able to resolve the crisis of desire that paradoxically they set in motion in the first place.

The final example has much the same structure but this time violence is more central than desire and the link to Jesus is much more explicit. It is the movie *In Bruges*, written and directed by Martin McDonagh. The story tells of two hitmen sent to the Belgian city of Bruges after a job; they are to await further instructions from their boss, Harry. The younger of the two, Ray, has accidentally killed a little boy while—for reasons unexplained—carrying out the assassination of a priest.

The two criminals spend their time sightseeing the canals and churches of the medieval city. They visit a church in which is kept a phial of Jesus' blood, brought back from the Holy Land by a knight of the Crusades. This blood is said to liquefy in times of great stress and

34. Ibid., 136.

it fascinates the older of the pair, Ken. He invites Ray to join the queue to touch it. Ray responds, "Do I have to . . . ?" Ken explodes, "Of course you don't (expletive) have to. It's only the blood of Jesus of (expletive) Nazareth . . ."

The episode provides the key to Ken's later actions. He is ordered by Harry to kill Ray as the necessary consequence of Ray's killing the boy; the purpose of their being in Bruges was Harry's wish to give the young man one last happy time in the "fairytale city." Ken is first in two minds but cannot go ahead with the hit. He then puts the young man on a train out of the city, to get him away from Harry and the old criminal life. Harry comes to Bruges to finish the job himself, but first he has to settle with Ken. They meet in the great bell tower of the main plaza of the old city. Ken refuses to fight, saying he's prepared to take the consequences but he had to give the young man another chance. Harry then is unable to kill Ken because he's "gone all Gandhi on him." However, he shoots him in the leg saying, "Do you think I'm going to do nothing to you just because you're standing around like Robert (expletive) Powell." "Who?" groans Ken. Harry answers: "Robert Powell out of Jesus of (expletive) Nazareth."

The dialogue ties the incident to the visit to the church of Jesus' blood, and on that basis the further action gains gospel quality. A struggle ensues when Ken finds out that Ray is in the piazza below, and he is shot again by Harry who hurries off to kill Ray. Ken hauls himself back to the top of the tower leaving a trail of very liquid blood. He then pitches himself from the tower in order to warn and save Ray. The story ends in a highly expressionist scene, a film-set of medieval mummers, into which Harry and Ray stumble and where Harry continues his killings. The strong visual implication is that contemporary violence is a simple continuum with medieval violence, a matter of being stuck eternally "in Bruges." Meanwhile the "blood of Jesus" cries out for a very different resolution. The effect in the movie is accomplished purely by visual and narrative links, but they are mobilized at their heart by the cross itself and the infinite transformative effect it has introduced to culture.

The three examples that I have given serve to illustrate the argument made first philosophically and theologically. The world has been mobilized toward the Holy Mystery by the cross of Christ. On the one hand this shows itself in an intensified crisis of violence. On the other, there is steadily clarifying and transformative focus on the nonviolence, forgiveness, and life at the heart of the crisis. This is a cultural process or evolution that always has to be chosen, but that does not make it less real or inevitable at the level of historical anthropological disclosure.

In the Heideggerean understanding that we have seen underlying both Rahner and Balthasar this means that ontologically the accent has shifted from objective metaphysics to the visible in the sense of a dynamic or kinetic unveiling of love. In a word—in a full Christian expression—the world sees Jesus. It is the image of his extraordinary life that is slowly but surely changing our relationship to the object. This sign cannot be in the world after so many years of painful labor, without leaching through all the old constructs, rendering them invalid, in crisis, and in the very same moment (in the true sense of movement) suggesting its own restorative transcendence.

In short the Crucified is in the world not simply or primarily as an agent of exposure of the old but as the declaration of the new. Every time the cross springs the joints of the sacred order it shows itself as the possibility of the new and pulls the universe toward itself, and this is eschatology. The cross re-creates *to on hēi on*, being *as* being, what is *as* what is conceived, i.e., in terms of our human imaginations, of our action, of our fundamental relationality.

Eschatology is therefore transformative ontology, something that Heidegger understood but inverted, something that infuses the structure of Girard's thought but remains unspoken, something that Rahner and Balthasar grasped yet need Girard to give flesh to. His anthropology saves them from a too-Greek style of speculation. But in the end all these thinkers simply give voice to the kinetic power of the cross, the iconochrony at work in our world.

12

A Kinder, Gentler Apocalypse?

René Girard, the Book of Revelation, and the Bottomless Abyss of the Unforgettable Victim[1]

STEPHEN FINAMORE

INTRODUCTION

ONE OF THE DIFFICULTIES with the standard introductions to the thought of René Girard is that they focus on some aspects of his thought at the expense of others.[2] The issues that are to the fore tend to include the imitative nature of desire, the scapegoat mechanism, and Girard's reading of Scripture, especially the canonical gospels. It may well be that these are truly the most interesting and significant aspects of Girard's thought and the areas into which general readers require some initiation. Each is certainly worthy of consideration. However, there are other features which are sometimes given rather cursory treatment or which sometimes go unmentioned. These include Girard's dependence on structuralism, his engagement with Nietzsche, his denigration as "sacrificial"[3] of some traditional church teaching which he designates "Historical Christianity," and the apocalyptic dimensions of his thought.[4] The last of these is denied by some,[5] ignored by others, and underrated

---

1. The essay summarizes part of the argument of Finamore, *God*.

2. See for example Alison, *Knowing*; Kaptein, *On the Way*; and Kirwan, *Discovering*.

3. E.g., Girard, *Things Hidden*, 224–62.

4. Alison, *Living*, uses Girard's ideas to consider things eschatological.

5. Nemoianu, "René Girard," denies that Girard's ideas, with one or two limited exceptions, are apocalyptic.

by most. Furthermore, some of Girard's interpreters are optimistic about the future of humanity while it is not always clear that Girard himself always shares their expectation.[6]

The fact that attention is now being drawn to the apocalyptic and eschatological dimensions of Girard's thought is therefore to be welcomed. It is intriguing that the title *Compassionate Eschatology* has been chosen for a conference and a collection of essays that engages with these aspects of his thought.

While I hope that what follows will prove a helpful contribution, I confess that I personally see little grounds within Girard's own thinking for the appropriateness of such a title. The fact that the coming apocalyptic upheavals will turn out to be of human origin, rather than being the direct work of God, does not necessarily entail the idea that they will be experienced by those affected as compassionate. The God of Girard's thought may be gentle, loving, and wholly without violence, but the same cannot be said for God's creation, least of all for that part of it that we call humanity.

STRUCTURALISM, MIMESIS, AND SOCIAL DIFFERENTIATION

Under the influence of structuralism, Girard understands human cultures to be based on systems of differentiation that are ultimately arbitrary. This is the presumed philosophical basis for much of the discussion in *Violence and the Sacred* and *Things Hidden Since the Foundation of the World*.[7] However, unlike those structuralists who failed in their quest to uncover a transcendental signifier, one that grounds or anchors the systems of human cultural exchange,[8] Girard understands that the first signifier is the primary victim. He argues that human language and all other manifestations of human culture have their origins in the scapegoat mechanism, the all-against-one violence of the primal horde that is transformed by the social and psychological impact of the death of

6. In his foreword to Williams, *Bible*, Girard carefully understates the differences saying of the book's author, "My general outlook is perhaps a little less optimistic than his," x.

7. In the introduction to *Gospel*, Robert Hamerton-Kelly calls Girard's method "radical structuralism." Elsewhere, in "Religion," he calls the theory *poststructuralist* in the sense that it assumes the insights of structuralism.

8. See the discussion in *Things Hidden*, 102–3.

its victim. The original difference is the one between the killers and the killed. All other cultural differentiation is derived form this.

Human societies, in particular those that lack a judicial system, maintain their systemic differentiation in two ways. Firstly, cultural prohibitions, for example the incest taboo, sustain difference and imbue it with a sacred significance. Secondly, the system is periodically renewed through the re-enactment of the founding murder in rituals, that usually take the form of a sacrifice, and the retelling of it in the stories that we commonly designate myths. Thus, in contrast to those former structuralists who concluded that there is no transcendental signifier as such and made the journey into poststructuralism, with its profound scepticism about the capacity of language, or of any other signs, to refer to anything other than other signs within the system of which they are a part, Girard concluded that systems of differentiation take their beginning from the scapegoat mechanism and so do refer, albeit in a distorted way, to a reality beyond themselves.

Of course, humans inevitably misconstrue the events that lead up to and that follow the operation of the scapegoat mechanism so that memory of the events concerned is distorted. The myths that retell the story are lies, though necessary lies, but they are lies told about a real event. Myths and rituals are recollections of something real.

One impact of *mimesis*, the human propensity to imitate others, especially in their desire, is to generate a tendency in people to aspire to appropriate the same things. These things may be tangible, such as property or sexual access to a partner, or they may be intangible, such as status or prestige. In the end, the things desired are secondary for it is the *being* of the *other* that is sought. The consequence of this is that cultural differentiation is constantly threatened. A part of this process is that prohibitions against mimetically induced behaviour become weakened leading to a greater and greater tendency for people to desire and to seek to acquire the same things. Humans become rivals for the same objects and this generates the potential for violence. Where a culture possesses sacrificial resources these violent inclinations may be directed away from the rival and find instead an outlet in ritual.

However, there comes a point in the cycle of a culture's existence when the myths and rituals lose their efficacy. The truths they purport to contain are doubted and so they are rendered less and less effective. Their ability to redirect violence becomes more limited and their capacity to restate the founding story in a way that reinforces cultural differentiation is lost. When this happens, there is no brake available on the power of mimesis to erode differentiation and to promote rivalries and hence violence. This process can culminate in the all-against-all violence of a social crisis and the effect may be described as one of undifferentiation; the loss of social differences. This is experienced by humans, who rely on differentiation to enable them to interpret the world, as *uncreation*: the unmaking of the ordered world and the emergence of a world experienced as monstrous. This is a return to the stage in which myths are generated, the time when the animals talk, land has yet to emerge from the sea, and the day and the night are yet to be separated from one another. This is the stage often referred to as *chaos* out of which order has yet to be summoned.

Girard has argued that the chaos images of mythology are a representation of the experience of social undifferentiation undergone in the course of violent primitive social crises. Language, being a system of differences, cannot directly express undifferentiation and so non-difference, which cannot be signified, is expressed in terms of the monstrous,[9] plagues,[10] floods,[11] and images of chaos. Thus, Girard claims, "The original chaos of the Greeks, the *tohu wa bohu* of Genesis, Noah's flood, the ten plagues of Egypt, and the companions of Ulysses turned into swine by Circe are all examples of mythical undifferentiation."[12]

The order that emerges from chaos in creation myths is a reflection of the new or renewed structural, cultural differentiation that arises when the crisis is resolved. Girard believes that this resolution is achieved by violence, by the murder of one or more members of the community by the other members of the community. Therefore, in mythology, order emerges from chaos through violence. Girard says,

> Everywhere, in "primitive" texts, the collective murder is associated with the confusion of day and night, of the sky and the earth,

9. Girard, *Violence*, 64, 160–61; Girard, *Scapegoat*, 33. Girard discusses hallucination and the experience of monsters and doubles in crises and in corresponding rituals in *Violence*, 119–68.

10. Girard, *Violence*, 77; *Things Hidden*, 12–13; "To Double," chapter 8: "The plague is universally presented as a process of undifferentiation, a destruction of specificities," 136; "The distinctiveness of the plague is that it ultimately destroys all forms of distinctiveness," 137.

11. *Things Hidden*, 12–13.

12. Girard, "To Double," 156.

of gods, men and animals. Monsters swarm. Everything begins
with the abolition of differences.... the mixing of what should
be distinguished.[13]

Only when the play of mimesis transforms the all-against-all violence of the horde into the all-against-one violence of the mob is there
the prospect of a killing out of which new or renewed order can emerge.
Of course, the stories that come to be told about this killing will distort
the truth. The arbitrariness of the victim will be forgotten and he or she
will turn out to have been selected for a reason; the killing will be shown
to have been both necessary and justified for it will become clear that
the victim had breached some known taboo or boundary. On this basis
a new form of cultural differentiation will emerge.

To this extent, human societies may be understood as being cyclical. They emerge from disorder and they end in disorder. They endure
so long as the lies on which they are founded and on which their cultural differentiation depends, can be sustained by prohibitions against
the effects of mimesis and by the renewal of the culture and its systems
of differentiation through the re-presentation of the founding event in
myth and ritual.

It is interesting to note the relationship between order and truth
in this understanding. At the beginning of the cycle, in the period when
the effects of the founding murder are strongest, cultural differentiation
is clearly pronounced and rituals are effective in strengthening it; as a
result cultural order is stable. At this point in the cycle the founding lie
is firmly believed. As the cycle progresses and imitative mimesis slowly
undermines cultural differentiation, the cultural order becomes weaker
and the founding myths start to appear less self-evidently true and the
mythological and ritual victims less self-evidently guilty. These hints of
the truth limit the effectiveness of myth and ritual and so serve to further undermine the cultural order.[14] Thus, in Girard's system, order and
truth appear to be incompatible; to expose the truth about cultural order
is to contribute to its collapse.

When Girard turns his attention to our current history his analysis changes; there is no possibility of return. Any new collapse into
all-against-all violence is likely to be final. This is not simply because

13. Ibid., 235–36.

14. "During periods of crisis and widespread violence there is always the threat of
subversive knowledge spreading." *Scapegoat*, 100.

humanity's capacity of mutual destruction is greater than ever, but because something is at work within human history which is eroding our capacity to renew culture in the ways that we have in the past. He contends that we have embarked upon the stage within the life of our culture when differentiation is being undermined. The truth about human cultural origins and our tendency to seek scapegoats to help renew our culture are exposed and consequently social order is threatened; we are no longer able to believe in or to act upon the lies that we have told about ourselves.

ENGAGEMENT WITH NIETZSCHE

It is here that Girard's engagement with Nietzsche becomes especially significant.[15] Girard conflates his cyclical view of cultures with Nietzsche's concept of the *eternal return*.[16] However, Girard suspects that Nietzsche harbours doubts that the process will continue permanently. Something new has been introduced. It seems that the message of Christianity has the capacity to discredit the collective murder that generates the eternal recurrence. With this in mind Girard asserts,

> Far from taking Christianity to be just another sacrificial religion, Nietzsche reiterates several times that its great fault is to "prevent sacrifice," to render impossible the acts of violence necessary to the smooth functioning of society.

In fact Nietzsche is undecideable on this point and Girard continues,

> One finds the same ambiguity at the conclusion of the Twilight of the Idols. One does not know if the colossal finish marks the end of the cycle only, the promise of a thousand renewals, or if it is truly the end of the world, the Christian apocalypse, the bottomless abyss of the unforgettable victim.[17]

15. See, e.g., the following writings of Girard: "Dionysus;" "Nietzsche"; "To Double"; "Founding."

16. Girard, "Founding."

17. Ibid., 246.

THE IMPACT OF THE GOSPELS

For Girard the situation is a little clearer. The gospels account for the state of Western culture in our day. Girard suggests that it is the gospels that have generated our awareness of the innocence of the scapegoats of others and even of our own victims. The gospels have spread the subversive knowledge that is preventing the operation of the scapegoat mechanism. We have reached the point where our knowledge of the truth will prevent us from restoring a cultural order of the kind we have had in the past. Girard writes,

> Mankind has become, for the first time, capable of destroying it-
> self. . . . The whole planet now finds itself, with regard to violence,
> in a situation comparable to that of the most primitive groups
> of human beings, except that this time we are fully aware of it.
> We can no longer count on sacrificial resources based on false
> religions to keep this violence at bay. We are reaching a degree
> of self-awareness and responsibility that was never attained by
> those who lived before us.[18]

So, the history of human culture has, until now, been cyclical. However, the effects of the gospels have now given it a linear trajectory. Now humans must find a means to escape the influence of the way in which our cultures are founded and on which all our systems of representation are built, for these make us imitate acquisitive acts, react to crises by searching for scapegoats, and respond to violence with more violence. In other words, we must find the means to found a nonviolent cultural order. And, since mimesis is inescapable, we must find a new model to imitate; one based on truth rather than upon a lie so that it has the prospect of being stable.

Girard's suggestion is found in the gospels; it is the kingdom of God as proclaimed and exemplified by Jesus. It involves the universal renunciation of violence, the elimination of every form of vengeance, retribution, and reprisal from human relations.[19] To do this is to escape from the realm of violence, which involves enslavement to the pervasive lie, into the domain of God.[20] The gospels tell us "all that people must do in order to break with the circularity of closed societies, whether they be

18. Girard, *Things Hidden*, 260–61.
19. Ibid., 197–98.
20. Ibid., 197.

tribal, national, philosophical or religious."[21] To escape from the realm of the lie to the kingdom of God is possible; "Mankind can cross this abyss, but to do so all men together should adopt the single rule of the Kingdom of God."[22] This is a call to conversion, to secede from the mimetic consensus.[23]

SACRIFICIAL CHRISTIANITY

Of course the world was not confronted immediately with this crisis. The act of revelation has taken time to have this impact. Girard suggests that one of the reason for this is that historic Christianity has interpreted the New Testament texts in sacrificial terms.[24] This (mis)reading provided enduring sacrificial resources which are only now becoming exhausted. However, the reading could not postpone forever the crisis generated by the diffusion of the gospel text and its penetration into human awareness.

THE MARTYRS

Those who seek to follow Jesus contribute to the subversive effect of the gospel story. This is most especially true of the martyrs of whom Girard says, "Dying in the same way as Jesus died, for the same reasons as he did, the martyrs multiply the revelation of the founding violence."[25] Elsewhere he insists that it is the fact of martyrdom rather than the words of the martyrs that has the decisive effects;

> What the martyrs say has little importance because they are witnesses, not of a determined belief, as is imagined, but of man's terrible propensity, in a group, to spill innocent blood in order to restore the unity of their community. The persecutors force themselves to bury their dead in the tomb of their representation of persecution, but the more martyrs die the weaker the representation becomes and the more striking the testimony.[26]

21. Ibid., 198.
22. Ibid., 199.
23. Girard, "Anti-Semitism?" 348–50.
24. Girard, *Things Hidden*, 224–62.
25. Ibid., 197.
26. Girard, *Scapegoat*, 212.

Thus the gospel drives humanity towards the eschaton and this end is open. It could be self-destruction in reciprocal violence or it could be the kingdom of God. There is a choice to be made between destruction and the renunciation of violence.

The gospels thus offer an alternative to established human means of interaction. However, communities built around the representation of the death of Jesus can inevitably offer only indications and anticipations of the kingdom of God. Existing human languages are derived from the scapegoat mechanism and any concept expressed in them will be tainted by sacrificial thinking; they cannot fully articulate a social world in which violence is wholly renounced. They cannot state absolute truth.

That is why the Word that states itself to be absolutely true never speaks except from the position of a victim in the process of being expelled. There is no human explanation for his presence among us.[27]

GIRARD AND THE APOCALYPSE

Girard has suggested that the book of Revelation is not the surest guide to this true Word. He calls it "a text which is clearly less representative of the gospel inspiration than the apocalyptic chapters in the Gospels themselves."[28] This may or may not be true, but the purpose of this paper is to suggest that the Apocalypse is wholly amenable to an evangelical interpretation when read in the light of Girard's thought. In particular, Girard has identified a thread of texts within the Scripture that have taken the perspective of the victim as their own. If the peak of God's revelation of Godself to humanity is, as Christian theology has usually acknowledged, found in the story of Jesus of Nazareth, and the peak of that peak has been found in the passion narratives, then it may be reasonable to propose a canonical reading of Scripture that approaches every text from the perspective of the dying Jesus, on the understanding that this is where God's clearest Word to a violent humanity is spoken.

THE DEATH OF JESUS IN REVELATION

The book of Revelation understands the death of Jesus in a number of ways. Firstly, it is a testimony to the truth that may be emulated by the book's hearers. Secondly, it is a means of unmasking the false ideolo-

27. Girard, *Things Hidden*, 435
28. Ibid., 188.

gies that allow the violence of the powerful to be regarded as legitimate. Next, it liberates the followers of Jesus from such ideologies. Finally, it is the means by which the eschatological plans of God are initiated. These things are present in the death of Jesus, are re-actualized whenever the event is represented in the gospel and are reinforced when a believer maintains his or her testimony to the point of martyrdom.

WITNESS

It cannot be insignificant that Revelation constantly describes Jesus as a witness and one who testifies. This suggests that he is understood to embody truth and that the Christian is called to a similar role. The word for witness is often linked in the text to death and it is clear that in Revelation the word used for witness carries connotations of the English word *martyr* that is derived from it.

The idea that the suffering of Jesus' followers might have similar significance to his own is found in the New Testament, particularly in the Pauline corpus.[29] This idea gained some currency within the early church. Origen states that the deaths of the martyrs have atoning significance.[30] In Revelation the deaths of the martyrs are understood to have a similar effect to that of their model, Jesus.

This idea is already present in the exegesis of a number of scholars whose work is independent of Girard. John Sweet, for example, discusses the relationship between the testimony of Jesus and the sufferings and victory of Christ and his followers. He concludes that one aspect of the ministry of Jesus and of Christians is to witness to the truth of God's word and against the illusion that grips the world. Such a witness torments and provokes the world that responds with persecution. The Christians die but are regarded as victors although why this should be so is, for Sweet, an unexplained mystery.[31]

Adela Yarbro Collins argues that in Revelation the martyrs are depicted as playing a part in bringing about the end of the world. She writes, "the deaths suffered by members of the community are thought to play a role in bringing about the turning point, the eschatological battle," and also that "martyrdom is part of the eschatological process." She says,

29. E.g., 2 Cor 1:6, Eph 3:13, Col 1:24, 2 Tim 4:6.

30. *On Numbers* 10.2.

31. Sweet, "Maintaining."

The faithful are to suffer persecution and death in the present. They expect a violent resolution of the conflict in which heavenly forces will defeat their adversaries. Their contribution to this outcome may be made in the form of a martyr's death, which hastens the end, because a fixed number of martyrs must die before the eschatological battle can be initiated. The value of the martyr's death is greatly enhanced by the example of Christ.[32]

Richard Bauckham makes a number of observations on this theme. He claims that the messianic army are followers of the Lamb "who participate in his victory by following his path to death." And he argues that when Christians "maintain their witness even to death and are seen to be vindicated as true witnesses, then their witness participates in the power of his [Christ's] witness to convert the nations." He also notes "how it was possible for the death of Christ to be such a victory is not explained."[33]

Of course, as Alison Trites says, "the testimony of the martyrs in life and death is valued only in so far as it is a repetition or continuation of the testimony of Christ."[34] As such a continuation of Jesus' own work, the testimony of the martyrs contributes to its consequences; it witnesses to the truth and is an agent of the eschatological process. As G.W.H. Lampe puts it, "Christ's death is re-presented in each martyrdom."[35] Girard comments on the Johannine Paraclete,

> When the Paraclete comes, Jesus says, he will bear witness to me, he will reveal the meaning of my innocent death and of every innocent death, from the beginning to the end of the world. Those who come after Christ will therefore bear witness as he did, less by their words or beliefs than by becoming martyrs and dying as Jesus died.[36]

These observations are reinforced by noting the role played by the two witnesses of 11:3–13. They prophesy, give testimony and are killed in a way that is linked to the death of Jesus. The life, death and resurrection of Jesus bring testimony of God's truth to the world. His followers are expected to witness to the truth in the same way as he did and their testimony will augment the consequences of his.

32. Yarbro Collins, "Political," 256
33. Bauckham, *Climax*, 229, 281, 185.
34. Trites, *New Testament*, 162.
35. Lampe, "Testimony," 258.
36. Girard, *Scapegoat*, 212.

CONQUER

There is another very significant word within Revelation and that is the verb usually translated "conquer," especially in those instances, only ever applied to God or God's agents and people, where it is used in a distinctive way; without an object. The word when used in this sense is defined in Rev 5:9, interpreting 5:5, and 12:11. It refers to the idea of maintaining faithfulness to the truth in the face of any opposition and strongly suggests that such faithfulness should be maintained to the point of death. Certainly, key theologians in the early church believed that conquering was achieved through martyrdom. Tertullian discusses the use of the verb in Revelation and writes, "Who, pray, are these so blessed conquerors, but martyrs in the strict sense of the word?"[37] The verb has become almost a technical term for maintaining faith in Jesus in the face of the prospect of martyrdom.

Furthermore, there seems to be a possibility that the formula found at 13:8 alludes to the tradition preserved at Luke 11:50. The latter suggests that the blood of the prophets has been shed from the foundation of the world. Perhaps Jesus is to be understood as standing at the end of a long line of murdered prophets whose witness to the word of God is now vindicated. It suggests that the Lamb is the archetypal victim, the one who represents all the silent and innocent victims killed and expelled by violent humanity. It is even possible that Jesus represents the primal victim who, according to Girard's understanding of human social life, lies dead at the beginning of every human culture. God, acting through this Jesus, has exposed the truth and the vindicated Lamb, slain from the foundation of the world, now stands in judgement over all the works of humanity. If Girard is right in asserting that no society can long withstand the knowledge that its scapegoats are innocent then the Lamb, vindicated by God, may be seen, along with his followers, as the agent of God's eschatological process. Conqueror indeed!

REVELATION 4–5

This eschatological process is, from one perspective, the wrath of God, or the wrath of the Lamb. It is not that God is active in the violence, although it does depend on God's initiative in the Christ event. It is at

---

37. *Antidote* 12.

this point that the exegesis of the book of Revelation, especially chapters 4, 5 and 6, becomes significant.

One of the major problems with existing readings is that scholars have often relied too heavily on interpretative frameworks derived from outside the text. Some have used history for this purpose and have imported as a frame of reference the Jewish War; or the events of the first century in Palestine, Asia Minor or the Empire as a whole; or the history of the European and Near Eastern world and church to date; or a framework of salvation history derived from the rest of the Bible and systematic theology; or a framework of future events or of eschatological events divined from an understanding of prophecies from other parts of the Bible. All can be used to understand Revelation. Others have found the framework from elsewhere: the pattern of ancient myth or ritual; the structure of the liturgy of the early church; the shape of Greek tragedy; a pattern derived from Jewish apocalyptic texts; sometimes even a structure that purports to be internal to the text but into which the text must to some extent be forced: in every case the framework determines the subsequent meaning found in the text.

Of course, some form of framework is necessary if a text is to be interpreted at all. It provides a limit to the infinite range of possible referents that any given symbol might otherwise possess. However, most frameworks prove too inflexible; they treat the text as though it were an elaborate code or allegory, the key to which has been lost. They attempt to impose a pattern on the text and then require that every image be interpreted in accordance with it. Many work adequately for some elements of the text but strain to provide adequate explanations of others so that the interpretations of some of the text's symbols can appear arbitrary. The results are therefore speculative. All exegesis will involve some form of decoding, but the "this is that" approach required by most readings may prevent the reader from engaging imaginatively with the text as a whole.

In addition, there has been relatively little work on how the plague sequences relate to the rest of the book. In particular, it is clear that the first sequence at least flows out of the events described in 5:1–13. Yet few discussions of the text connect the interpretation of the seal openings to the nature of those events as they have been explicated. Few attempts have been made to explain why the events of 5:1–13, for example the opening of a scroll or the worship of a lamb, should have such consequences. The exegesis of 5:1–13, and of 4:1–11 to which the vision is linked, is a vital first step towards an appropriate understanding of the subsequent plagues.

Something has happened that leads to chaos, but the nature of the event and the reason for its consequences remain unclear. Furthermore the explanations of the plagues so far encountered offer no explanation of why God, who elsewhere in the biblical tradition acts in the world to bring order out of chaos, should here be the source of disorder. God casts chaos upon the world and it is hardly surprising that some have found this difficult to reconcile with Christian theology.

All that need be presumed is that this is a Christian text and that the first hearers would have been aware of the primitive *kerygma* concerning the life, death, resurrection, ascension and *parousia* of Jesus. Given such an approach and the ideas of Girard as a heuristic device, a fresh reading of the text becomes possible.

Revelation 4 is often regarded as a depiction of the timeless worship of heaven. There are however, a number of reasons for believing that heaven is here represented as anticipating an act that will bring profound change. Firstly, God is described (for the last time in the book) as being "to come." Secondly, the key verbs in verses 9 and 10, while usually translated as present continuous, are in fact futures. They are surely a promise of what is to come and so, in chapter 5, the elders sing a new song. On these and other grounds, Eugenio Corsini argues that the move from 4 to 5 takes the reader from the Old Testament to the New.[38] This accords with the view of Christopher Rowland that there is nothing within 4 that is distinctively Christian.[39] What we have is a description of "the situation in heaven before the advent of Christ."[40] Revelation 4 depicts heaven on the verge of a new happening. As Richard Bauckham argues:

> Chapter 4 is primarily a revelation of God's sovereignty, as it is manifest and acknowledged in heaven. Only a little acquaintance with prophetic-apocalyptic literature is required for a reader to infer that this vision prepares for the implementation of God's sovereignty on earth, where it is presently hidden and contested

38. Corsini, *Apocalypse.*
39. Rowland, *Open,* 222.
40. Ibid., 425.

by the powers of evil. In other words, the kingdom of heaven is to come on earth as it already exists in heaven.[41]

The scroll of Revelation 5, however it is best understood, contains the promises of God, both of judgment and of salvation. Heaven anticipates seeing the beginning of the fulfilment of those promises. When John believes that this expectation is false, for none is found who can open the scroll, his tears are the inevitable response. However, he is soon corrected and sees the slain Lamb who can open the scroll, who, we may understand, has done what is necessary to inaugurate the process by which the promises of God find their fulfilment. The new song clarifies the means by which this has been achieved: the Lamb, that is Messiah Jesus, has been slain; he accomplishes his purpose by being a victim.

This is the moment for which heaven has been waiting. The actions promised in 4:9–10 take place. In a series of concentric circles around the throne, starting with those closest, all creation acknowledges what has happened. By the end of the chapter no voice is silent. This can only be a description of the *eschaton* when all things are in agreement and all things acknowledge the rule of God and of the Lamb.

Revelation 4 is best understood as a representation of the primitive Christian *kerygma* concerning Jesus who died and ascended to the right hand of God and whose status as Lord will one day be recognized by all things.[42] This one scene therefore depicts both the ascension and the *eschaton*. The latter is the consequence of the former. The process of fulfilment inaugurated by the Christ event culminates in the agreement of creation. From one perspective, these events are one and the same; all that God needs to do to bring about the end has been accomplished. It was believed that the heavenly beings, the angelic powers, became subject to Jesus at his exaltation.[43] Perhaps the image of elders leaving their thrones to cast their crowns before the throne signifies this. The eschatological process is the vindication of the victim.

If Revelation 4 depicts heaven awaiting the work of the Messiah to be accomplished and Revelation 5 the exaltation of the Messiah in heav-

---

41. Bauckham, *Climax*, 249. Elsewhere Bauckham suggests that Revelation should be understood as a description of the fulfilment of the first three petitions of the Lord's Prayer, *Theology*, chapter 2. This position was adopted in some medieval exegesis. See Matter, "Apocalypse," 49.

42. E.g., Acts 2:22–36; 5:28–32; 7:51–56, Rom 8:34, Eph 1:20, Heb 1:3; 10:12; 12:2.

43. Eph 1:20–23; 1 Pet 3:22 and, especially, Phil 2:6–11.

en and the fulfilment of his work at the *eschaton*, the succeeding chapters may be read as commentary on it; an account of the means by which the *eschaton* derives from the accomplished work of the Messiah.

REVELATION 6

One effect of Jesus' death, according to both Girard and the book of Revelation, was to witness to the truth. The victim is vindicated. This event, the death and exaltation of Jesus, and its representation in the proclaimed gospel and in the life of the followers of Jesus, now has its inevitable impact upon human cultures; it reveals their violence, the innocent blood on which they are founded and which sustains them; it summons them to a new way of being; it provokes a crisis of differentiation but prevents its resolution by former methods. The sign of the slain Lamb stands over the world, judging it by exposing it to the truth of its own nature; as a result the eschatological process is inaugurated.

The effects of non-differentiation and the related cultural crisis can only be described in symbolic language, in particular the kind associated with myth.

On this reading the anticipated effects of the death and exaltation of Jesus are firstly, the representation of his story and the imitation of his way by those who follow him, a crisis of differentiation expressed in terms of cosmic chaos, and futile attempts to restore order through scapegoating, especially the persecution of those who are associated with this new story and who secede as a result from the mimetic consensus. These phenomena are described in Revelation beginning at the start of 6.

The interpretation of the rider of 6:1 is widely debated in the literature. Most of the proposals interpret the text by importing an external framework rather than interpreting the figure in terms of Revelation itself and by presuming that the hearer knows the rider is part of the group that follows and should be understood as such. In fact the rider is the first consequence of the turn of the ages and is best understood as the continuation of the work of Jesus by those who follow. As he conquered, so they conquer. The majority of commentators reject this view but something similar was the unanimous view of the early church. The oldest extant commentary is that of Victorinus of Pettau who argues that the first act of the ascended Jesus is to send the Spirit so that the word about Jesus may be made known:

> After the Lord ascended into heaven and opened all things, He
> sent the Holy Spirit, whose words the preachers sent forth as
> arrows reaching to the human heart, that they might overcome
> unbelief. . . . Therefore the white horse is the word of preaching
> with the Holy Spirit sent into the world.[44]

That the first rider is positive is borne out by a number of factors: the parallels with 19:11–16; the fact that every other instance of the word *white* within Revelation refers to something associated with God or his agents or people; that only those on God's side have crowns, though his enemies may have headgear that is *like* crowns; while there are no other references to a bow in Revelation, the weapon was associated with God and his people, for the prince of Psalm 45, a Psalm interpreted in messianic terms, shoots arrows and so must be understood to bear a bow, and God himself hangs up his bow in Genesis 9; finally and significantly the verb "to conquer," when used without an object, only ever describes the actions of the people of God. It is the defining act of Christ as we see at 5:5. As J. S. Considine acknowledges, the first rider is "the progressive and continuous effect of Christ."[45]

However, as has been suggested, the consequences of the exaltation of Jesus are not all beneficent. With the next few riders it is not so much that the Christ event generates warfare and oppression as that it reveals its true extent. The false claims about order, peace and justice have been exposed and the riders reveal the truth. This is the same function as the riders in Zechariah from where this motif is probably derived.

Inevitably, the exposure of the truth has consequences because it does not give only intellectual knowledge about the world, it changes the way in which people and institutions behave. Attempts are made to suppress the truth by silencing and persecuting those who witness to it. This action is counterproductive because each innocent death simply confirms the truth that has been revealed and so accelerates the cultural breakdown and worsens the effects of the things symbolized by the last three riders.

The scene changes with the fifth seal when the souls under the altar are revealed. Whether these are to be understood as Jewish or Christian or both or neither, and whether they lived and died before or after the time of Jesus are not especially important. They are those who have died

44. See Haussleiter, *Victorini*, 68.

45. Considine, "Rider," 421.

because of their witness to truth and they are revealed by the death and exaltation of Jesus because these events have exposed the truth about the victims of every human culture.

As we have seen, the deaths of the martyrs play a role in the eschatological process. In Girardian terms, they reinforce the awareness of the scapegoat mechanism achieved by Jesus. The persecutors become increasingly aware of the innocence of their victims until their violence loses its culturally acceptable outlet and becomes redirected in ways that provoke vengeance and other forms of reciprocal violence. This process, or the conversion to the way of Jesus of their victimizers, is the vindication for which the martyrs pray.[46]

The moment the persecutors recognize that the grounds for their actions are baseless, lies in the future. As the text indicates, the number of the martyrs is not yet complete. The deaths of others will be necessary before the cultural crisis that has been generated reaches the stage where participants are forced to abandon their belief in the guilt of their victims. When they do they will be forced to choose between the way of Jesus and uncontrolled violence. The victims sit in judgement over the culture that sought to silence their witness to the truth.[47]

The sixth seal is then opened. The language is derived from Old Testament images of Holy War and the Day of Yahweh.[48] The origins of this language are disputed,[49] but Sweet notes its nature; it is expressed, "in terms of God undoing his work of creation: bringing back chaos."[50] One of the biblical understandings of creation sees it in terms of differentiation; the process by which order emerges from chaos.[51] On the Day of Yahweh this process is undone and creation reverts to its primeval state. Evidence of this is found at the opening of the sixth seal. The changes to the sun, moon and stars mean that the difference between night and

---

46. Sweet, *Revelation*, 142, proposes the translation *vindicate* as at Luke 18:8, in place of the more usual *avenge*. The martyrs long to have their innocence made known to their killers.

47. Wisdom 2–3 suggests that the just will be victimized by the wicked but will become their judges.

48. See Isa 34:4, 8; Joel 2:11, 20–21; Amos 8:9; Nah 1:6; Mal 3:2.

49. See Von Rad, "Origin," and *Holy War*.

50. Sweet, *Revelation*, 143.

51. See Gunkel, *Schöpfung*.

day is abolished. When the sky rolls up as a scroll, the difference between heaven and earth is lost and the one lies fully exposed to the other.[52]

The removal of mountains and islands means that all the principal means of orienting oneself on land and sea are lost. Verse 15 suggests that all seven types of human are not only equally affected but reduced to the same condition; all cultural hierarchy and difference is gone.[53] In other words, humans find themselves disoriented both physically and culturally. All this is brought about by the great earthquake that, as Bauckham has demonstrated, is traditionally the herald of God's coming in judgment.[54] And of course, like the preceding seal openings, this is a consequence of the death and exaltation of Jesus.

A Girardian approach to language of this kind offers a new way of interpreting it.[55] It avoids the difficulties of literalism and those associated with treating it as an intentional metaphor. It reads the eschatological language as a representation of the experience of participants in a crisis of cultural differentiation. Cosmogonies tell the story of the origins of culture in terms of the origins of the cosmos. The cosmic chaos is an expression of the social chaos that is perceived by those involved in cosmic terms and articulated after the event in myths of cosmic origin. The threat of a future crisis finds expression in the same language but this time the process is reversed and order breaks down into chaos. The renewal of chaos is a necessary precursor to the re-establishment of a renewed cultural order. This chaos, brought about by the exposure of human culture to the truth, is, according to the Girardian reading, the phenomenon that the Bible calls the wrath of God.

While the ontologically existing cosmos beyond the earth is not necessarily affected greatly by human behaviour, the same is not true for the cosmos as it is experienced by humans. A number of studies suggest that what is perceived as reality is a social construct. Human perception of reality may therefore be affected by human behaviour; social chaos could be perceived as cosmic chaos. In the ancient world the link was of-

---

52. Here the loss of differentiation results in anguish. In the closing chapters, after the destruction of the forces of negative mimesis, the loss of differentiation is a part of the New Jerusalem.

53. Harrington, *Apocalypse*, agrees that the text depicts the abolition of all forms of social difference.

54. Bauckham, *Climax*, 199–209.

55. See Schwager, "Theory."

ten made between social disorder and cosmic chaos.[56] This idea is found in the Old Testament; Psalm 74 links the destruction of the temple with the chaos that preceded creation and Psalm 72 links the fertility of the land to the justice done by the king. These themes are explored by Robert Murray who suggests that the link between the state of the cosmos and justice in human society is the subject of a cosmic covenant.[57] Human disobedience fractures the cosmic order and chaos is come again.

On this basis this text may be understood to offer an insight into the perceptions of those who are involved in the final cultural crisis; the one that is a consequence of the exaltation of the Lamb, the one brought about by the ministry of Jesus and the representation of that ministry by his followers. During the crisis of differentiation, the perception of the cosmos by those involved is affected. In one sense the events are not literal; the stars do not fall out of the sky. In another sense, this language is the closest that human speech can come to articulating the experience of those who go through the trauma of such a crisis.

Past crises of this kind have always been resolved by the operation of what Girard calls the surrogate victim mechanism; the killing of a scapegoat. In the final crisis, there can be no such resolution. The revelation of the truth of the innocence of the victim means that the mechanism cannot operate for the participants can no longer be deceived by the process. They murder the martyrs but their action is to no avail. All are aware that the crisis and their inability to resolve it are related to Jesus. It is in this sense that the process described can be called "the wrath of the Lamb."

The sixth seal opening is a part of the response to the plea of the martyrs at 6:10.[58] The action of Jesus in revealing the truth and the ministry of his followers in witnessing to the truth have provoked the crisis. These followers are also the victims of the violence generated by the crisis. The word of God spoken in the exclusion of victims brings the wrath of God upon the human world. The violence is human but it has been brought about by God and the Lamb because the human mimetic consensus constrains people to engage in reciprocal violence unless and until they respond to the gospel's offer of an alternative.

56. See Cohn, *Cosmos*, chapters 1–2.
57. Murray, *Cosmic*.
58. Gilles Quispel says that in 6:12–17 the Lamb stands up for the martyrs, see his *Secret*.

The visions of chapter 7 stand alongside these scenes of crisis, depicting the state of those who follow the way of Jesus. These are the victims of the violence of the crisis but, paradoxically, are also, in one way, those who avoid it; they do not participate in the violence generated by the cultural crisis for they have understood the true nature of human society and have chosen a different way of being. They escape from the wrath and enjoy the presence of the Lamb. Their experience foreshadows that of the New Jerusalem.

CONCLUSIONS

Space does not permit further exegesis of the text, but the foregoing may offer some suggestions about the way in which a fuller reading might proceed. In chapter 5 Jesus, the innocent victim, is vindicated. The series of plagues that afflict humanity flow from this; they are the consequence of the exaltation of the Lamb. They could be avoided if humans changed their way of being and abandoned the mimetic consensus derived from acquisitive mimesis and embraced the mimesis of renunciation at the heart of Jesus' teaching about the kingdom of God. In other words, the wrath would be avoided if humans repented.[59] The series of plagues describe the process by which humans enter a crisis of differentiation from which they prove unable to emerge by the usual means. The cosmos itself is experienced as being affected.

Yet Revelation offers the possibility of hope. Whether its message holds out the prospect of a universal salvation may be doubted,[60] but the promise is made that the crisis will be resolved by the victory of truth over the one who deceives the whole world. Throughout Revelation the enemies of God are portrayed as parodies of God and God's agents; they are engaged in a false mimesis of God motivated by a desire for God's being. This has been noticed by a number of scholars.

Sophie Laws speaks of God's adversaries as being a parody of God and God's co-workers.[61] Dieter Georgi claims that Revelation teaches that the Roman state and cult ape the authentic eschatological conviction caused by Jesus.[62] J. Massyngberde Ford actually uses the idea of

59. See 9:20–21; 16:10.
60. See Bauckham, *Climax*, 238–337 for a discussion of the issue.
61. Laws, *In the Light*, especially 36–46.
62. Georgi, "Who Is?" 124.

mimetic rivalry, deriving the language from her reading of Hamerton-Kelly. She argues that in Revelation this rivalry is at the root of idolatry, economic sanctions, and murder.[63] So, the final visions in the closing chapters of the book are of a world in that the forces which generate human violence, mimetic rivalry, and mimetic desire are defeated and destroyed and a new human way of social being is envisaged.

The day of the Lord begins with the opening of the sixth seal and its consequences are depicted in terms of cosmic and social chaos in the subsequent sequences of plagues. The plagues do not refer to specific historical events nor are they literal future events. The text uses traditional material to depict the sensations of humans caught up in the extended and final cultural crisis that the exaltation of the Lamb is bringing upon the world. The crisis will bring about the transfer of sovereignty over the earth to God from God's adversaries. The process begins at Calvary, it continues in the representation of the life and death of Jesus in the words and lives of his followers, and culminates in a new kind of human social life. The agency that achieves this change is God's apocalypse, his revelation or disclosure, the truth, the word of God, living and active, the sharpest of two-edged swords; it brings things into being and accomplishes the things of which it speaks. It breaks into the human world and promises judgement and salvation, the end of the present age and the life of the age to come, the destruction of the existing human social world and a new type of human community.

63. Ford, "Construction."

13

The Final Judgment

Sunrise of Christ's Liberating Justice

JÜRGEN MOLTMANN

FUTURE EXPECTATIONS AND PRESENT WORLDVIEWS

OUR LIFE IS NOT only shaped by memory and tradition but by future expectations in anxiety and hope as well. There is always a correlation between personal life expectations and our way of life, and between public future perspectives and our present worldviews. Let us review some of the spirits of our times.

The American way of life was and still is shaped by trust in an irresistible and incessant progress into a glorious future of unlimited possibilities and inexhaustible resources. The future is always better than the past, and the past is at best a prologue to the future. Because a happy life is destined for us, the *pursuit of happiness* is a fundamental human right in the U.S. Constitution.

Belief in progress was not different in Germany at the beginning of modern times. "I shall lead you into glorious times," promised Kaiser Wilhelm II to his subjects in the German Reich. Two years later he sent them into World War I, where the most advanced nations of humankind destroyed each other with the most advanced weapons of mass annihilation: poison gas. Belief in unending progress in science, technology, economy, and last but not least in morality is nothing but secularized millennialism. The religious expectation of the millennium of Christ was translated into the future golden age of humankind. Because in the Christian expectation Satan was bound for a thousand years (Rev 20:2), a secular moral optimism shaped the modern culture of the nineteenth century. The founding fathers of the United States had a strong messianic faith: the "New World Order" of peace and democratic self-government of the people were their global vision. On the one-dollar note we still read *novus ordo seclorum*, the new world order.

Europeans today no longer share this dream of perfection. The fear of catastrophes is much more deeply rooted in our souls. The twentieth century was for us an *age of anxiety*, with innumerable crimes against humanity, mass murder, and displaced persons in prison camps, refugee camps, concentration camps and the Gulag Archipelago. Our existential question is no longer: How can we complete God's unfinished future by progress in science, economy, and education? But much more: Is there a justice higher than inhuman brutality and crimes?

With wounded memories of human catastrophes in mind many are saying, "No, there was and there is no higher justice." The law of the jungle is that the stronger win, the weaker are lost. The reckless and cynical will to power justifies all means, and success sanctifies every brutality. There is no God; therefore everything is allowed. In the times of Darwinism this was a justification for the supremacy of the white race, white racism, and colonialism. In our time of global turbo-capitalism, the "survival of the fittest" is the only law respected by all global players. There is no higher justice; the godless are victorious, the violent win.

But no, others would protest: God will not allow God to be mocked. God will destroy this godless world as God had done in Noah's time with the flood that came over a sinful generation. We have to expect the end of the world soon. *Doomsday* is near, as more crimes and catastrophes happen. The day of revenge is coming, because God is God. *Dies irae, dies illa. Solvet seclum in favilla*: Day of wrath, that day will dissolve the world to dust.

This was the most famous rhyme-verse in medieval times. This sinful world can take no good end. The world will go down in chaos or end up in fire or, in more modern terms, this world will destroy itself in a nuclear or ecological or terrorist catastrophe. People who expect this like to interpret natural or human catastrophes in history as signs and anticipations of the final world destruction by a wrathful God. God punished sinful Sodom and Gomorrah; God punished arrogant Babylon; on September 11, 2001, God punished the sinful—or was it the homosexual?—city of New York. Allah punished the Indonesian province of Aceh with the tsunami killing 200,000 people because of the too-soft and lax Islam of the people. False prophets and self-made repentance preachers are obscuring God as the dark power of a terrifying destiny. Is their God a world terrorist? Are suicide mass-murderers his obedient slaves?

When he was a boy, an American friend asked his Baptist grandmother about the end of the world. She answered only with the one mysterious, terrifying name Armageddon. In Rev 16:16 this is the valley for the final battle between God and the devils. Today the final battle is between the good and the evil, or us and the terrorists.

American fundamentalists illustrated their apocalyptic dualism with modern end-time scenarios, as in Hal Lindsey's *The Late Great Planet Earth* (1970) and Tim LaHaye and Jerry B. Jenkins's Left Behind series. People may be fascinated, entertained, or annoyed by these strange end-time fantasies, but they do shape present worldviews. They introduce and justify in politics the *friend-foe paradigm* as the one existential political category of a nation. Whoever is not for us is against us. President Ronald Reagan speculated on an Armageddon "in our generation," possibly a "nuclear Armageddon," because the Soviet Union was "the realm of evil." We are lucky to have a total change of affairs in 1990: instead of Armageddon, Mikhail Gorbachev came. George W. Bush applied this old political dualism in the form of an "axis of evil" from Iraq to Iran to North Korea. America is at war, he declared after September 11, and whoever is not for us is against us. What kind of war is this? Is the unending war against terrorists already the beginning of Armageddon?

We can see a similar effect on the present worldview in the traditional Christian and Muslim expectancy of God's final judgment. At the end of the world, God will separate the believers from the unbelievers, bring the first to heaven, the others to hell, and destroy the earth. Whoever is expecting such a final separation of humankind will develop a worldview of *religious friend-foe* for today: Here is the "house of God" for believers—there is the "house of war" for unbelievers. Unbelievers are enemies of God and so also our enemies, because we are on God's side. You can't trust an enemy of God. We may punish them already here and now with neglect or contempt, excommunication, or terror. Crusades and jihads against unbelievers are justified. To kill or be killed in holy wars makes true believers into martyrs of God. In short, the expectation of an exclusive final judgment justifies the exclusion of those who do not belong to us. Whoever is not for us or like us is against us—and we against them.

WHAT AWAITS US AT THE LAST JUDGMENT?

Throughout the ages, expectations of the great judgment at the end of time have plunged human beings into fear and trembling. The earliest pictures of this judgment known to us do not belong to the Christian world but come to us from the Egypt of the Pharaohs. Here the great judge Osiris pronounces judgment, and Anubis weighs the souls according to their good and evil deeds. A human being is nothing but the sum of his or her deeds, good and evil. In medieval Christian pictures, Christ in place of Osiris is seen sitting on the judgment throne with a double-edged sword in his mouth. The archangel Michael stands in front of him with the scales. Sometimes there is also a little devil who pulls down the scales on the side of evil, but a good angel keeps his hands on the other scale, so that no unjust judgment results. In this final judgment there are only two verdicts: eternal life or eternal death. On the right-hand side the angels carry off the righteous to heaven; on the left, devils drag the wicked down to hell.

Since no one knows how righteous he or she has to be in order to get to heaven, the expectation of judgment evokes more fear and trembling in human beings than it awakens trust in God—"Sinners in the hands of an angry God," as Jonathan Edwards preached. Fear of hell then increases the fear of death in the dying, because in our last hours it is no longer possible to put anything right. Everyone must appear alone before the divine judgment seat with his or her life just as it has been. *Suum cuique*: to each his or her own.

Modern interpretations of judgment have therefore put the personally responsible human being at the center, instead of the wrathful judging God: No one is sent to heaven or hell against his or her will. It is the person's own decision, which has one or the other consequence. Everyone has the chance finally to reject God and to enter the state of eternal God-forsakenness which used to be called hell. From this perspective—the perspective of the personally responsible human being—the last judgment appears to be simply a symbol for the ultimate endorsement of our free will. "God predestines no one to go to hell; for this, a willful turning away from God is necessary, and persistence in it until the end," says the new Universal Catechism of the Roman Catholic Church of 1992.[1]

Let us consider both ideas about the last judgment. If the judging God is at the center, no one knows how righteous he or she has to be. Everyone is delivered over to the unknown judgment of God. If the responsible human being is at the center, no one knows what future he or she will arrive at, because voluntary human decisions can vacillate. If the God of wrath is at the center of judgment, we must despair of God. If the freely deciding human being is at the center, each of us must despair of him- or herself. According to both ideas, human beings are really the masters of their own fate, or their own executioners. In both cases the role of God is reduced to that of executor or accomplice of the human being's free choice. Heaven and hell become religious images that endorse human free will. We are the Lord's, and God is our servant. Whether the judging God or the responsible human being is at the center, nothing Christian can be detected in these ideas. We find them in exactly the same way in the ancient Egyptian Book of the Dead, in the Qur'an, or in the Chinese myth of the Ten Judges of the Dead.

Our first question is: Who has the keys of hell and death in hand? We human beings? No. God? *No*. It is Jesus Christ who was dead, but is alive from eternity to eternity (Rev 1:18). What is he doing with these keys of death and hell? It is high time to Christianize our traditional images and perceptions of God's final judgment and to evangelize their present effects on our lives and worldviews, so that we may greet the coming judge of the world with joy: "Maranatha, come LORD Jesus, come soon"—and may live already here and now in the sunrise of God's justice on earth (Rev 21:20).

Is the expectation of a final judgment necessary, or a relic of times past? I believe it is a necessary expectation: Injustice cries out to high heaven. The victims who have suffered injustice and violence do not hold their peace. The perpetrators who have caused the suffering find no rest. The hunger for justice and righteousness remains a torment on both sides. The victims must not be forgotten; the murderers must not finally triumph over them. The expectation of a final universal judgment in which divine justice will finally triumph was originally a hope cherished by the victims of violence and injustice. It was their counter-history to the world of the triumphal evildoers. They hoped for the final Judge

---

1. Universal Catechism of the Roman Catholic Church, Article 1037.

who will establish justice for those who suffer wrong. To this the psalms of lament in the Old Testament are an eloquent witness. Here judging means saving lives, healing wounds, restoring dignity. It was only later and under other influences that this saving judge of the victims became the judge of a criminal court before whom evildoers had to appear. The expectation of saving justice oriented towards the victims turned into a moral judgment oriented towards the perpetrators on the motto of "measure for measure"—the retributive justice in which good is repaid by good, and evil by evil. To each his or her own. This was Roman law.

Who is the Judge? According to the Christian ideas of the New Testament, judgment day is the day of the Son of Man who came "to seek that which was lost" (Luke 19:10, KJV // Matt 8:11, KJV). Whoever thinks there are lost people Christ has not found is declaring him ineffective and rather unsuccessful. The day of judgment is in fact "the day of Jesus Christ" (Phil 1:6). It is to be the day when the crucified Christ will be manifest to the whole world, and the whole world will be manifest before the risen Christ. "We must all appear before the judgment seat of Christ" (2 Cor 5:10). On that day both will emerge from their concealment into the light of truth—the Christ who is now hidden in God, and the human beings who are hidden from themselves. The eternal light will reveal Christ and human beings to each other. And what is now still hidden in nature will also become clear and lucid, for as bodily and natural beings men and women cannot be isolated from nature, not even before the face of God and at the judgment.

But how will Christ appear? As divine avenger or as final retaliator? No, I believe Christ will appear as the crucified and risen conqueror and victor over sin, death, and hell. Christ shall be revealed as the first fruit of the dead and the beginning and leader of eternal life.

According to what righteousness will Christ judge when he comes and is manifested as the Son of Man, judge of the world? Surely this righteousness will be no different from the righteousness he himself proclaimed in his gospel and practiced in fellowship with sinners and the sick! Otherwise no one would be able to recognize him. The coming judge is the one who was put to death for many on the cross. The one who will come as judge of the world is the one "who bears the sins of the world" and who has himself suffered the suffering of the victims. When we look at the judge in many medieval pictures, by ourselves we would hardly arrive at the idea that he could be Jesus of Nazareth, the crucified one, and least of all if we look at that hero belonging to the ancient world in Michelangelo's famous picture in the Sistine Chapel.

The justice that Christ will bring about for all and everything is not the justice that establishes what is good and evil, and the retributive justice that rewards the good and punishes the wicked. It is God's creative justice, which brings the victims justice and puts the perpetrators right. The victims of injustice and violence are first judges so that they may receive their rights. The perpetrators of evil will afterwards experience the same justice that puts things to rights. They will thereby be transformed inasmuch as they will be redeemed only together with their victims. They will be saved through the crucified Christ, who comes to them together with their victims. They will die to their evil acts against their victims and the burden of their guilt in order to be born again to a new life together with their victims. Paul expresses this with the image of the fire through which every human work is proved: "If any man's work is burned up, he shall suffer loss, but he himself shall be saved, yet so as by fire" (1 Cor 3:15, KJV). The image of the end-time fire is an image of the consuming love of God and not an image of the wrath of God. Everything that is and has been in contradiction to God will be burned away, so that the person who is loved by God is saved, and everything that is and has been in accord with God in that person's life is preserved.

The purpose of vindicating the victims and correcting the perpetrators is not reward and punishment but the victory of God's creative justice over against all that is godless in heaven, on earth, and under the earth. Victorious divine justice will not separate humankind into blessed and condemned at the end of the world, but will unite them for God's great day of reconciliation on this earth. On this day all the tears will be wiped away from their eyes, the tears of suffering as well as the tears of remorse, for there will be no more suffering and pain nor crying (Rev 21:4). The earth will then be cleansed from the dirt of sin and death. The shadows of sin will disappear together with the night of death: "And death shall be no more." The powers of annihilation are annihilated.

It follows that the final judgment is not the ultimate thing, but only the penultimate. God's judgment is but one step on the transition from this corruptible to incorruption, and from this mortal to eternal life. What is final, ultimate, and everlasting is only the new creation of all things built on the foundation of divine justice. And because the judgment serves the new creation, justice deals not with the past only but is a healing and correcting act of God for the future of his kingdom. The final judgment is not standing in service of sin and death as a great "settlement of accounts," but serves the new creation of all things. The end of the old age of the world is nothing else but the beginning of the "life of the world to come." In my opinion, it was a fatal mistake of Christian tradition in doctrine and spirituality, images and concepts, to look only on the final judgment over the past of the world and not see through this horizon into the new world of God, not believe in the new beginning at this end.

Of course the evil committed and suffered is not always distributed between different people and separate groups of people. Victims can also become perpetrators, and in many people the perpetrator side of evil and the victim side are indistinguishably interlocked. It is all the more important to perceive that the coming judge casts us down as perpetrators and raises us up as victims, and in this way also reconciles us with ourselves. But his judgment is always a social judgment.[2] The accused do not stand solitary and alone before their judge, as they do in human criminal courts, and in solitary torments of conscience at night. The victims stand there together with the perpetrators and the perpetrators with the victims, Cain with Abel, Israel with the nations, the rich with the poor, the violent with the helpless, the martyrs with their murderers. The history of human suffering is indissolubly bound up with its history of guilt. The conflicts in which one becomes the victim and the other the perpetrator are always social and political conflicts which are unsolved or unsolvable.

In Israel's history with God, God's justice is invoked with the words: "May the Lord judge between you and me!" (Gen 16:5, 31:53; 1 Sam 24:12, NRSV). In these conflicts God is invoked as justice of the peace. That is the way he is to judge between the poor and the rich, the high and the low: "Behold, I shall judge between sheep and sheep, between rams and goats" (Ezek 34:17, NKJV), so that the herd can again live in peace. The petitioners in the Psalms are also calling for judgment in social life with their tormenting questioning of why everything goes right for the godless while those who are faithful to God are persecuted. God should judge between believers and the godless. A social judgment is to put right the relationship between human beings that has been disrupted

2. Volf, "Final."

through evil; the purpose is not to reward or punish individuals. God will "put things to rights."

Judgment does not have a merely negative sense but above all a positive one. That is, it will not only destroy but above all will save; it will not merely dissolve but will above all fulfill. It is the annihilating "no" to all the powers hostile to God, and is the dissolution of the world of evil. But it is also the saving and fulfilling "yes" of creation: "Behold, I make all things new!" (Rev 21:5, NKJV). "Arise, O God, judge the earth" (Ps 82:8, NKJV; cf. Ps 96:13).

If judging in the final judgment is a social judging, then it is also a cosmic judging too. All the disrupted conditions of creation must be put right so that the new creation can stand and endure on the ground of justice. That refers to the relations between human beings, but it also refers to the relations between humankind and the world of living beings on earth, and last but not least to the corruptions that let creatures suffer and long for redemption outside of human presence. According to Genesis 1, all creatures are created with a specific open space for their own activity, and this gives chaotic possibilities and possible corruption to them all.

Not least, "the first creation" is a creation threatened everywhere by chaos. According to the picture language of the Bible, chaos thrusts into the creation of light and the earth in the form of "night" and "the sea." These "first things" are to pass away (Rev 21:1, 5). According to John's vision, the new creation of all things will no longer know any "night" or "sea," because God's radiant glory will illumine everything and Christ is the light thereof, and all created being will participate in God's being and Christ's eternal liveliness. That is a fundamental change in the constitution of earthly life and of the cosmos itself. Psalm 96:10–13 describes this hopeful picture of the cosmic world judgment beautifully:

> Say among the heathen that the LORD reigneth:
> The world also shall be established that is shall not be moved,
> He shall judge the people righteously.
> Let the heavens rejoice, let the earth be glad,
> Let the sea roar, and the fullness thereof.
> Let the field be joyful, and all that is therein,
> Then shall all the trees of the wood rejoice before the LORD.
> For he comes, for he comes to judge the earth,
> He shall judge the world with righteousness,
> And the people with his truth. (KJV)

What will be annihilated is nothingness; what will be slain is death; what will be dissolved is the power of evil; what will be separated from all created beings is separation from God, sin. If death is no more and hell destroyed, the question of whether all or only a few shall be saved is irrelevant.[3] The ground is then prepared for the healing and the new creation of all things. To put it philosophically: The negation of the negative constitutes a position of the positive, which cannot be destroyed.

DIALECTICAL UNIVERSALISM: LOVE AND THE PREFERENTIAL OPTION FOR THE OPPRESSED

Anticipating God's final judgment through dividing humankind into believers and unbelievers (with the possible consequence of persecuting unbelievers as enemies of God) is wrong, because it is godless. The God of Jesus Christ is not an enemy of unbelievers and also not an executioner of the godless. "God has imprisoned all in disbelief so that he be merciful to all," declared the apostle Paul (Rom 11:32, NRSV). Whether they believe or not, whether they share our faith or have another faith, we respect and see every person being embraced by the mercy of God. Whoever they are, God loves them, Christ died for them, and the Holy Spirit is working in their lives. For God's sake, we cannot be against them.

Our inhuman and godless friend-foe thinking is overcome. We must not exclude. We may—as much as we can—embrace, because we and the others are embraced by God in Christ. We should not take their unbelief or other belief more seriously than the all-embracing mercy of God, who "makes his sun rise on the evil and the good, and sends rain on the just and the unjust" (Matt 5:45, NKJV). We should develop the habit of seeing every human being we meet as a believer, never doubting this and never dealing with them differently.[4] When a Marxist or a Muslim is coming, we should call them "believers," because God believes in them. God believes in me, and this is the objective belief. The universalism of hope in God's future for the whole universe opens us to love without limits.

3. Balthasar, *Dare*; Ansell, "Annihilation."
4. Blumhardt nach Ragaz, *Der Kampf*, 57; Barth, *Kirchliche*, 304–13.

But we live in an unjust, hostile, and divided world. We live and suffer in an ongoing struggle for power. We must therefore take sides with the poor, the weak, and the victims of violence, if we want to work for a universal redemption and anticipate the coming liberating and healing justice of God. God's justice is first of all for the victims of sin, and then and thereby also for the slaves of sin, to overcome sin on both sides. The liberation of the oppressed is the first option and includes as the second option also the healing of the oppressors. For overcoming the power of sin and evil we need liberation on both sides. It is God's own action in history to take sides with the victims and to redeem the perpetrators from their violence through this partisanship.

Listen to the Magnificat of Mary:

> He hath put down the mighty from their seats,
> And exalted them of low degree.
> He hath filled the hungry with good things
> And the rich he has sent empty away. (Luke 1:52–53, KJV)

Look into the gospel of Christ: Jesus turned to the sinners to redeem also the Pharisees; Jesus healed the sick to save the healthy too; Jesus was poor among the poor in order to liberate the rich as well.

And for the apostle Paul the Christian congregation is in itself a witness to the one-sided divine action for the benefit of all: "See your calling . . . how that not many wise men after the flesh, not many mighty, not many noble, are called. But God hath chosen the foolish things of the world to confound the wise, and God has chosen the weak things of the world to confound the things that are mighty . . . that no flesh should glory in his presence" (1 Cor 1:26–29, KJV). There was one man in this country who in his convincing way integrated the present engagement for the victims of oppression with the strong messianic hope in God's coming liberating justice for all. Liberating politics and messianic hope in the coming of God strengthened each other in Martin Luther King Jr.'s unforgettable dream that he proclaimed in Washington, DC on August 28, 1963:

> I have a dream that one day this nation will rise up and live out
> the true meaning of its creed: "We hold these truths to be self
> evident, that all men are created equal."

I have a dream that one day ... the sons of former slaves and the sons of former slave owners will be able to sit down together at the table of brotherhood.

I have a dream that one day every valley shall be exalted, and every hill and mountain shall be made low ... and the glory of the Lord shall be revealed, and all flesh shall see it together (Isa. 40:4–5).[5]

I am certain: All flesh will see the glory of the Lord—but only together.

5. King, "I Have."

14

Orthodox Eschatology and St. Gregory of Nyssa's
De vita Moysis
Transfiguration, Cosmic Unity, and Compassion

ANDREW P. KLAGER

INTRODUCTION

THE PURPOSE OF THE present volume is to introduce readers to a compassionate eschatology from the vantage point of various theological attitudes and traditions. What follows, then, is an outline of the eschatological themes that comprise an Orthodox Christian perspective. As we navigate through an Orthodox conception of the hope endowed to all creation when Christ "trampled down death by death," and which is assimilated by the Church through ascetic struggle, participation in the liturgical theodrama, and veneration of icons that depict and embody the eschaton, the sentiment that "compassion" is a worthy foil through which to apprehend an Orthodox eschatology is justified.

With the conviction that a dialogue on the validity of a compassionate eschatology should depend not only on the outcome of theological conjecture and syllogism, but must also include a historical precedent, especially from the Church fathers, to circumscribe and frame this dialogue, the present essay will also appeal frequently to St. Gregory of Nyssa's celebrated philosophical and ascetic treatise, *De vita Moysis*,[1] as a highly apposite patristic voice to guide our investigation.

1. For all English references, I will be using Gregory of Nyssa, *The Life of Moses*, translated by Ferguson and Mahlerbe (hereafter simply *Vit. Moys.*). Since this essay is appearing in a book whose audience is concerned more with Christian eschatology than with Gregory of Nyssa himself, all references to the original Greek will not be to

It has become whimsically aphoristic for Orthodox Christians to answer theological inquiries, and especially the more difficult ones, with, "It is ultimately a mystery!" But, this is true of its eschatology perhaps more than for any other theological issue. While the ecclesial schisms that have characterized much of Christianity's history over matters of Christology, Triadology, and the like are at least comprehensible on a primal level, it is utterly unfathomable the many more recent schisms that have compounded as a result of squabbles over events that have not yet even occurred![2] An Orthodox articulation of eschatology is therefore unique in its reticence, refusing to speculate beyond the creedal affirmation that Christ "is coming in glory to judge the living and the dead, and his kingdom will have no end," which motivates his Bride to "look forward to the resurrection of the dead and the life of the world to come."

Yet, very little if anything in Orthodox theology is untouched by its eschatological hope, so that Fr. Andrew Louth is able to claim, "[I]n the doctrine of *ta eschata*, 'the last things,' the whole of Christian doctrine—creation, incarnation, redemption, and deification—finds its fulfillment."[3] Consequently, in considering the innumerable attendant facets, teachings, and ontological embodiments of Holy Tradition, the daunting task ahead is made less so if we focus on those features that most pointedly manifest the compassionate character of Orthodox eschatology. With this in mind, we will limit our discussion to an Orthodox understanding of the parousia (second coming), bodily resurrection, and final judgment, all essentially a unified manifestation and suffusion of the cosmos with Christ's glory, which contributes deeply and emphatically to a compassionate eschatological outlook but that contrasts markedly the violent and retributive models that have dominated Western eschatology. Before this, however, we will explore the preparation of humanity here on earth for its encounter with Christ's final judgment. In this sense, the present essay concerns itself with both (1) the microcosmic manifestation of eschatological hope in personal ascetic struggle, communion with the Church, and liturgical observance of the present age, and (2) the macrocosmic, and *de facto* unity of humanity in the ineluctable encounter of

---

the usual *Gregorii Nysseni Opera*, on which the English translation is based, but will instead be to the much more accessible: Migne, *Patrologiae Graeca* (hereafter *PG*).

2. See Ware, *Orthodox Way*, 133f.

3. Louth, "Eschatology," 233.

the entire cosmos with the glory, mercy, and love of Christ at the final judgment in the age to come.

Although we will elaborate on this in more detail later, it is important to keep in mind throughout the essay that the Orthodox Church teaches an "eschatological monism" that opposes the notion that humanity is predestined, or destined in any respect, to undergo a transportation to one of two corporeal locations, but rather proposes that the "location," understood figuratively as a great mystery,[4] is actually monadic and uniform, yet subjectively experienced multifariously based on one's ontological composition in either passions (*pathē*)[5] or virtue (*aretē*).[6]

ONTOLOGICAL PREPARATION FOR THE FINAL JUDGMENT

An Orthodox understanding of the last things is incomplete if it does not first address humanity's and, perhaps more deliberately and faithfully, the Church's anticipation and preparation for the eschaton. It is this expectancy, and the attendant anthropological and soteriological characteristics, that ultimately elicits Christ's compassion as curative rather than retributive and that underscores the singularity and uniformity of Christ's final judgment as inexorably wrapped up in the uniformity of the Godhead and of humanity—indeed, the entire cosmos—that he has come "not to condemn . . . , but that the world might be saved through him" (John 3:17 RSV).

To begin, then, we must explore the role of free will that permits human beings to both prepare for the final judgment in this life and to continually reject in self-condemnation or else accept anew the Savior of the cosmos in the hereafter. Orthodox soteriology and eschatology are both intimately linked to the freedom of the human will,[7] which St. Gregory of Nyssa describes in terms of an equidistant *suspension* between two prospective and latent invaders: virtue and passions, life and death, God and the Evil One.[8] On the one end of the spectrum, virtue

4. *Vit. Moys.* 2.242: *PG* 405B.

5. See Smith, *Passion*, 62f., 68–72, 204–6. On ἀπάθεια or the suspension of passion, see Daniélou, *Platonisme*, 63ff., 92–103.

6. Ware, *Orthodox Church*, 262.

7. See *Vit. Moys.* 1.12; 2.3; 2.74: *PG* 301D; 328B; 348A-B.

8. For an exploration into the freedom of the will in Gregory's thought, see Blowers, "Perpetual Progress," 156; Geljon, "Divine Infinity," 162; Ferguson, "God's Infinity," 70; Meredith, *Gregory of Nyssa*, 24.

is voluntarily self-subdued and non-encroaching or is innately so since it is by nature love, which refuses to coerce, while on the opposite end Christ has conquered death, rendering it impotent through his incarnation, crucifixion, and resurrection. In his *De vita Moysis*, St. Gregory of Nyssa elucidates God's refusal to coerce by invoking the plague of darkness that the Hebrews nevertheless experienced as light: "It was not some constraining power from above that caused the one to be found in darkness and the other in light, but we men have in ourselves, in our own nature and by our own choice, the causes of light or darkness, since we place ourselves in whichever sphere we wish to be."[9]

This freedom, or equidistant suspension between the virtues and passions, factors into both humanity's preparation and future encounter with the universal divine judgment. With this in mind, Orthodox lay-theologian Paul Evdokimov claims, "The ability to refuse God" is not only "the pinnacle of human freedom," but also engenders "the necessity of hell, which comes from human freedom."[10] "We prepare our own hells for ourselves," Evdokimov states elsewhere, "closing ourselves in from the love of God who continues to dwell in us without change."[11] Metropolitan Kallistos Ware affirms a compassionate eschatology despite one's prerogative to reject Christ: "The best we can do, is to hold in balance two truths, contrasting but not contradictory. First, God has given free will to man, and so to all eternity it lies in man's power to reject God. Secondly, love signifies compassion, involvement; and so, if there are any who remain eternally in hell, in some sense God is also there with them."[12] In like manner, St. Isaac the Syrian maintains, "It would be improper for a man to think that sinners in Gehenna are deprived of the love of God. . . ."[13] We will later discuss how this free will also more positively factors into the possibility or hope expressed in Orthodox *theologoumenum* (theological opinion) for the *apokatastasis tōn pantōn*—the final restoration of all.

9. *Vit. Moys.* 2.80: *PG* 349A-B. Cf. *Vit. Moys.* 2:45–46; 2.56; 2.65; 2.216: *PG* 337D–340A; 341B–C; 344C–D; 397B–C. Cf. Denning-Bolle, "Mystical Flight," 108–11; and Robert W. Jenson, "Gregory of Nyssa," 536.

10. Evdokimov, "Eschatology," 32f.

11. Ibid., 31.

12. Ware, *Orthodox Way*, 135f. Cf. Louth, "Eschatology," 242.

13. St. Isaac, *Ascetical Homilies*, "Homily 28," 141.

For the Orthodox Church, soteriology, ecclesiology, and liturgy can never be separated from eschatological considerations. Accordingly, Fr. Andrew Louth observes, "The last things are not remote future events, but events made present in the risen Christ, and in the risen Christ the boundaries between death and life have been broken down, as has the separation implicit in our experience of space and time."[14] This is why St. Gregory of Nyssa writes about "the Preparation for the Sabbath," this being "the present life in which we prepare for ourselves the things of the life to come,"[15] and in other works expounds on the mystery of the eschaton as the eighth day, which is more indigenous to Orthodox eschatological discourse.[16] Similarly, St. Symeon the New Theologian teaches that "[i]n this present life, . . . by repentance, we enter freely and of our own will into the divine light" and, "owing to the divine love and compassion," are placed under a "judgment [which] is made in secret, in the depths of our soul, to purify us," so that we do not become like "those who hate the light, [for whom] the second coming of Christ will disclose the light which at present remains hidden, and will make manifest everything which has been concealed."[17] It is important to note therefore how the freedom of the will also enables human beings to prepare for the final judgment in this life before our repose, prompting Ivan Ilyin to synopsize the ascetical life as a "school of preparation for death."[18]

Although the Orthodox teaching on free will ostensibly exposes a heightened vulnerability to divine retribution since it absolves both God and the Evil One from direct manipulation, it instead both assists in one's preparation for the final judgment as a divinely devised anthropological maneuver and underscores the arduousness (and in its deified *telos*, near impossibility) of this preparation. On the one hand, humanity's *mutability* and susceptibility to progress in virtue exhibits the positive value of free will. For instance, with respect to Gregory of Nyssa, Gerhart Ladner remarks, "Only if man received mutability . . . would mankind as a whole, be able to reach its pre-ordained *pleroma* [fullness], only thus would it have the opportunity to return to God." Otherwise, "man would

14. Louth, "Eschatology," 236.

15. *Vit. Moys.* 2.144.

16. *Inscr. Ps.* 2.5.52–3, p. 136f.: *PG* 44.504D–505A.

17. Quoted in Lossky, *Mystical Theology*, 233f.

18. Quoted in Sakharov, *Love*, 224.

have remained fixed in spiritual aversion from God, together with the fallen angels."[19]

This mutability permits what the Orthodox Church teaches as *theosis*, or deification. Recalling the eschatological character of theosis, Nicholas Berdyaev avers, "Paradise is theosis, deification of the creature."[20] With the final judgment in mind, Fr. John McGuckin explains, "Deification in Orthodox theology ... [means] ... that the grace of God 'conforms' the saints to his presence so that they can see and enjoy the divine radiance which is impossible for the unclean to witness except as a torment."[21] Elsewhere, McGuckin equates the Holy Tradition of the Church with theosis rather than a mere system of doctrines and canons, and refers to it as the "eschatological sign of salvation."[22]

The event that links this present ascent in theosis and the future parousia is the transfiguration of our Lord, which gives content to both the *telos* of one's preparation in this life and the glory of Christ's mercy emanating at his parousia and final judgment. Fr. Sergei Bulgakov, for instance, notes the soteriological significance, with theosis as its goal, of the transfiguration, in which "Christ becomes visible for all in the radiance of divinity in glorified humanity: God in man and Man in God, the God-man, drawing to Himself all the tribes of the earth."[23] Fittingly, therefore, Andreas Andreopoulos recognizes the "relationship between the transfiguration and paradise, or eschatological glory" in the impressive mosaic engulfing the apse of the Basilica of Sant'Apollinare Nuovo in Classe, Ravenna, and remarks that "[A]lthough most scholars have identified the mosaic as primarily a depiction of the transfiguration, ... [t]he overall depiction is an eschatological scene"[24] since it includes several "symbols of paradise."[25]

Our ascetic struggle toward theosis in this life has as its stage the post-Pentecostal epoch, at the commencement of which the Holy Spirit, reminiscent of the kenosis—or self-emptying—of God in the incarnate Christ, descends to the earth and infuses the cosmos more covertly

19. Ladner, "Philosophical Anthropology," 84.

20. Berdyaev, *Destiny*, 287.

21. McGuckin, *Church*, 198.

22. Ibid., 96.

23. Bulgakov, *Lamb*, 395.

24. Andreopoulos, *Metamorphosis*, 118.

25. Ibid., 120.

in contrast to the patently visible glory of Christ's future parousia.[26]
Reflecting the singularity of Christ's final judgment as love is the oneness of the Church, to which Pentecost gave witness as tongues of fire.
In a post-lapsarian world, the fragmentation of humanity and all the
cosmos—the severed relationships plaguing all of creation—gives way
to the unity of Christ's body, the Church, as a manifestation of eschatological healing and fullness in the present life. Because salvation is communal, reflected in the unity of humanity and the cosmos that we will
explore in more detail later, theosis is attained more fully in communion
with the Church as a manifestation of this unity.

In this way, our own individual theosis is a microcosm of the fullness or catholicity of the Church as *sobernost*—the relinquishment of
individualism, or one's self-will, to emphasize what is in common—and
the unity of the Church is a microcosm of the eschatological, yet mysteriously also the present *de facto*, unity of all humanity and creation.[27]
It is this all-embracing and exhaustive unity that elicits a monistic final
judgment, informed by the singularity of the divine essence, as love,
which therefore characterizes Orthodoxy's compassionate eschatology.
With this unity squarely in site, McGuckin claims, "[T]he church is itself
the Eschatological Mystery"—the "holy of holies in the eschatological
order, and the quality of its life of prayer, intercession, and charism is
inextricably related to the eschaton."[28]

The theater for the manifestation of the eschaton in the present life
is the Divine Liturgy. Although the performance of an eschatological
theodrama is reflected in the symbolism of the liturgy, the movement
toward partaking the eucharistic body and blood of Christ is itself an authentic ascension into the spiritual realm and a genuine co-participation
in heavenly worship with the angels and saints who reside there. The
Liturgy begins with the proclamation, "Blessed is the Kingdom of the
Father and the Son and the Holy Spirit, now and ever and unto ages of
ages. Amen." With this, the parishioners wait eagerly in anticipation of
the liturgical parousia of Christ, after which they gain entrance into the
heavenly banquet so that they may partake of the Holy Gifts.

The parousia is represented variously in patristic literature by the
bishop's descent from his throne for the gospel reading in St. Maximos the

26. Bulgakov, *Lamb*, 394.

27. See Sakharov, *Love*, 135f.

28. McGuckin, "Eschatology," 133.

Confessor's *Mystagogia*[29] and in the *Ecclesiastical History* of St. Germanos I, Patriarch of Constantinople,[30] while St. Symeon of Thessaloniki believed that the Great Entrance of the Holy Gifts represented the second coming.[31] This is the reason parishioners stand during the liturgy facing East when they pray—in anticipation of Christ's parousia—and the liturgy unfolds in such a way that the eucharistic banquet is enjoyed *after* the second coming represented in either the bishop's descent from his throne or the Great Entrance. Further, when the parishioners exit the nave into the narthex, typically they are greeted by an icon of the final judgment on the west wall to remind them of their need for ontological refinement through the purity of heart initiated by repentance.

Indeed, the ascetic struggle toward ontological purity of the communicant is requisite for participation in Holy Communion.[32] This preparation for Holy Communion, typically comprised of pre-Communion prayers and the cultivation of a life in Christ, further informs the eschatological character of the liturgy. Fr. Alexander Schmemann also considers the communal character of this precondition:

> [W]e must understand that what "happens" to bread and wine happens because something has, first of all, happened to us, to the Church. It is because we have "constituted" the Church, and this means we have followed Christ in his ascension; because he has accepted us at His table in His Kingdom; because, in terms of theology, we have entered the Eschaton, and are now standing beyond time and space; it is because all this has first happened to us that something will happen to the bread and wine.[33]

To understand the need for attentiveness to the purity of one's heart and communion with the Church before receiving the eucharistic Gifts, Mary, who is portrayed in icons of the final judgment as standing to the right of Christ interceding to him on behalf of all humanity, and her role as Theotokos, or God-Bearer, is of paramount importance. Of the many Old Testament types that the Orthodox Church uses to explain Mary's salvific role, the burning bush is most germane to our purposes. Mary, divinely chosen as the pinnacle of obedience and purity that God ex-

29. Wybrew, *Liturgy*, 97.

30. Ibid., 124.

31. Ibid., 168f. See also ibid., 182 and Louth, "Eschatology," 234–36.

32. McGuckin, "Eschatology," 133.

33. Schmemann, *World*, 37.

pected of his people after generations of apostasy, was uniquely worthy to bear within her womb God himself and therefore was not consumed in the same way that the bush was suffused with the divine fire without being consumed. As St. Gregory of Nyssa observes, "From this we learn also the mystery of the Virgin: The light of divinity which through birth shone from her into human life did not consume the burning bush, even as the flower of her virginity was not withered by giving birth."[34]

Similarly, Orthodox Christians offer up pre-Communion prayers, among them for instance the observations of St. Simeon Metaphrastes who, after noting that Christ's blood was generated by the "pure blood of the Virgin," describes the mingling of his blood with our own during Holy Communion with further allusions to the divine fire: "Freely, you have given your body for my food, you who are a fire consuming the unworthy. Do not consume me, O my Creator, but instead enter into my members, my veins, my heart. Consume the thorns of my transgressions.... Cleanse me, purify me and adorn me.... Show me to be a temple of your one Spirit ... as I become your tabernacle through Communion."[35]

Moreover, the degree to which one becomes worthy to partake of the Holy Gifts during the eschatological heavenly banquet is experienced multifariously much in the same as is the final judgment. St. Gregory of Nyssa, for instance, illuminates the implications of the uniformity of the manna, which is understood by Orthodox to represent the Eucharistic Gifts,[36] when he observes, "In appearance the food was *uniform*, but in quality it was varied, for it conformed itself to each person's desire,"[37] which exhibits the manifold function of the manna depending on the need of the one receiving it. All of these liturgical elements, from our preparation to its culmination, mysteriously share in the actual unfolding of the last things that themselves transcend the temporal world, which are attested to by our attentiveness to the purity of heart that calibrates not only our reception of the Eucharistic Gifts at the heavenly banquet after the parousia but also our encounter with the final judgment of Christ as merciful love.

34. *Vit. Moys.* 2.21.
35. Quoted in Evdokimov, "Eucharist," 253.
36. Wybrew, *Liturgy*, 63.
37. *Vit. Moys.* 2.137: *PG* 368A–B.

This attentiveness to the purity of one's heart cultivates an ontology that manifests itself in the same compassion—merciful love—that the final judgment offers intuitively. Our preparation in the present life therefore contains an ethical component, of equity with wealth and abstention from violence, in proportion to our ontological purity and attainment of *theosis*. It is a compassionate eschatology, therefore, because our own transfiguration through ascetic struggle cultivates compassion for the world in coincidence with the mercy of God that we encounter at the final, universal judgment—as the divine Light.[38]

This compassion has an eschatological character not only in our present incomplete participation in what we anticipate for the future in its fullness, but also in the way it harmonizes with the final judgment of Christ as mercy in the eschaton. McGuckin puts it this way: "[T]he Christian ethic clearly emerges as the mainspring of the church's eschatological awareness, and it will serve as the leaven to bring about the fulfillment of its eschatological calling in any generation."[39] By fleshing out the details a bit more, McGuckin continues,

> The struggle for ethical purity, then, will be perfected only in the lively sense of repentance consequent on the acknowledgment of its "weakness of the flesh." In becoming a virtuoso of repentance the church learns how the finite stands before the Infinity, and becomes skilled in teaching a broken world about the "quality of mercy"—both its own and that of the Lord whom it manifests. In this, the church fulfills its fundamental eschatological duty to the world as laid upon it in Luke 24:47: the preaching of repentance for the forgiveness of sins.[40]

Moreover, this compassion involves an eternal solicitude beyond the grave made possible by death's impotence and made evident in the intercessory prayer of the saints on their behalf. A more recent Russian ascetic from Mount Athos, St. Silouan, manifests this tenderness perfectly, not only when he "wept with pity for the poverty-stricken people, and felt compassion for the whole universe and every living creature,"[41] but with a more eternal focus when he observed, "There are people who desire the destruction, the torment in hell-fire of their enemies, or the

---

38. Louth, "Eschatology," 236.
39. McGuckin, "Eschatology," 133.
40. Ibid., 133.
41. Silouan, *Silouan*, 374.

240 COMPASSIONATE ESCHATOLOGY

enemies of the Church. They think like this because they have not learnt divine love from the Holy Spirit, for he who has learned the love of God will shed tears for the whole world."[42]

However, we have yet to answer why the freedom of the will staves off juridical retribution from God if he and the Evil One have been absolved from any interference. First, the arduousness of participation in virtues is underscored by the infinity of the ascent in coincidence with the infinity of the Godhead—resumed even posthumously—that Gregory of Nyssa terms *epektasis*,[43] which therefore deems at least some deficiency inevitable.

Moreover, this arduousness also attests to the constraints and disadvantage of the human situation. For instance, Gregory of Nyssa remarks, "[T]he gnawings of desire are frequently active even in the faithful"[44] and, using medical terminology, observes, "[H]uman nature is especially drawn to this passion, being led to the disease along thousands of ways."[45] Therefore, while the freedom of the will ideally places humanity in a position to unite with Christ,[46] it simultaneously asks humanity to perform the impossible rendering inevitable at least some degree of failure.[47] Accordingly, our environment creates a "conflict in us, for man is set before competitors as the prize of their contest,"[48] while ultimately "free will [has an] inclination to evil"[49] so that "[i]t was only to be *expected* that some . . . would be filled with lust."[50]

The *expected* or *inevitability* of sin and the arduousness of one's ascetic struggle are what elicit a remedial rather than juridical response

43. On *epektasis* in Gregory's though, see Blowers, "'Perpetual Progress,'" 151–71; Daniélou, *Platonisme*, 309–326; Meredith, *Gregory of Nyssa*, 13f., 22; 318f.; Smith, *Passion*, 11f., 18f.; and Balthasar, *Presence*, 37f. On the ultimate infeasibility of the complete purification of the soul or ascent of the holy mountain, see *Vit. Moys.* 1.5–8; 2.220; 2.224–26; 2.230; 2.235; 2.238–39; 2.242: *PG* 300C–D–301B; 400A–B; 400D–401B; 401C–D; 404B; 404C–405A; 405B.

44. *Vit. Moys.* 2.277: *PG* 416A–B.

45. Ibid., 2.271: *PG* 413B–C.

46. Ibid., 2.5–6. Cf. Ferguson, "God's Infinity," 71.

47. On the ineluctability of sin, see Balthasar, *Presence*, 71–87. Cf. *Vit. Moys.* 2.299: *PG* 424A.

48. *Vit. Moys.* 2.14: *PG* 329D–332A. Cf. 2.276: *PG* 416A.

49. Ibid., 2.76: *PG* 348B–C. Cf. 2.271: *PG* 413B–C.

50. Ibid., 2.299: *PG* 424A.

from Christ inherent to a compassionate eschatology. The reason why the dualism of a juridical response is not sufficient is because, as Evdokimov avers, "[t]here is no separation not between good and evil people, but such a dividing line, rather, runs through the heart of every one of us."[51] "Far be it," declares St. Isaac the Syrian, "that vengeance could ever be found in that Fountain of love and Ocean brimming with goodness! The aim of His design is the correction of men."[52] The image of fire is therefore "not as torture and punishment, but as purification and healing,"[53] for "[t]he Eastern Church remains a stranger to every penitential principle."[54] This is the fire that St. John Climacus says burns those who "still lack purification, . . . [but] enlightens [those who guard the heart] in proportion to the perfection they have achieved."[55]

In agreement with the inevitability of participation in the passions, as unavoidable and evoking the same feeling of helplessness as contracting a disease, *De vita Moysis* is replete with medical images of healing which are antithetical to juridical measures that generate the reverse outcome. Gregory therefore labels both pleasure and passions as an "illness" or "disease"[56] and three times designates Christ, the lawgiver, as the "physician [who] accommodated the remedy to what the evil had produced."[57] In a particularly expressive passage, Gregory relates how "the physician induces vomiting by his medicines,"[58] and elsewhere insightfully outlines the role of the incarnate Christ to minister "to the condition of those who had become ill" when he enlists Moses, as a type of Christ, to co-suffer with humanity as one who "even besought God for mercy on their behalf."[59] This truly demonstrates "the divine concern for us"[60] and appreciation of the inexpedient circumstances with which humanity must contend.

51. Evdokimov, "Eschaology," 27.

52. St. Isaac, *Ascetical Homilies*, "Homily 48," 230.

53. Evdokimov, "Eschaology," 27.

54. Ibid., 30.

55. St. John Climacus, *Ladder*, "Step 28," 280.

56. *Vit. Moys.* 2.70–71; 2.79; 2.303: *PG* 345B–D; 348D–349A; 424C.

57. Ibid., 2.278: *PG* 416B. Cf. 2.87; 2.172: *PG* 352A–B; 380C–D

58. Ibid., 2.87: *PG* 352A–B. Cf. 2.277: *PG* 416A–B.

59. Ibid., 2.261: *PG* 412A–B.

60. Ibid., 2.214: *PG* 396D–397A.

Culpability, therefore, does not circumscribe human guilt and criminality to incite a proportionate execution of divine retribution, but instead identifies the infirmed in need of God's healing and restoration by determining who is proximate to the offense.[61] Accordingly, Dunstone claims that for Gregory, "Humanity is thus pitiable, rather than culpable,"[62] and further suggests that both St. Paul and the Nyssen bishop are "more concerned with the culpability of the disease and . . . with the misfortune of those who suffer from it."[63] Sin, Evdokimov explains, "is a sickness to be healed even if the cure is the blood of God."[64] Consequently, Gregory of Nyssa lists the casualties in both the ascetical struggle and the Triune God's eschatological restoration of humanity as one's "trespasses,"[65] "irrational envy,"[66] "idolatry,"[67] "injustice,"[68] "arrogance,"[69] "passion,"[70] and "lust of the flesh."[71] Indeed, "[s]in is the real serpent, and whoever deserts to sin takes on the nature of the serpent."[72] So much does Gregory sympathize with the unenviable situation within which humanity finds itself that the only time he uses the word "blame"[73] is in reference to the devil, "whom the history blames ($\kappa\alpha\tau\eta\gamma o$) [for] producing evil in men [which] leads them to the subsequent sin."[74]

ESCHATOLOGICAL MONISM AND THE FINAL JUDGMENT

The Orthodox Church teaches that a human being enters an intermediate state after death and receives a particular, individual judgment in anticipation of the final, universal judgment at the second coming. The Orthodox conception of how this individual judgment unfolds after one

61. Ibid., 2.193; 2.206: *PG* 389B–C; 393C–D.

62. Dunstone, *Atonement*, 10.

63. Ibid., 16.

64. Evdokimov, "Eschaology," 30.

65. *Vit. Moys.* 1.62: *PG* 321C.

66. Ibid.

67. Ibid., 2.15: *PG* 332A.

68. Ibid.

69. Ibid.

70. Ibid., 2.78: *PG* 348D.

71. Ibid., 2.276: *PG* 416A.

72. Ibid., 2.275: *PG* 413D–416A.

73. Gk. $\kappa\alpha\tau\eta\gamma o$.

74. *Vit. Moys.* 2.279: *PG* 416B–C.

has reposed is incomplete and serves less to accurately describe what will actually occur and more as a commentary on other, more enshrined teachings from the vantage point of a human being's preparation for death and communion of the saints. The consensus of the Church fathers on the matter is fragile, so that the liturgical rites performed upon and after one's death, the experiences of the saints, and popular belief of a later origin inform Orthodoxy's conception of this intermediate state.

For instance, the "Trisagion for the Departed" in Greek churches and the "Panikhida" among the Russians is celebrated at the funeral, and then on the third, ninth, and fortieth days after death, each commemorating a component in the narrative of the afterlife.[75] The first three days are reserved for the acclimation of the soul to its separation from the body, which itself functions as a passive judgment to the extent that the departed was attached to earthly vanities. Between the third and ninth days, the soul is thought to gain passage through a series of toll houses, each occupied by an angel and demon who decide the state in which one will be situated before the final judgment based on one's collusion with the various vices. However, "[d]uring this passage," Louth observes, "the soul is assisted against the efforts of the demons not just by the angels of the toll houses, but also by its guardian angel, the prayers of the saints, and the prayers of those living on earth,"[76] which not only demonstrates the universality of the cosmos that we will elaborate on soon, but also reveals a compassionate disposition even during this intermediate state.

As less of a precise description of what will actually occur, "The passage of the toll houses represents, in a vivid way, what is required for someone to pass from the sin and temptations of this world ... to the holy presence of God,"[77] and therefore narrates what is proper to one's preparation for the final judgment—the love and mercy of God. The remaining days up until the fortieth are spent visiting the abodes of the afterlife, about which very little is known or taught explicitly. Upon the completion of the forty days, the soul awaits the final judgment in its assigned state based on the accumulation of its passage through the toll houses and assistance from the angels and saints. Revealing again God's compassion during this life and in the next, Louth concludes, "The temporal dimension of the services may have more to do with the

75. See Louth, "Eschatology," 239–41.
76. Ibid., 240.
77. Ibid.

temporal process of grieving and remembrance than with tracking the departed soul's progress in a state after death, about which little has been revealed to us save God's sure love and Christ's triumph over death in his resurrection."[78]

The universal bodily resurrection at Christ's parousia is better suited to convey a compassionate eschatology. Much like the uniformity of the final judgment as divine mercy, "The resurrection itself," observes Vladimir Lossky, "will reveal the inner condition of beings, as bodies will allow the secrets of the soul to shine through."[79] This is because, as Louth informs us, "It is not just that we have souls *and* bodies, but rather that what we are, even our spiritual capacities, are bound up with our bodies."[80] The resurrected body, then, will function as a portrait of the ontological ascent of the Holy Mountain, i.e., theosis, during one's earthly life through the degree to which it shares "in the qualities of Christ's human body at the transfiguration and after the Resurrection."[81]

Lossky expresses this notion of the bodily resurrection as both an implicit judgment on one's earthly preparation and the import of the transfiguration: "At that time, everything which the soul has stored up in its inner treasure, will appear outwardly, in the body. All will become light, all will be penetrated by uncreated Light. The bodies of the saints will become like the glorious body of the Lord, as it appeared to the apostles on the day of the transfiguration."[82] In this sense, the bodily resurrection is a foretaste of how one will react to God's merciful love at the final judgment.

We now turn our attention to Christ's final judgment as mercy, which is the culmination of one's preparation in the earthly life. First, we recognize the parousia and final judgment as in some sense a single event. As Bulgakov observes, "[T]he parousia, the coming of Christ in glory, that is, in the manifestation of the Holy Spirit, is, as such, already the judgment."[83] This is the initial encounter with Christ's glory, mercy, and love—*as* love and truth in ontological fullness.

---

78. Ibid., 241.

79. Lossky, *Mystical Theology*, 234.

80. Louth, "Eschatology," 244.

81. Ware, *Orthodox Way*, 136.

82. Lossky, *Mystical Theology*, 235.

83. Bulgakov, *Lamb*, 455.

Moreover, although the parousia and final judgment are very real events, it is important to acknowledge also· the "location" of one's final destiny—heaven or hell—as being figurative. Bulgakov, for instance, maintains, "The eternal fire is not some place in creation but only a *state* of a certain part of creation."[84] St. Isaac the Syrian likewise maintains that "[s]in, Gehenna, and Death do not exist at all with God, for they are effects, not substances."[85] With respect to the popular conception of eternity, Bulgakov further avers, "[H]ere, one must first completely exclude the conception of eternity as time and temporality. Let us state more precisely that time and eternity are by no means related in the way that is usually postulated, because eternity is not a temporal but a *qualitative* determination."[86] In like manner, Gregory of Nyssa gives an explanation of God's pronouncement, "Here is a *place* beside me."[87] "In speaking of 'place,'" Gregory maintains, "he does not limit *the place* indicated by anything quantitative (for to something unquantitative there is no measure). On the contrary, by the use of the analogy of a measurable surface he leads the hearer to the unlimited and infinite."[88]

Gregory of Nyssa eventually asserts that this place is God himself, who, of course, is One;[89] it is here, in this one "place," confronted with the fullness of his glory, that all those who God created will be transfigured according to their need, ever increasing from glory to glory. God's oneness intrinsically outlines the uniformity of his operations, of his essence, and of his final judgment, which therefore reveals the *content* of this uniform final judgment as merciful love universally offered. Evdokimov, for instance, observes, "God is eternally identical to himself. He is not the fearful Judge but he is Love and the very love which subjectively 'becomes suffering among the outcasts and joy among the blessed.'"[90]

The monadic, immutable, and ceaseless object of eschatological encounter is therefore the love and mercy of God, his glory which infuses the heavenly temple, and it is the subjective human reaction that engenders multiplicity or any division of experience. St. Isaac the Syrian again

84. Ibid., 502.
85. St. Isaac, *Ascetical Homilies*, "Homily 27," 133.
86. Bulgakov, *Lamb*, 470.
87. *Vit. Moys.* 2.241: *PG* 405A–B. Exod 33:21.
88. Ibid., 2.242: *PG* 405B.
89. Ibid., 2.249: *PG* 408B–C.
90. Evdokimov, "Eschatology," 27.

wonderfully describes the operations of love at the final judgment: "I also maintain that those who are punished in Gehenna, are scourged by the scourge of love. . . . The power of love works in two ways: it torments sinners . . . [as] bitter regret. But love inebriates the souls of the sons of Heaven by its delectability."[91] Perhaps Fr. Thomas Hopko's appraisal of Bulgakov on this matter can be considered, if not the definitive, at least a characteristically Orthodox eschatological instinct:

> [I]t is precisely the presence of God's mercy and love which cause the torment of the wicked. God does not punish; he forgives. . . . In a word, God has mercy on all, whether all like it or not. If we like it, it is paradise; if we do not, it is hell. Every knee will bend before the Lord. Everything will be subject to Him. God in Christ will indeed be "all and in all," with boundless mercy and unconditional pardon. But not all will rejoice in God's gift of forgiveness, and that choice will be judgment, the self-inflicted source of their sorrow and pain.[92]

The variety in experience is not, however, a reflection of God's transactions with humanity but of our own self-condemnation. This self-condemnation intimates that what one experiences in the next life is not a reflection of who God is and what his operations are, and this because his operation is singular, *viz.*, merciful love whose objective is the purification and restoration of the image of God in all humanity.[93] Self-condemnation, as the term itself implies, reflects the impurity of one's soul upon her or his encounter with the singular operation of the indivisible and immutable Holy Trinity. "The judgment and separation," Bulgakov observes, "consist in the fact that every human being will be placed before his own eternal image in Christ, that is, before Christ. And in the light of this image, he will see his own reality, and this comparison will be the judgment. It is this that is the Last Judgment of Christ upon every human being."[94]

St. Gregory of Nyssa also explains that "even if one says that painful retribution comes directly from God upon those who abuse their free will, it would only be reasonable to note that such sufferings have

91. St. Isaac, *Ascetical Homilies*, "Homily 28," 141.

92. Fr. Thomas Hopko, "Foreword," in Bulgakov, *Orthodox Church*, xiii.

93. *Vit. Moys.* 2.318: *PG* 429A.

94. Bulgakov, *Lamb*, 457.

their origin and cause in ourselves."[95] When he writes about the plagues unleashed on the Egyptians, Gregory further warns his audience, "[L]et us not draw the conclusion that these distresses upon those who deserve them came directly from God, but rather let us observe that each man makes his own plagues when through his own free will he inclines toward these painful experiences."[96] In like manner, St. Maximos the Confessor depicts the soul as analogous to either clay or wax, depending "upon its own will and purpose." Under the same rays of "the Sun of righteousness," every soul that "deliberately cleaves to the material world, hardens like clay and drives itself to destruction. . . . But every soul that cleaves to God is softened like wax and, receiving the impress and stamp of divine realities, it becomes 'in spirit the dwelling-place of God.'"[97] St. Basil of Caesarea, Gregory's elder brother, also notes the property of self-condemnation inherent to the episode of the three youths in the fiery furnace and those outside the furnace who felt its heat, concluding that "those worthy of the fire will feel its caustic quality and those worthy of the lighting will feel the illuminating property of the fire."[98]

In addition to the figures of the "stream of faith,"[99] the Red Sea,[100] and the episode of the water from the rock,[101] the most striking image that Gregory cites to represent the future hope taught in eschatological monism, the presence of God for and in all, is light.[102] For example, Gregory observes that during the plague of darkness that God had inflicted on Egypt, "the eyes of the Egyptians were not in darkness because some wall or mountain darkened their view and shadowed the rays, but the sun cast its rays on all equally. Whereas the Hebrews delighted in its light, the Egyptians were insensitive to its gift."[103] Therefore, the light is uniform, but is again experienced diversely, not because of the quality or

---

95. *Vit. Moys.* 2.87: *PG* 352A–B.

96. Ibid., 2.86: *PG* 349D–352A. Cf. 2.76: *PG* 348B–C.

97. St. Maximos the Confessor, "First Century (on Theology)," *Philokalia*, 2:116.

98. St. Basil of Caesarea, "Homily 13: On Psalm 28," quoted in Hierotheos (Vlachos) of Nafpaktos, *Life After Death*, 257.

99. *Vit. Moys.* 2.66: *PG* 344D345A.

100. Ibid., 2.126: *PG* 364B–C. Cf. 2.124: *PG* 361D.

101. Ibid., 2.136: *PG* 368A. Cf. 2.244; 2.248: *PG* 405C–D; 408B. Cf. O'Connell, "Double Journey," 319.

102. See, for instance, Denning-Bolle, "Mystical Flight," 111f.

103. *Vit. Moys.* 2.81: *PG* 349B. Cf. 2.80: *PG* 349A–B.

composition of the light itself, but because of the subjective preparedness of the one encountering the light. The experience of this light *as* light is an indication of closer proximity to the archetype, Christ, of a higher altitude in one's ascent of the holy mountain and recalls the transfiguration of Christ, typologically revealed when "Moses was transformed to such a degree of glory that the mortal eye could not behold him."[104]

The mystery of the final judgment is compounded if we consider also the unity of humanity and the cosmos reflected in the communal nature of salvation and thus of the final judgment itself. As Christ's judgment is uniformly offered as merciful love, so is the *de facto* unity of humanity taken into account concurrently. It therefore first becomes imperative to acknowledge that the final judgment is universal. "This encounter with God," suggests Bulgakov, "this entering into the realm of the divine fire, is not something optional for human beings. It is inevitable."[105]

The inevitable and universal final judgment is also absorbed by all humanity and the entire cosmos in unison. Because it is impossible to distinguish between the culpability of individuals due to the social and cosmic unity and interconnectedness of humanity, Orthodoxy teaches that each person is responsible for the sins of another. This concept is expressed wonderfully by Alyosha's staretz, Fr. Zosima, in Dostoevsky's *The Brothers Karamazov*:

> Everything is like an ocean, everything flows and intermingles, you have only to touch in one place and it will reverberate in another part of the world.... Take yourself in hand, and be answerable for the sins of all men. My friend, this is actually true: you need only make yourself sincerely answerable for everything and everyone, and you will see immediately that it is really so, and that it is you who are actually guilty of the sins committed by each and every man."[106]

Similarly, Archimandrite Sophrony (Sakharov) comments on the "ontological unity of humanity"[107] in St. Silouan's teachings, averring that it is specifically "Christ-like love ... [that] ... makes all men ontologically one."[108]

104. Ibid., 2.217: *PG* 397C-D. Cf. Laird, "Darkness," 598.

105. Bulgakov, *Lamb*, 455.

106. Dostoevsky, *Brothers Karamazov*, 401.

107. Archimandrite Sophrony, *Silouan*, 222.

108. Ibid., 123.

With the eschatological import of this teaching in mind, Bulgakov observes that "in discussing heaven and hell, one should remember that, although this judgment is personal, is rendered upon every person, it is also universal ('all nations'), for Christ's humanity is one, and the destiny of everyone is connected with the destiny of all; everyone is responsible for all."[109] The unity of humanity and all the cosmos suggests that Christ's uniform judgment of mercy is experienced as bliss by some and torment by others only in degree and extent, for even the sorrow that St. Silouan felt in the quote above for those experiencing torment in hell is in some sense suffered alongside eternal bliss. Archimandrite Sophrony, for whom St. Silouan was a spiritual father on Mount Athos, also describes the eschatological import of this cosmic unity that his Staretz taught, claiming that rather than interpreting "justice in the juridical sense, ... Christian love speaks otherwise, seeing nothing strange but rather something natural in sharing the guilt of those we love. Indeed," Sophrony continues, "it is only in this bearing of another's guilt that the authenticity of love is made manifest and develops into full awareness of self."[110] Therefore, "every separate individual overcoming evil in himself inflicts such a defeat on cosmic evil that its consequences have a beneficial effect on the destinies of the whole world."[111]

To explain this phenomenon, St. Gregory of Nyssa appeals to the episode when "Moses armed the Levites against their fellow countrymen," which resulted in "one thrust of the hand equally for everyone," regardless of innocence or guilt. In Gregory's spiritual interpretation:

> It is like someone punishing a person caught in an evil act by whipping him. Whatever part of the body he may hit, he tears to shreds with the scourge, knowing that the pain inflicted on that part extends throughout the whole body. The same thing happens when the whole body united in evil is punished: The scourging inflicted on the part chastens the whole.[112]

This description reflects what John Sachs calls Gregory's unique espousal of a "*communal* nature of salvation," which is "[c]entral to Gregory's eschatological vision of a final and universal restoration in the

109. Bulgakov, *Lamb*, 477.
110. Archimandrite Sophrony, *Silouan*, 120.
111. Ibid., 222.
112. *Vit. Moys.* 2.205: *PG* 393C. Cf. *Oratio Catechetica*, *NPNF2* 5:496.

good" where "the image of God ... comes to its fullness or *pleroma* only in the human race as a whole."[113] Indeed, this unity of humanity and of the universal encounter with Christ's judgment is reflected also in the intercession of the saints on behalf of all humanity, which is again how the Theotokos is depicted in icons of the final judgment.

The unity of humanity and the entire cosmos also gives cause to reflect more seriously on the *apokatastasis tōn pantōn*—the final restoration of all. The reason why Origen taught the final restoration of all was, as Louth explains, because "it is inconceivable that Christ is to remain in sorrow for all eternity, on account of the failure of any rational creature to respond to his love and to benefit from his sacrifice"[114] Gregory also makes clear the temporality of Gehenna when he interprets the light after the three days of darkness that the Egyptians experienced as revealing "the final restoration (*apokatastasis*) which is expected to take place later in the kingdom of heaven of those who have suffered condemnation in Gehenna,"[115] while the fires of Gehenna are for the purification of those who endure it.[116]

Gregory seems to have developed his teaching on *apokatastasis* more deliberately, in more detail, and in a more thoroughly Orthodox manner separate from the interpretations in the past that relied too heavily on Stoic and Plotinian Neoplatonist conceptions of humanity's restoration to Goodness or Oneness.[117] Such a "pretended apokatastasis" that envisaged the restoration of the spirits alone to their alleged pre-existent state is usually thought to be justly rejected at the fifth ecumenical council held in Constantinople in 553 CE,[118] the same council that simultaneously affirmed and commended Gregory's Orthodoxy. This is

113. Sachs, "Apocatastasis," 637. See also Hart, "Vestigia Trinitatis," 548f. and Ladner, "Philosophical Anthropology," 82.

114. Louth, "Eschatology," 245.

115. *Vit. Moys.* 2.82: *PG* 349B–C.

116. Ibid., 2.84: *PG* 349D. For more on Gregory's teaching on *apokatastasis*, see Andreopoulos, "Eschatology," online: http://www.theandros.com/restoration.html; Barrois, "Gregory of Nyssa," 7–16, esp. 14–16; Daley, *Hope*, 85–9; Ludlow, *Universal Salvation*; Sachs, "Apocatastasis," 617–40, esp. 632–38; Tori, "Apokatastasis," 87–100; and Tsirpanlis, "Gregory of Nyssa," 41–56.

117. Sachs, "Apocatastasis," 633.

118. See *NPNF2* 14:318. For alternative views, see Bulgakov, *Orthodox Church*, 185; Idem, *Lamb*, 482; and Daley, *Hope*, 84, 190. Cf. Barrois, "Gregory of Nyssa," 8; and Sachs, "Apocatastasis," 639f.

the case because Gregory's understanding of *apokatastasis* relies more on scriptural motifs and centers around an eschatological *hope* that is consistent with typical Orthodox discourse on the subject, and indeed with its life of prayer. What makes Gregory's espousal of the final restoration less objectionable are the contextual items that not only regulate his understanding but give it purpose and a content that is more consistent with typical Orthodox epistemological and eschatological discourse, while simultaneously ensuring the integrity of this mystery by avoiding over-analysis.

Bulgakov also notes, "From most ancient times doubts have existed as to the eternal duration of these torments; they are sometimes vied as a provisional pedagogic method of influencing the soul, and a final restoration is hoped for."[119] More specifically, Fr. Andrew Louth notes Sts. Maximos the Confessor and Isaac the Syrian's reflection on the final restoration of all and lists Olivier Clément,[120] Metropolitan Kallistos Ware,[121] and Bishop Hilarion Alfeyev[122] as sympathetic to this teaching as well. However, in his seminal work, *The Orthodox Church*, Ware affirms the predominant perspective in Orthodoxy is a median position of *hope* and an intercessory and earnest *desire*, not as false hope but in confidence of the possibility that all will taste salvation: "It is heretical to say that all *must* be saved," and, I would submit, that some *must* be tormented without end, "for this is to deny free will; but," Ware continues, "it is legitimate to hope that all *may* be saved."[123] Evdokimov, also avers, "The Savior's plan, *that all be saved* (1 Tim 2:4; Rom 8:32) is infinitely more mysterious and *impenetrable* than predestination which is so human and so impoverished in its rectilinear logic. The 'complex of the elect' is a morbid state, symptomatic of an unhappy conscience, and anxiety about hell."[124]

CONCLUSION

In Orthodox teaching, Christ's final judgment exhibits a compassionate eschatology, for it does not discriminate between those who need love

119. Bulgakov, *Orthodox Church*, 185.

120. Clément, *Mysticism*, 296–307.

121. Ware, "Salvation," 193–215.

122. Alfeyev, *Mystery*, 212–23.

123. Ware, *Orthodox Church*, 262.

124. Evdokimov, "Eschatology," 18. See also Bulgakov, *Lamb*, 482, 506.

and those who invite condemnation; it only adjudicates between those who need love and those who need *more* love, if it could be imagined for a brief moment that God could love inequitably. St. Gregory of Nyssa and some Orthodox theologians could envisage the *apokatastasis tōn pantōn* because the calibration of human culpability authorizes mercy to take precedence over retribution and because salvation is communal concurrent with the unity of humanity and the entire cosmos.

The *inevitability* and *ineluctability* of sin—of disobedience, sedition against God, a lack in virtue and purity, and an ontological distortion of the image of God—renders inconsistent any principle or ideology that encourages divine retribution or that adduces the expediency of avenging that which cannot be avoided. Therefore, instead of sentencing a portion of humanity to suffer eternal torments as punitive retribution and the remainder to their meritoriously earned heavenly reward, God's eschatological response to the inevitable mutability of his creation, exhibited in varying degrees of sinfulness, is uniformly one of merciful, therapeutic love. Just as it would be imprudent to exact vengeance on a human being suffering under an illness, the Great Physician in his co-suffering love and inherent mercy effectuates healing, which at times includes the pain of purification and a clearer consciousness but includes the hope of restoration and reconciliation with the Triune God. And with this, Evdokimov is given the final word:

> [T]he God who seems unable to suffer nevertheless does suffer. God sees the sadness ahead, and his love is no less vigilant, because man is able to refuse him and build a whole life upon this rejection, upon an atheistic revolt against him. Which is more important, love or freedom? The two are infinite and hell bears this question in its fire.[125]

125. Ibid., 20.

15

Prophecy, End-Times, and American Apocalypse

Reclaiming Hope for Our World

BARBARA R. ROSSING

A N ARTICLE IN THE October 2006 *New York Magazine* led off with the question, "What do Christian Millenarians, Jihadists, Ivy League professors, and baby-boomers have in common? Answer: They're all hot for the Apocalypse."[1]

Hot for the Apocalypse: The whole notion of Apocalypse, of catastrophic future scenarios, and end-times is prominent on American cultural radar screens these days. A new Christian video game, "Left Behind: Eternal Forces," released just before Christmas, invites players to "Command your forces through intense battles across a breathtaking, authentic depiction of New York City. Recover ancient scriptures and witness spectacular Angelic and Demonic activity as a direct consequence of your choices." An online ad for the game shows gun-wielding soldiers marching through New York City, helicopters exploding overhead, accompanied by the music of "Amazing Grace."

So is this how God's unfinished future is about to end? Is this the Apocalypse? We must say "no" to the "Left Behind" fictional version.

A SENSE OF AN "END"

We are faced with experiences of a sense of an "end" from all kinds of quarters—whether from global climate changed caused by carbon dioxide levels higher than any time in the past 500 million years; or the prospect of peak oil (the gradual or sudden depletion of the supply of

1. Andersen, "End."

the elixir that has fueled world expansion these past hundred years); or from escalating violence and the threat of nuclear weapons. We cannot just say an easy "no" to apocalyptic questions anymore, much as I would like to. There *is* a sense of an end right now in our culture. Christians need to address that.

When Hurricane Katrina hit New Orleans, I was in the Middle East, attending a conference in Bethlehem, the city of Jesus' birth. I had seen some television images but hadn't grasped the full magnitude of the disaster. A reporter from Ohio emailed me that she wanted to interview me for a story on Katrina and the book of Revelation, to get my take on whether this hurricane was predicted in the Bible. Since I had very limited Internet access, I emailed my husband, "Can you check on LeftBehind. com, Pat Robertson, etc., to see if the right-wing American Christians are really saying Hurricane Katrina is the Apocalypse? Because of course I need to say that it isn't."

My husband emailed me back in capital letters: "What do you mean this isn't the Apocalypse? Isn't that always what you have been saying is the root meaning of the world Apocalypse: 'pulling back a curtain to reveal something'?"

If Apocalypse means "revealing," as my husband reminded me— and that *is* the meaning of the Greek word—then the question is: What curtain did Hurricane Katrina pull back to reveal for us? What do other events—the accelerating melting of Greenland ice, the war in Iraq—you name them—unveil for us today? How do we read the signs of the times?

This is of course where Christian millenarians, jihadists, Ivy League professors, and baby-boomers disagree about the signs of the times— even if all can be said to be hot for the Apocalypse.

I was struck by a 2005 column from an unexpected quarter, by Peggy Noonan, *Wall Street Journal* columnist and former Reagan speech-writer, who coined the phrase "Morning in America" (so she's normally no apocalypticist). Noonan wrote a column entitled "A Separate Peace," suggesting that we may be living at the end of something: "I was chatting with friends about the sheer number of things parents now buy for teenage girls—bags and earrings and shoes. Someone said, 'It's affluence,' and someone else nodded, but I said, 'It's also the fear parents have that we're at the end of something, and they want their kids to have good memories.'"[2] The fear parents have that we're at the end of something.

Here's how Noonan describes the larger sense of the end:

> I think there is an unspoken subtext in our national political culture right now. In fact, I think it's a subtext to our society. I think that a lot of people are carrying around in their heads, unarticulated and even in some cases unnoticed, a sense that the wheels are coming off the trolley and the trolley off the tracks. That in some deep and fundamental way things have broken down and can't be fixed, or won't be fixed any time soon.

Noonan goes on to ask about our response as a culture, as a nation, as leaders:

> If I am right that trolley thoughts are out there, and even prevalent, how are people dealing with it on a daily basis?
>
> I think those who haven't noticed we're living in a troubling time continue to operate each day with classic and constitutional American optimism intact. I think some of those who have a sense we're in trouble are going through the motions.
>
> And some—well, I will mention and end with America's elites. Our elites, our educated and successful professional, the ones who are supposed to dig us out and lead us. I have a nagging sense that many of these people have made a separate peace. That they're living their lives and taking their pleasures and pursuing their agendas; that they're going forward each day with the knowledge, which they hold more securely and with greater reason than non-elites, that the wheels are off the trolley and the trolley's off the tracks, and with a conviction, a certainty, that there is nothing they can do about it.
>
> I suspect that history, including great historical novelists of the future, will look back and see that many of our elites simply decided to enjoy their lives. And that they consciously, or unconsciously, took grim comfort in this thought: I got mine. Which is what the separate peace comes down to, "I got mine, you get yours."

"I got mine; you get yours." But as Christians, that cannot be our message.

---

2. Noonan, "Separate."

THE END OF *WHAT* WORLD?

In this essay, I talk about reading the Bible for the future, maybe even for the end of the world, since end-times discourse is to prominent in our culture and in the Bible.

But the question is: the end of *what* world?

Jürgen Moltmann speaks about resurrection hope, eternal life, and eschatology. His work has been important on other themes as well. He developed a Christology in the book *The Crucified God*, that opened up a framework on which many feminist and liberation theologians have built. I also want to underscore Moltmann's ecological commitments— with which I deeply resonate—laid out in the preface to his book *God in Creation*, in which he calls the ecological crisis "a crisis so comprehensive and so irreversible that it can . . . be described as apocalyptic" and also in a 1996 retrospective, in which he says: "If I could start all over again I would link my theology with economic questions; the next century will be the age of ecology."[3]

So that's the context in which I frame the question of God's unfinished future today: How can we find a biblical vision for the future that addresses the ecological crisis of global climate change, the crisis of global warming?

As we think about God's unfinished future, I will make the case for reclaiming the Bible, even the Apocalypse, as a diagnosis of the illness of the imperial world, and as an urgent wake-up call about the future— a vision for hope for this planet earth and for every one of us.

Using the paradigm of illness and healing from Jesus' healings of people in the gospels, and also from the final chapter of Revelation, "the leaves of the tree of life are for the healing of the nations" (Rev 22:2), I suggest that our world is ill, very ill. The wheels may indeed be off the trolley and the trolley off the tracks, to use Noonan's words. The Bible helps us face that illness.

The Bible also proclaims God's vision of hope and healing, ecological healing as well as spiritual healing, physical healing, political healing, economic healing—healing for all the deepest wounds we carry.

We do face a sense of the end today. What may be ending, in my view, is our unsustainable way of life—even our empire—but not the earth itself. Like the early Christians in the New Testament, our task may

---

3. Moltmann, *God*, xi. Moltmann's comments about "ecological economics" are in response to Meeks, "Jürgen Moltmann," 105.

be to help people envision a way of life beyond empire, articulating God's joyful and compelling vision for the future.

CRITIQUING RAPTURE THEOLOGY

In order to make a case for apocalyptic hope and healing, we must first deal briefly with some popular but problematic interpretations of Revelation and the Bible—and I'll leave aside the aging baby-boomers as well as the jihadists and Ivy League professors and others mentioned by that *New York Magazine* article, in order to focus my critique especially on the Christian millenarian interpretation made so popular by Hal Lindsey's *The Late Great Planet Earth* in the 1970s and more recently by the "Left Behind" theology of Tim LaHaye and Jerry B. Jenkins: that of rapture and Armageddon politics.

That's the version of Revelation most people are getting in the culture, on Christian television and radio, and indeed that has been spilling over into our political life in multiple and very dangerous ways.

Is the goal of biblical apocalypses to spell out a recipe for Armageddon as many Christian fundamentalists claim? Does Revelation furnish us with a roadmap for the end-times in which America's war in Iraq plays a divinely ordained role? Does the Bible predict a countdown of events of ever-escalating violence, all prophesied in advance, including earthquakes, tsunamis, plagues of bird flu or *E. coli*, hurricanes and floods of greater intensity, all leading up to the mother of all battles, a divinely ordained World War III? Does the Bible snatch Christians off the earth to escape the suffering, and then mandate Jesus' future return to earth seven years later as an avenging warrior on a white horse to do battle with his enemies—after the so-called rapture and after three quarters of the world's people have been killed—to fight the bloody battle of Armageddon on the plains of northern Israel and then take up residence on David's throne in Jerusalem?

That's what the best-selling Christian *Left Behind* novels and televangelists want you to think—novels in which the heroes are an elite band of born-again Christians called the "tribulation force" who drive gas-guzzling Hummers and carry Uzis as they battle the Antichrist during the earth's seven last years.

Listen to the almost pornographic description of Christ's second coming by today's popularizers in *Glorious Appearing* (2004) from the interminable *Left Behind* series: "Men and women, soldiers and horses seemed to explode where they stood. It was as if the very words of the Lord had superheated their blood, causing it to burst through the veins and skin"; "Even as they struggled, their own flesh dissolved, their eyes melted and their tongues disintegrated"; "Jesus merely raised one hand a few inches, and . . . they tumbled in [to hell], howling and screeching."[4]

My specialty as a New Testament scholar is the book of Revelation, and I am alarmed at how Revelation, indeed the entire biblical apocalyptic tradition, with its important critique of imperial injustice, has been hijacked to provide a platform for violence, even voyeurism—a cavalier use-it-or-lose-it mentality that risks dismissing long-term issues such as peace and even the environment on the grounds that the earth only has to last seven more years. It's a theology that one Jewish scholar has aptly decried as "God so loved the world that he sent World War III."[5]

Revelation is the foundational text for this militant prophecy industry. Not Revelation's critique of empire and its healing vision for a renewal for the world, which I believe is the heart of the book, but rather the violent story of Armageddon, of a supposed countdown to tribulation and destruction in which only a few individuals are saved out of the world, a story of how the planet must be decimated before the wrathful lion-like Jesus can return to earth to fight a battle in which blood will flow up to the horses' bridles. (Let me make clear: the *Left Behind* novels can be fun, thrilling, exciting, even spiritually renewing, if you have a stomach for violence. But they're fiction, not only the plot and the characters, but also the theology on which they're based.)

The so-called rapture that forms the basis for the *Left Behind* novels is not traditional biblical teaching, but was rather a nineteenth-century invention of the British pastor John Nelson Darby, founder of the Plymouth Brethren.[6] Rapture theology "sounds biblical," as Roman Catholic bishops of Illinois have warned. But it is not biblical. Nowhere does the Bible say that born-again Christians will be snatched up to heaven while they watch God inflict tribulation and disasters on earth, although believers can piece together a chain of Bible verses to construct the rapture chronology. Already in the nineteenth century, when this rapture theology first came out, the former slave Sojourner Truth, cri-

---

4. LaHaye and Jenkins, *Glorious*, 225, 273, 380.

5. Landau, "President," 475.

6. Boyer, *When*, gives a succinct overview of Darby and his legacy.

tiqued both its escapist framework and its violence—a critique that is amazingly timely today also:

> You seem to be expecting to go to some parlor *away up* some-
> where, and when the wicked have been burnt, you are coming
> back to walk in triumph over their ashes—this is to be your New
> Jerusalem!! Now I can't see any thing so very nice in that, coming
> back to . . . a world covered with the ashes of the wicked. Besides,
> if the Lord comes and burns—as you say he will—I am not going
> away; I am going to stay here and stand the fire, like Shadrach,
> Meshach, and Abednego! And Jesus will walk with me through
> the fire, and keep me from harm.[7]

Going to a "parlor away up somewhere" to watch the destruction, and then coming back to earth to walk on the ashes seven years later is an apt description for the pre-tribulation rapture premillennial dispensational-ist system.

The program is especially dangerous for the Middle East—for both Israelites and Palestinians. While the Middle East is not my focus here, let my just note that Christian fundamentalists have become a major lobby regarding U.S. policy in the Middle East, with some extreme voices going so far at to promote a U.S. nuclear strike on Iran—this, in order to fulfill God's prophetic plan. Very scary stuff, a complete reversal of Jesus' blessing of peacemakers and Jesus' teaching of love for enemies.

Roman Catholics, Lutherans, Episcopalians, Presbyterians, Metho-dists, and most evangelicals all reject such violent rapture theology. But institutional religious criticism has a hard time gaining much traction against such an incredible popular culture and mass media pheno-menon.

REASONS *NOT* TO REJECT THE APOCALYPSE

So what do we do? In the face of such problematic fundamentalist in-terpretations of Apocalypse, the logical solution might seem to be to reject the apocalyptic strand of the Bible altogether. After all, it is dan-gerous cultural stuff, open to wildly misguided interpretations, as early Christians realized already in the second century when a grassroots movement called New Prophecy or Montantism began to claim that Revelation's prophecies were coming to life in their own time.

---

7. Quoted in Griffith, *War*, 193.

But can we reject the Apocalypse today? Is such a move helpful or even possible? No, because the Apocalypse is part of our public rhetoric as well as part of our Bible, and has been for centuries. Mainline Christians have tried ignoring Revelation—I know I did when I was pastor of a Lutheran congregation in the 1980s. But while we mainline Christians were busy ignoring this apocalyptic book, fundamentalists came in with a vengeance to tell Christians what it "really" means.

Moreover, I believe the Apocalypse can help us today. It can help us face seriously that our world is ill, very ill—ill with what Seattle film-maker John de Graaf calls "affluenza," a combination of affluence and influenza; ill with what nature writer and Methodist Bill McKibben calls the disease of "More" with a capital M, a carbon-devouring lifestyle that is not sustainable; ill with what Chalmers Johnson calls the "sorrows of empire," manifested in many different and interrelated ways—militarily, economically, ecologically, spiritually.[8] The voice of the earth and the voice of the poor are crying out to us with two parallel cries, writes Brazilian theologian Leonardo Boff.[9]

What we need to do is reclaim the important biblical apocalyptic voice of protest and hope away from the problematic violent readings that have become so dominant in America today. The heart of Revelation and other apocalypses is a prophetic message very different from what we're being told by the fundamentalist program of the *Left Behind* novels or others seeking to precipitate Armageddon in the Middle East. The heart of the Bible and even of the book of Revelation is not rapture and imperial violence against the earth. It's a message that Sojourner Truth and so many others have lifted up in struggles for justice through the centuries, whether in the struggle against slavery in the U.S. or more recently in South Africa or Latin America.

As my husband reminded me that day in Bethlehem, the word *apocalypse* means "unveiling." Apocalypses pull back the curtain—like the movie *The Wizard of Oz*, where Dorothy's dog Toto is the one who pulls back the curtain to expose Oz for how he really is. Apocalypses unveil and expose; they help us see the truth. They take us on a journey behind the curtain, a journey into the heart of our world, a journey to the throne of God.

---

8. DeGraaf, Wann, and Naylor, *Affluenza*; McKibben, *Coming*, 10; Johnson, *Sorrows*.
9. Boff, *Cry*, 104.

So what, if anything, does Revelation unveil for us today? That is the question we need to ask and consider together. Revelation doesn't predict events in the twenty-first century. It is prophecy, but prophecy doesn't mean prediction.

If we can take ourselves back to the first century to hear its message for the original hearers to which it was written, then we can ask about analogies to today, places where that first-century message might also be God's word for today.

For churches living in first-century Roman Asia Minor, the original audience of the book, Revelation's core unveiling was an urgent pronouncement of the end of the imperial world—it diagnosed the illness, the sickness of the Roman world. And here I draw a distinction between three different Greek words for "world." Revelation unveils not the end of the physical created world (the Greek words *kosmos* or *ge*) but the end of the imperial world, the *oikoumene*.

The Roman Empire had its own imperial eschatology, the message of *Rome aeterna*, "world without end," bombarding people every day through imperial propaganda and iconography, inscriptions, magnificent triumphal arches, victory parades, coins showing conquering divine emperors on one side and weeping captives on the other. The message was everywhere that Rome had conquered the whole *oikoumene*—the lands, the seas, the ends of the earth, geographically as well as temporally. Any resistance was futile.

This theology is perhaps best captured by one famous imperial scene, exquisitely carved in sardonyx on a tiny cameo, called the Gemma Augustea, now in the museum in Vienna. It shows a personified figure of *Oikoumene* placing a crown on the head of Emperor Augustus, signifying the whole imperial world, the whole *oikoumene*, giving its allegiance to the empire. That's the top tier of the two-tiered cameo. Below, figures of Roman soldiers abuse bound captives in Abu Ghraib-like scenes, graphically reminding viewers of how the whole Roman imperial system rested on the backs of conquered peoples and lands. It is to this Roman imperial eschatology of "empire without end" that the New Testament says "no." Jesus, the gospels, Paul, Revelation: all counter Rome's claims of eternal domination with a strong sense of an end, an end to the *oikoumene*.

I find it striking that the New Testament refrains from referring to the *oikoumene* in any positive sense—probably because *oikoumene* had come to mean the imperial world, as signified in the Gemma Augustea's depiction. In the Gospel of Luke's Christmas story, for example, when Caesar Augustus decrees that the whole world should be enrolled in a census, the word for world is *oikoumene*. Similarly, what Satan offers Jesus in the temptation stories in both Luke and Matthew is the kingdoms of the world—the *oikoumene*—the imperial world. There are no positive references to the word.

Two other Greek words, for earth (*ge*) and world (*kosmos*), are used more positively. The earth certainly suffers judgment and tribulation, but God is the one who created the earth, both *ge* and *kosmos*, a claim that is absent for *oikoumene*. Moreover, a number of New Testament texts proclaim that the earth will be renewed in God's future world, as God's dwelling place (Rev 21:1). A key verse is Rev 11:18 in which God says, "I'm going to destroy the *destroyers* of the earth," not "I'm going to destroy the earth."

In this Roman imperial eschatological context, the core vision of Revelation for first-century Christians was a choice between two cities, two competing political economies, two ways of life—God's economy of justice and well-being versus the Roman Empire's way of life.

The book takes us on two tours led by the same angel: first, a tour of Rome—called the whore of Babylon—to see and experience the terrors of the unjust imperial world; and second, a tour of God's New Jerusalem. The plagues are part of the first tour, projecting out into the future the logical consequences of the trajectory of the Roman Empire so that people can see where it will all end before it's too late. These plagues are not predictions but rather warnings, like Scrooge's visionary journeys in Charles Dickens's *Christmas Carol*, where Scrooge is shown horrifying future scenarios not because they must happen, but so that he can alter the course of his life.

Even nature itself participates in this warning, crying out to oppressors about the consequences of their own deadly actions. When waters and springs turn to blood, the angel (messenger) of the waters interprets this through the logic of natural consequences, as a boomerang-like effect, in Rev 16:6: "You are just, O Holy One . . . for you have judged these things. Because they shed the blood of saints and prophets, you have given them blood to drink. It is axiomatic" (*axios estin*; Rev 16:5–6). It is not the language of punishment so much as the language of axiomatic consequences. The messenger of Revelation's waters seems to be saying that oppressors who commit acts of violence will eventually unleash their own destructive consequences upon themselves.

Such biblical plagues, therefore, are meant to be not predictions but rather urgent warnings, like the Exodus plagues, part of the book's diagnosis of the illness of the imperial world, to wake us up to the consequences of our actions before it is too late. Revelation 17–18 shows the catastrophic end of that empire, its way of life, as merchants, kings, shipping magnates all lament the destruction of their world trade center.[10]

But Revelation doesn't end there. It doesn't just take you to Armageddon, to the smoke rising from burning Babylon. It also offers the vision of hope—the alternative.

The entire book of Revelation leads up to the wondrous vision of New Jerusalem in chapters 21–22, the incredible city of beauty, welcome, and ecological renewal. This is the most important vision of the book to which the whole tour has been leading: "And I saw the holy city, the new Jerusalem, coming down out of heaven from God, prepared as a bride. . . . And I heard a loud voice from the throne saying, 'See, the dwelling of God is among mortals. God will dwell with them as their God; they will be his people, and God's very self will be with them'" (Rev 21:2–3).

Heaven is not mentioned again after Rev 21:2, a fact especially striking for a book in which heaven has been so central. This is because God's throne moves down to earth, to be with us.

The New Jerusalem of Revelation 21–22 is a wonderfully earth-centered vision of hope for this world. Contrary to the escapism and "heavenism" that dominate many fundamentalist interpretations, the picture of Revelation emphasizes that our future dwelling—and God's—will be on earth, renewed, in a radiant, thriving city landscape. The core vision of Revelation, and a vision that we need for today, is not of people being "raptured" away to heaven, but rather, if anything, of God being "raptured" down to earth (Rev 21), to dwell with us in what is called New Jerusalem.

That's why I think it can even be an ecological vision. In every way, this beloved city is the very opposite of the toxic political economy of the Roman Empire. Whereas Rome was built on deforestation, mining, slavery, unjust global trade—all critiqued in the amazing cargo list of Rev 18:12–13—New Jerusalem centers around a Tree of Life. In chapter 22, my favorite part, John sees a paradise of green space right in the middle of the city, a river of life, flowing through the city of God from

10. Catherine Keller describes living in Manhattan and thinking of the line in Revelation 18: "The smoke goes up from its burning." *God*, 3.

the throne. What a wonderful image for our rivers![11] On either side of the river grows the Tree of Life, a wondrous canopy of shade. And the leaves of the tree are medicine, like those of so many trees in traditional religions. The leaves of the tree "are for healing of the nations," John says.

Oh, how we need those healing leaves! As I think about the message of Revelation for our political life, for ecology, for global warming, for violence in the Middle East, I keep coming back to this medicinal tree of life, with its wondrous "leaves for the healing of the nations." God wills not to destroy our world but to heal it. That's the final word of the Bible. Healing comes in Revelation not directly from God but from the leaves of a tree, from the creation. The tree of life is an image common to Christianity, Judaism, Islam, and to so many other religious traditions.

TAKING REVELATION'S TRUE MESSAGE TO HEART

The question for us is: How can we take to heart that healing tree and those medicinal leaves today? How can we reclaim our vision for planet earth, our political vision, our spiritual vision, to be shaped not by Armageddon and war, but by this healing vision?—a vision of Jerusalem and all cities as places of justice and beauty, with a river of life flowing through the middle, welcoming all.

Contrary to the dispensationalist claims, New Jerusalem is not re-served for a far-off future, an event on a chronology after Armageddon and other destructive events. Rather, New Jerusalem is a vision that was intended to guide the ethical life of Revelation's readers even now. It is a future vision, yes, but also God's life-giving vision for justice for our whole wounded world. Revelation invites marginalized people, those who hunger and thirst for justice, to come for healing to the tree, to come to the river: "Let everyone who thirsts take the water of life as a gift, without price" (Rev 22:17).

Our world is ill. We all feel that. It is a sickness, this warmongering. The planet is heating up with a fever, the fever of global warming that we all must urgently address. The Arctic has suffered another record loss of sea ice. As the Arctic region absorbs more heat from the sun, causing the ice to melt still further, the relentless cycle of melting and heating

11. The Roman Catholic bishops of the Pacific Northwest used this image for a pas-toral statement on the Columbia River, calling on parishioners to view this river as a watershed of life. See: *Columbia River Watershed.*

will shrink the massive land glaciers of Greenland and dramatically raise sea levels. Scientists tell us that the Greenland ice sheet is ill, sliding the length of a football field each day. Soon we may cross a critical threshold beyond which the climate cannot recover, scientists tell us. How do we find healing?

What would it mean if Revelation's core message is a message of hope for the world, embodied in those leaves of the tree of life? What would it mean if Revelation wants to lay on each one of the wounds of the world—the shrinking glaciers, the Iraq war, the aftermath of Hurricane Katrina—leaves from the tree of life, to save those glaciers, to downsize our ecological footprint before it is too late, to help heal and reconcile the war and brokenness of our world? Can the Apocalypse play such a healing role for our culture today, rather than beating the drum for rapture and Armageddon?

I'm not a novelist, but that's the version of the story that urgently needs to be written. People are hungry for narratives of how God is alive and at work in the world, as *Left Behind* reminds us. Stories hold great power to shape our worldview.

We need a novel that tells the story of the Bible and Revelation not as escape from earth or earth's destruction, but as a story of hope, of renewal for the planet. We need a novel whose heroes are not hiding out in underground bunkers, or flying around in attack helicopters, or driving gas-guzzling Range Rovers and Humvees, as in the *Left Behind* novels, but whose heroes are rooted on the earth, living in sustainable communities, maybe practicing permaculture gardening—sharing in the river of life, tending the nation-healing tree of life. Such a story could be just as thrilling as the *Left Behind* story—but instead of carrying guns to battle the Antichrist and his forces, our little band of heroes carries seedlings, or solar panels; they rescue farmers about to be bulldozed by developers; they foil the evil forces of polluters and greenhouse emitters—today's most dangerous manifestations of the Antichrist.

We need a novel based on the book of Revelation in which the earth itself—the feminine figure of *Ge* from chapter 12 of Revelation and eighty-some other references—plays a starring role, first crying out for justice on behalf of all the victims of imperial oppression, both human and non-human, and then becoming the hero. In Revelation 12, the Earth comes to the rescue of a mythic "woman clothed with the sun," who represents us, God's people, in danger of being devoured by the

Satanic dragon of empire. Now that's a story! The earth opens its mouth to save us from our own captivity to empire!

It's all there in the Bible. I'm not making it up. We need a novel that helps us envision the promise and renewal of chapters 21–22. It needs to be a gripping, daring story of God's love for the earth, for the whole world, a world that will not be left behind—the story of God's dwelling on earth with us, with the glaciers, with every beloved species, with every endangered salmon, everything God created, taking part in an urgent plot, and most of all, the story of the healing tree of life, that amazing tree at the very center of our world.

Salvation from empire, from Armageddon, from our own destruction. The tree of life. The River of Life. Who will write the novel of that Apocalypse?

16

Vincent Van Gogh's Compassionate Eschatology

W HEN VINCENT VAN GOGH left the Belgian coalmining district after
three years as an evangelist he looked more like a man emerging from the wilderness than a representative of the respectable Belgian
Missionary Society. He had given his all in service to the destitute miners
and was now totally depleted. He looked the part of one in need of help
rather than one who helps. This is the way he thought that one should
serve Christ and that is what he felt called to do even if it took his last
portion of energy. He looked more like a madman, but some thought he
was a saint.

EARLY INFLUENCE

Vincent Van Gogh was born into a well-established and respectable
Dutch family. Many of his immediate forebears had achieved high
standards in their respective careers, some of which included theology
and art dealing. Much worldly success was expected of the eldest son of
Pastor Theodorus Van Gogh. Vincent's early family life gifted him with
the experiences of life as a preacher's son that would once lead to his
profoundly lived vocation. But because Vincent took his vocation to the
extreme he became the antithesis of what his family (with the eventual
exception of his brother Theo) envisioned him to be.

He spent his boyhood in Southern Brabant, Netherlands, where his
father served small rural parishes. Vincent and his siblings were edu-
cated in a moderate faith. Parables of Jesus told around the table during
family meals were lessons about acts of charity, about finding the kingdom here on earth and about attaining eternal life. Vincent accompanied

his father on pastoral visits to the poor peasants and it was there that the lessons the family read about from the Bible became vivid reality. It was in the interaction with the rural poor where he grew up seeing and believing that human beings manifested God's indwelling spirit through their compassionate care for one another.

A sensitive child, he spent much of his free time alone, roaming through the heath absorbing the deep lessons he witnessed in nature— the cyclical rhythms of the seasons, the tilling, sowing and harvesting, the birthing and dying. When Vincent left his parental home at age fifteen, he carried within himself the seeds that would later grow into a life of compassionate purpose. Throughout his years as an art dealer apprentice in his uncle's art gallery, Vincent spent much time studying the Bible and other religious books with great intensity. He gradually immersed himself so completely into his religious studies that he distanced himself more and more from fulfilling the duties of his apprenticeship. Consequently he was dismissed and set adrift with doubts and many unanswered existential questions.

Vincent's fervor and passionate desire to live as he believed Christ admonished his followers to live lead him to finally choose to take up theological studies to prepare himself for the ministry. Failing, however, at passing his preliminary theological exams, he was directed to try missionary training instead. He chose as his mission field the impoverished Belgian mining district called the Borinage. Here Vincent found tremendous human need. He responded by bringing comfort and hope, at first through words, then through deeds. For three years Vincent immersed himself in the lives of the miners and their families. He bonded with them and became their friend and caregiver. He spent time in the mineshafts. He used his last shirt to bandage a miner wounded so seriously in an explosion that he had been given up for lost. Vincent nursed him back to health. He entered the miners' homes and helped the worn-out miners' wives with their daily chores in order to alleviate their struggles, free from the distractions of religious doctrine and societal and parental authority.

Vincent lived bearing others' burdens and thus fulfilling the law of Christ. This downward path into utmost solidarity with desperate people on the lowest scale of society led him to the upward path of his spiritual awakening and his true vocation. The Mission Society, however, did not take kindly to Vincent's devotion and dedication. So thoroughly did he identify with the needs of the people that he gave away everything he had, sacrificing his own health and comfort. The missionary supervisors felt that such an unrespectable looking man with such zeal could not adequately represent them. So they dismissed Vincent who was a disgrace and an embarrassment to them.

TRANSITION FROM MISSIONARY EVANGELIST TO EVANGELICAL ARTIST

At the time of his departure from the Borinage, Vincent was twenty-seven years old. He had reached the lowest point of his already failure-ridden life. He managed to persevere in part because of his deep love for Christ and because of an intimate connection to his brother Theo. Thanks to the resources of art and literature and his love for nature that were the "soul ingredients" he had incorporated into his life, Vincent found consolation and hope and a new direction. With these internal founts of wisdom and beauty to sustain him, he instinctively began to make sketches.

> I should like to begin making rough sketches of some of the many things I meet on my way, but as it would probably keep me from my real work, it is better not to start. . . .[1]

He was still reluctant to give in to this desire to draw for fear it would keep him from his real work of caring for his parishioners. For his strong sense of duty to live with a purpose was gratified by his work among the miners. He wrote,

> When one lives with others and is united by a feeling of affection, one is aware of a reason for living and perceives that one is not quite worthless and superfluous, but perhaps good for something.[2]

But as he gave in more and more to his desire to pick up his pencil and make hasty sketches, he felt a stirring within himself. At the same time as he cried out during his deepest moment of despair, "My only anxiety is, how can I be of use in the world? Can't I serve some purpose

---

1. Letter 126. All quotes are from Van Gogh, *Complete Letters*. All the letters quoted are written by Vincent to his brother Theo.

2. Letter 132.

and be of any good?"[3] he came to the transformative realization that he would fuse his love and knowledge of art with his desire to follow Jesus. When he emerged from the Borinage, one door closed and a new vocational path opened. Vincent would henceforth embark upon a journey to become what he was born to become. No longer would he be the evangelist of the word, but with will-empowered determination he would seek to establish a new and modern religious language. It would be Rembrandt's language:

> There is something of Rembrandt in the Gospel, and something of the Gospel in Rembrandt. . . . Rembrandt is so deeply mysterious that he says things for which there are no words in any (spoken) language.[4]

He would seek to express his faith, freed from the dogmas of the religious institutions that had rebuked him. He shed the social standing of his family heritage and henceforth called himself only "Vincent." He would strive intensely for a deeper grasp on how to live a life of faith, continuing to believe that the essence of Christianity was to be found in the person of Christ—not in doctrine. His faith was experiential.

Rooted in the daily struggles of life, Vincent reasoned that he had successfully graduated from a free course in "the great university of misery"[5] that was the education that would propel him forward. So he reflected upon the miners in the Borinage and his solidarity with these forgotten and destitute laborers. The mining district was the fertile ground where his character was tested, his beliefs affirmed, and where his artist's mission was born. He now began to emerge from a chrysalis of obscurity with something to say to the world that he could do with authority based upon his own sacrifice and struggle. He could remain in solidarity with the poor through artistic expression that consoled and comforted. He could shine rays of light in the darkest corners through his art. He would communicate out of love and with love to those who needed comfort and hope with his artist's tools and vocabulary.

3. Letter 133.
4. Ibid.
5. Ibid.

VINCENT'S NEW CREED

Vincent collected art prints by the social realist artists he had admired while an apprentice in England. He, as always, derived inspiration and inner balance through long walks in the countryside where he delighted in the sights, sounds, and smells of the earth. He recorded his impressions of windswept landscapes, of rain puddles reflecting the sky, and of the perpetual motions of the sowers and reapers in long vividly descriptive letters to his brother Theo. He read books by the Romantic writers of the preceding generation whose views of nature as a sacred incarnation of the Divine resonated with his own deep love and reverence for all creation. And he became absorbed by the new French novels that dealt with the existential quandaries of the poor as they struggled to survive in the new industrial society. He compared the stories of these novels to the messages about love and redemption found in the New Testament, messages that he had internalized during the years of his intense study of biblical scripture. And he found inspiration in and resonated with the art of the Japanese whose woodblock prints celebrated everyday life as a source to achieve enlightenment.

To all his reading, studying, writing, collecting art, and going for long walks through the countryside and cities, Vincent added the discipline of practicing the fundamentals of drawing and painting. His devotion to living fully as an artist was equal to his devotion to his missionary work in the Borinage. He found that his life needed to unify his great love for literature (reading *and* writing), for art (art appreciation *and* painting), and for nature (*all* of creation) as necessary components for his spiritual journey. He synthesized these elements into his life's new creed:

> I think that everything which is really good and beautiful—of inner moral, spiritual, and sublime beauty in human beings and their works—comes from God ... *But I always think that the best way to know God is to love many things.* Love a friend, a wife, something—whatever you like—you will be on the way to knowing more about Him; that is what I say to myself. But one must love with a lofty and serious intimate sympathy, with strength, with intelligence and one must always try to know deeper, better and more. That leads to God, that leads to unwavering faith.[6]

6. Ibid.

A person must pay attention, he writes,

> to the things he sees with his eyes and hears with his ears, and
> think them over; he, too, will end in believing, and he will per-
> haps have learned more than he can tell. To try to understand the
> real significance of what the great artists, the serious masters, tell
> us in their masterpieces, *that* leads to God; one man wrote or told
> it in a book; another, in a picture. Then simply read the Gospel
> and the Bible: it makes you think, and think much, and think all
> the time. Well, think much and think all the time, it raises your
> thoughts above the ordinary level without your knowing it.[7]

NATURE AS VINCENT'S "OPEN BIBLE"

Throughout the ten years of his life as an artist he remained faithful to
Christ and the messages of Scripture that he had deeply internalized.
Now those words became more real to him as he immersed himself into
the landscape of the Provence, in France. Nature, the golden sun, the
strong mistral wind, the gentle rain, the starry heavens, all spoke of the
creative force, of truth and beauty, and of God's presence. He wrote to
Theo,

> At times there is *something indescribable* in those aspects—all
> nature seems to speak; and going home, one has the same feeling
> as when one has finished a book by Victor Hugo, for instance. As
> for me, I cannot understand why everybody does not see it and
> feel it; nature or God does it for everyone who has eyes and ears
> and a heart to understand.[8]

From this open Bible of nature he struggled as an artist to describe and
express in his work the "something indescribable," the "secret" of nature
as he called it.

> In any case, whether people approve or do not approve of what
> I do and how I do it, I personally know no other way than to
> wrestle with nature long enough for her to tell me her *secret*.[9]

The "secret" nature told Vincent was, *ce qui ne passe pas dans ce
qui passe*—that which is invisible (eternal) is revealed in that which is
visible (temporal). He strove to express this secret by trying to paint

7. Ibid.
8. Letter 248.
9. Letter 393.

what he perceived as the essence of things, of the blooming orchards of Arles, of the groves of gnarled olive trees and of the upward reaching cypress trees around the asylum in St. Remy. He struggled to grasp this secret and "translate" it with emphatic brush strokes and expressive colors so that others could understand it too. Vincent hoped that his images would elicit in the viewers of his work the same realization he experienced—that God spoke to him through His creation. His realizations and insights were painted into the portraits of the citizens of Arles and into the images of peasants laboring in the vast fields of wheat, and most of all into the brilliantly shining suns over the landscapes of the Provence. With all the physical and mindful strength he could muster he attempted to record what he absorbed through all his senses during every intensely lived moment of each sun-drenched or mistral-swept day or starlit night.

> I see that nature has told me something, has spoken to me, and that I have put it down in shorthand. In my shorthand there may be words that cannot be deciphered, there may be mistakes or gaps; but there is something of what wood or beach or figure has told me in it, and it is not the tame or conventional language derived from a studied manner or a system rather than from nature itself.[10]

He came to realize that nature spoke a revelatory language to all who listen and see and feel. The visible in nature became for him a symbol for that which was not discernable to the eyes—the Divine, the Eternal.

VINCENT'S ART AS MODERN LANGUAGE— ITS SYMBOLISM AND MISSION

A tenet of Calvinism, the religious climate of the time and place of Vincent's childhood, was for artists to paint only those things that their eyes were capable of seeing. Vincent would paint only what he saw—the ordinary things of life. But seen through his temperament and passionate relationship with the earth and humanity, he imbued the images with a personal sentiment and deeper meaning. His brushstrokes and vibrant colors were his own interpretations of what he saw and felt. This made Vincent's art uniquely personal and a new trend in the art of his time. His paintings and drawing were not merely the traditionally recorded

10. Letter 228.

historic moments, or portraits of specific persons, or picturesque landscape scenes.

With his art Vincent wanted to communicate, to engage the viewer
on a deeper level. He also wanted to challenge the religious language of
the past so that modern men and women could experience the biblical
messages in a new way—not through scriptural translations, but through
the universal language of visual art. Vincent understood that the vibra-
tory quality of color elicits in each person an unconscious response.
He understood the psychology of line. With studied as well as intuitive
knowledge Vincent used expressive lines and color as a language that
would speak to the soul. Vincent sought to express his own understanding of the lessons nature and life taught him. His contemporaries were
not quite able to comprehend Vincent's art language, but the wisdom
inherent in his paintings gained significance.

Once Vincent felt that he mastered the skills of using the vocabulary
of his new language, he strove to capture on his canvasses the "essence" of
the things he saw. He believed that the essence of something, or of some-
body, was the quality that reflected God's presence—that "something indescribable." He strove to create images of the visible world that pointed
to the invisible presence of the Divine. The ripening wheat containing
within it the force of germination touched upon that essence. Vincent
felt that within each grain of wheat there existed a force, the germinating
force, which was empowered by the energy of the sun. Vincent likened
this force within a grain of wheat to the force of Love that enlivens human beings. In Vincent's famous image of the sower sowing seeds into
the fertile soil with the ripe wheat field in the back ground under the
pulsating rays of the all-present and all-powerful sun, he tried to express
that God's presence, his Love, pervades all of life, a life beyond death. The
Sower's fertile seeds, the ripening and dying wheat containing the new
seeds, the sun energizing both life and death in an eternal cycle, this all
affirmed that the source for the germinating power within the seed was
eternally present.

Vincent's art was meant to be a means through which people would
gain a better understanding of their covenantal relationship to the whole
of creation. He also wished to bring beauty and comfort into the homes
of the poor through paintings that were affordable and attainable—
unlike the art of the galleries that could only be afforded by people of
means. Vincent hoped that some day the images of his wheat fields, of

the ordinary men and women portrayed as saints, would point people to the deeper meaning that underlie the temporary, ordinary things of everyday existence.

As with the parables that seek to reveal the truth through simple stories of widows and mustard seeds, so Vincent's paintings of blooming peach trees and plowed fields were meant to reveal deeper truths. His starry nights point to the vast mystery of God's omnipresence throughout the cosmos. The luminous images of the sun spreading intense yellow rays over the wheat fields, permeating the whole sky, symbolize the Source of all being, constantly there, even after going down behind the Alpilles [little alps] of the Arlesian landscape.

VINCENT'S GOD—A GOD OF COMPASSION

Vincent understood the Creator of all nature to be a compassionate God, a God who came to live among his own. When Vincent gave up his comfortable dwelling to go and live in a dirty hovel in the Borinage, his hostess voiced her dismay at his decision. But Vincent replied, "Esther, one should do like the good God; form time to time one should go and live among His own."[11]

Vincent's ministry emphasized that it was through human acts of compassion that God's presence was manifested. Vincent could see this presence in the simple faith of the miners and of the peasants of his rural Holland and in the acts of kindness by the people he met in the South of France. He was always aware that his concrete experiences of solidarity and intimacy with these people contained the mystery of what he sometimes called "Something on High." Vincent was compelled to live in such a way that God's love could be made visible in whatever way possible. All that he did was an experiment in gospel living.

> .... the truth is, there is no real independence, no real liberty, no steady self-reliance, except through Love. I say, our sense of duty is sharpened and our work becomes clear to us through Love; and in loving and fulfilling the duties of love we perform God's will.[12]

He wrote to Theo in 1881,

11. From a letter to Mr. V. W. van Gogh from P. Driutte. Van Gogh, *Complete Letters*, 230.

12. Letter, 161.

> You must not be astonished when, even at the risk of your tak-
> ing me to be a fanatic, I tell you that in order to love, I think it
> absolutely necessary to believe in God (that does not mean that
> you should believe all the sermons of the clergymen . . . far from
> it). To me, to believe in God is to feel that there is a God, not
> dead or stuffed, but alive, urging us toward steadfast love with
> irresistible force.[13]

In Vincent's copy of *The Raising of Lazarus* (one of his few explicitly religious paintings) by Rembrandt, the image of the sun replaces the
figure of Christ. He copied this painting essentially to console himself
during a time of intense discouragement due to his painful seizures. In
Vincent's version, the sun is shining upon Lazarus as he awakens in his
tomb—and Lazarus' face has the unmistakable resemblance to Vincent
himself. The sun, symbolizing the source of all Being, has the power to
heal and resurrect, to germinate new life. In that force, called Love, God
is present.

ETERNITY—HERE ON EARTH

Vincent felt that the visible world that is grasped through our senses
inherently links us to that part of life we can't see, that which is eternal.
He questioned, "is the whole of life visible to us, or isn't it rather that this
side of death we see only one hemisphere?"[14] He likened eternal life to a
sphere, something that was complete—and that one's fragmented view
of life showed "life to be flat" [or to be just one hemisphere]. Vincent felt
that the works of a painter would continue speaking to generations to
come even if they, the artists, had disappeared to the "other side of the
hemisphere." When the painters themselves were no longer amongst the
living, their life's work could still be seen. As it is with the setting sun—
the rays still linger, and after the sun has set the knowledge remains that
the sun is still there, though unseen, on the other side. Vincent wondered, then, whether death was so difficult. He himself didn't really know
anything about that other side of the hemisphere, but

> looking at the stars always makes me dream, as simply as I dream
> over the black dots representing towns and villages on a map.
> Why, I ask myself, shouldn't the shining dots of the sky be as ac-
> cessible as the black dots on the map of France? Just as we take

13. Letter, 189.
14. Letter, 506.

the train to get to Tarascon or Rouen, we take death to reach a
star. One thing undoubtedly true in this reasoning is that we cannot get to a star while we are alive, any more than we can take the
train when we are dead. So to me it seems possible that cholera,
tuberculosis and cancer are the celestial means of locomotion,
just as steamboats, buses and railways are the terrestrial means.
To die quietly of old age would be to go there on foot."[15]

The sowers and reapers, woven into the wheat fields as they partake
in the cycles of birth and death, are empowered by the gleaming vitality
of the sun.

....For I see in this reaper—a vague figure fighting like a devil in
the midst of the heat to get to the end of his task—I see in him the
image of death, in the sense that humanity might be the wheat he
is reaping. So it is—if you like—the opposite of that sower I tried
to do before. But there's nothing sad in this death, it goes its way
in broad daylight with a sun flooding everything with a light of
pure gold ....it is an image of death as the great book of nature
speaks of it—but what I have sought is the "almost smiling."[16]

Vincent's *Starry Night* is the celestial map of a skyscape vibrant with
the life force that permeates the whole universe—this and the other side
of the hemisphere. Eternity is there, to be reached by celestial means. But
Vincent felt in order to partake in eternity it was up to each individual
to be permeated with that life force, called love, here on earth. Living
a compassionate and purposeful earthly life would make eternal life
within that web of the life force attainable. He felt that it was the same
with people as it was with the wheat he saw swaying in the fields around
Arles, St. Remy, and later on Auvers. Human beings had to be sowed into
the earth, grow and live their purpose, die to their own egos, so that they
could then germinate into new life, as part of the cyclical rhythms of
creation. And he understood that the power that drove him on was that
"germinating force" in a grain of wheat—Love. Both birth and germination are "necessary and useful, as well as death or disappearance ...it is
so relative—and life is the same."[17] Eternity, Vincent felt, was hinted upon

15. Ibid.
16. Letter, 604.
17. Letter, 607.

in the ordinary things of life, like seeing "the infinite in the eyes of a baby in its cradle."[18]

VINCENT—MADMAN OR SAINT?

Vincent's passion for sacrifice and solitude and his eccentricity are translated by our culturally conditioned view of life as neurotic and as a deviation of human nature. His deep intuition to strive for a higher purpose in life at the expense of comfort and social standing are at odds with today's view of normalcy. His role as prophet or even as a modern mystic caused him to suffer, to struggle and to give up his own personal yearning for a family life. He lived in order to tell an old story through a new language. Most of us are fascinated by this "crazy artist who cut off his own ear." His prophetic writing in his hundreds of letters, his kinetic painting style, the mission and passion and intensity expressed in his paintings, his unconventional lifestyle, set him apart from the rest of us. It is as if he was fulfilling the role of prophet, healer, mystic, sage, and fool, all in one. Such figures are known throughout time as shamans or "medicine men."

> Shamans embody the crazy wisdom that strikes among humankind as unpredictably as lightning and has nothing to recommend itself but the sheer personal authority of the one who voices (or babbles or sings or dances [or paints]) its word of power. So strange and solitary is the life way of shamans, so dangerously close to what social convention regards as disease or madness, that it is almost as if they were of another species; mutants who live among visionary landscapes, obedient to a different order of necessity, their eyes forever on the movements of invisible things.[19]

Vincent's drive, bordering on frenzy, to record what he saw by translating it in "shorthand" has the power to enthrall us today, a hundred years later. It is as if his work casts a spell over us or, as indigenous peoples would call it, has a "strong medicine."

What Vincent and other artists, sages, and healers have seen and understood, we too are enabled to experience through their intercession. We listen and look, and inexplicably the world around us becomes *more* than it has been during our common, everyday awareness. Looking

18. Letter, 518.

19. Roszak, *Unfinished Animal*, 85.

at Vincent's wheat fields, olive groves, peasants at work elicits in many of his viewers a deepened sense of connectedness with reality. Vincent's imagery has become a revelatory symbol. His art work enables us to look into the heart of things, to see and hear the rhythmic heartbeat of matter, so to speak. Vincent often thought that his art would produce the comforting effect of music. Colors to him were the visual equivalent of sound and tone. The rhythmic quality of his brushstrokes mirrors the rhythms of music. Some of his landscapes produce the effect of a whole symphonic extravaganza. Vincent's brush strokes are tangibly visible and evoke the image of a conductor's baton bringing color harmonies and rhythmic punctuations onto the canvas. Standing before one of his paintings involves more than just our sense of sight.

Vincent—madman or saint, or both? Vincent could be regarded as mad if "mad" implies being an extraordinary visionary and prophet. But because he lived in such a way so as to fulfill and embody his vision, which was to help others see and understand and grasp life more fully, he could be called a saint.

CONCLUSION

Vincent's decision to become a missionary after his failed attempt at theological studies led him to a place where he physically, mentally, and spiritually broke away from all that had determined his life up to the moment he entered the Borinage. In this most desolate mining region he found himself utterly alone. It is here that Vincent finally realized that in order to survive he had to reject the narrow-mindedness of the institutional church and the academically respectable expectations of his family. In the God-forsaken mining district it was completely up to him how he would respond to the living conditions and personal needs he witnessed around him. Jesus was the one guide and companion whose admonition "to love unconditionally" he strove to follow and with whose suffering he could identify.

What Vincent realized through the years in the Borinage was that God could not be a distant being represented by pious clergy preaching eloquent words from the safe enclosures of church pulpits. God was not one to be limited and defined by church authorities and established dogma. According to the Gospels, God had sent his Son, Himself, to live amongst his own. Vincent felt that to live the faith he had been exposed to in his youth, he had to do what God had done with Himself. Vincent had to go amongst the people, especially those who needed solace and a consoling presence. Christ was his example. No well-articulated sermon could equal a true, selfless act of charity.

> It certainly is true that it is better to be high-spirited, even though one makes more mistakes, then to be narrow-minded and over-prudent. It is good to love many things, for therein lies true strength; whosoever loves much, performs and can accomplish much, and what is done in love is well done.[20]

A suffering miner needed to feel the physical embrace and support of a comforter, rather than hear the words spoken by a man of the cloth. The cloth had to become the bandage to ease the woundedness, rather than clothe and separate the healer from the wounded. God through Christ embodied this compassionate outreach. Compassion was the quality that gave his life purpose. And this purpose was expressed through his art. His art was the language through which Vincent sought to comfort people by enabling them to sense that God's Love is present and made manifest in creation. He wanted people to understand that the ordinary things and moments of everyday existence are sacred and imbue life with depth, meaning, and purpose. Vincent's art speaks to those who are willing to listen about a God of Compassion who is present in every grain of wheat, blossoming fruit tree, and table where ordinary peasants share a simple meal.

20. Letters, 121.

Bibliography

Alfeyev, Bishop Hilarion. *The Mystery of the Faith: An Introduction to the Teaching and Spirituality of the Orthodox Church.* Translated and edited by Jessica Rose. London: Dartman Longman & Todd, 2002.

Alison, James. *Knowing Jesus.* London: SPCK, 1993.

————. *Living in the End Times: The Last Things Re-Imagined.* London: SPCK, 1997.

Allison, Dale C. *Jesus of Nazareth: Millennarian Prophet.* Minneapolis: Fortress, 1998.

Andersen, Kurt. "The End of the World as They Know It." *New York Magazine* (October 2006).

Andreopoulos, Andreas. "Eschatology and Final Restoration (apokatastasis) in Origen, Gregory of Nyssa and Maximos the Confessor." *Theandros* 1:3 (2004). Online: http://www.theandros.com/restoration.html.

————. *Metamorphosis: The Transfiguration in Byzantine Theology and Iconography.* Crestwood, NY: St. Vladimir's Seminary Press, 2005.

Ansell, Nicholas John. "The Annihilation of Hell: Universal Salvation and the Redemption of Time in the Eschatology of Jürgen Moltmann." PhD diss., The Free University of Amsterdam, 2005.

Aulen, Gustaf. *Christus Victor.* New York: MacMillan, 1969.

Aune, David E. *Revelation.* 3 vols. Word Biblical Commentary. Dallas: Word, 1997; Nashville: Thomas Nelson, 1998.

————. *Revelation 17–22.* Nashville: Thomas Nelson, 1998.

Badillo, David A. *Latinos and the New Immigrant Church.* Baltimore: Johns Hopkins University Press, 2006.

Baillie, Gil. *Violence Unveiled.* New York: Crossroad, 1997.

Balthasar, Hans Urs von. *Dare We Hope "That All Men be Saved?": With a Short Discourse on Hell.* San Francisco: Ignatius, 1988.

————. *The Glory of the Lord.* Vol. 1: *Seeing the Form.* Translated by Erasmo Leiva-Merikakis. Edinburgh: T. & T. Clark, 1982.

————. *The Glory of the Lord.* Vol. 4: *The Realm of Metaphysics.* Translated Oliver Davies et al. Edinburgh: T. & T. Clark, 1991.

————. *Presence and Thought: An Essay on the Religious Philosophy of Gregory of Nyssa.* San Francisco: Ignatius, 1995.

Barr, David L. "Doing Violence: Moral Issues in Reading John's Apocalypse." In *Reading the Book of Revelation: A Resource for Students,* edited by David L. Barr, 97–108. Atlanta: SBL, 2003.

Barrois, Georges. "The Alleged Origenism of St. Gregory of Nyssa." *St. Vladimir's Theological Quarterly* 30:1 (1986) 7–16.

Barth, Karl. *Kirchliche Dogmatik* IV/2. Zuirich: Evangelischer Verlag, 1955.

Bauckham, Richard. *The Climax of Prophecy: Studies on the Book of Revelation.* Edinburgh: T. & T. Clark, 1993.

————. *Jude, 2 Peter*. Waco, TX: Word, 1983.

————. "Judgment in the Book of Revelation." *Ex Auditu* 20 (2004) 1–24.

————. *The Theology of the Book of Revelation*. New York: Cambridge University Press, 1993.

Beale, G. K. *The Book of Revelation: A Commentary on the Greek Text*. Grand Rapids: Eerdmans, 1999.

Belsey, Catherine. *Poststructuralism: A Very Short Introduction*. New York: Oxford University Press, 2002.

Berdyaev, Nicolas. *The Destiny of Man*. Translated by George Reavey. London: Geoffrey Bles, 1938.

Bieler, Andrea, and Luise Schottroff. *The Eucharist: Bodies, Bread, and Resurrection*. Minneapolis: Fortress, 2007.

Blount, Brian K. *Can I Get a Witness? Reading Revelation through African American Culture*. Louisville: Westminster John Knox, 2005.

————. *Revelation: A Commentary*. Louisville: Westminster John Knox, 2009.

Blowers, Paul M. "Maximus the Confessor, Gregory of Nyssa, and the Concept of 'Perpetual Progress.'" *Vigiliae Christianae* 46:2 (1992) 151–71.

Blumhardt, Christoph, and Leonhard Ragaz. *Der Kampf um das Reich Gottes in Blumhardt, Vater and Sohn—und weiter*. Zurich/Munich: Rotapfel, 1922.

Boff, Leonardo. *Cry of the Earth, Cry of the Poor*. Maryknoll, NY: Orbis, 1997.

Borg, Marcus J. *Reading the Bible Again for the First Time: Taking the Bible Seriously but Not Literally*. San Francisco: HarperSanFrancisco, 2001.

Boring, M. Eugene. "Narrative Christology in the Apocalypse." *Catholic Biblical Quarterly* 54 (1992) 702–23.

————. *Revelation*. Louisville: John Knox, 1989.

———— "The Theology of Revelation: 'The Lord Our God the Almighty Reigns.'" *Interpretation* 40 (1986) 257–69.

Boxall, Ian. *Revelation: Vision and Insight*. London: SPCK, 2002.

————. *The Revelation of Saint John*. Black's New Testament Commentaries. London: A. & C. Black, 2006.

Boyer, Paul. *When Time Shall Be No More: Prophecy Belief in Modern American Culture*. Cambridge: Harvard University Press, 1992.

Braidotti, Rosi. *Nomadic Subjects: Embodiment and Sexual Difference in Contemporary Feminist Theory*. New York: Columbia University Press, 1994.

Bredin, Mark. *Jesus, Revolutionary of Peace: A Nonviolent Christology in the Book of Revelation*. Carlisle: Paternoster, 2003.

Brenneman, James E. "Missional Practice: A Pasadena Mennonite Church Story." In *Evangelical, Ecumenical, and Anabaptist Missiologies in Conversation*, edited by James R. Krabill et al., 158–66. Maryknoll, NY: Orbis, 2006.

Brown, Raymond. *An Introduction to the New Testament*. New York: Doubleday, 1997.

Brown, Tom. *The Quest*. New York: Berkley, 1996.

Bulgakov, Sergius. *The Bride of the Lamb*. Translated by Boris Jakem. Grand Rapids: Eerdmans, 2002.

————. *The Orthodox Church*. Crestwood, NY: St. Vladimir's Seminary Press, 1988.

Bundang, Rachel A. R. "Home as Metaphor, Memory and Promise in Asian/Pacific American Experience." *Semeia* 90:91 (2002) 87–104.

Büsing, Gerhard. "Ein alternativer Ausgangspunkt zur Interpretation von Jer 29." *Zeitschrift für die alttestamentliche Wissenschaft* 104 (1992) 402–8.

Cadbury, Henry. *The Peril of Modernizing Jesus*. 1937. Reprint, Eugene, OR: Wipf & Stock, 2007.

Cahill, Thomas. *The Gift of the Jews: How a Tribe of Desert Nomads Changed the Way Everyone Thinks and Feels*. New York: Doubleday, 1998.

Caird, G. B. *A Commentary on the Revelation of St. John the Divine*. London: A. & C. Black, 1966.

Caputo, John D. *Demythologizing Heidegger*. Bloomington: Indiana University Press, 1993.

————. *Prayers and Tears of Jacques Derrida*. Bloomington: Indiana University Press, 1997.

Carrell, Peter R. *Jesus and the Angels: Angelology and the Christology of the Apocalypse of John*. New York: Cambridge University Press, 1997.

Carroll, John T., et al. *The Return of Jesus in Early Christianity*. Peabody, MA: Hendrickson, 2000.

Castro-Gómez, Santiago. "(Post) Coloniality for Dummies: Latin American Perspectives on Modernity, Coloniality, and the Geopolitics of Knowledge." In *Coloniality at Large: Latin America and the Postcolonial Debate*, edited by Mabel Moraña et al., 259–85. Durham, NC: Duke University Press, 2008.

Chomsky, Aviva. *"They Take Our Jobs!" and Twenty Other Myths about Immigration*. Boston: Beacon, 2007.

Clément, Olivier. *The Roots of Christian Mysticism*. Translated by Theodore Berkeley. London: New City, 1993.

Clifford, Anne. "When Being Human Becomes Truly Earthly: An Ecofeminist Proposal for Solidarity." In *In the Embrace of God: Feminist Approaches to Theological Anthropology*, edited by Ann O'Hara Graff, 173–89. Maryknoll, NY: Orbis, 1995.

Clouse, Robert G. "Eschatology and the Lord's Supper: Hope for the Triumph of God's Reign." In *The Lord's Supper: Believers' Church Perspectives*, edited by Dale R. Stoffer, 129–39. Scottdale, PA: Herald, 1997.

Cobble, James F., Jr., and Charles M. Elliott, editors. *The Hidden Spirit: Discovering the Spirituality of Institutions*. Matthews, NC: Christian Ministry Resources, 1999.

Cohn, Norman. *Cosmos, Chaos and the World to Come: The Ancient Roots of Apocalyptic Faith*. New Haven, CT: Yale University Press, 1993.

Collins, John J. "The Zeal of Phinehas: The Bible and the Legitimation of Violence." *Journal of Biblical Literature* 122 (2003) 3–21.

The Columbia River Watershed: Caring for Creation and the Common Good: An International Pastoral Letter by the Catholic Bishops of the Watershed Region. Online: www.columbiariver.org.

Confession of Faith in a Mennonite Perspective. Scottdale, PA: Herald, 1995.

Considine, J. S. "The Rider on the White Horse; Apocalypse 6:1–8." *Catholic Biblical Quarterly* 6 (1944) 406–22.

Corsini, Eugenio. *The Apocalypse: The Perennial Revelation of Jesus Christ*. Wilmington, DE: Michael Glazier, 1983.

Cosgrove, Charles H. *Appealing to Scripture in Moral Debate: Five Hermeneutical Rules*. Grand Rapids: Eerdmans, 2002.

Crossan, John Dominic. *God and Empire: Jesus against Rome, Then and Now*. San Francisco: HarperSanFrancisco, 2007.

"Current Immigration in Perspective: Never Before Has Immigration from One Country Been So Massive." Online: http://www.fairus.org/site/PageNavigator/facts/research _current_immigration/.

Daley, Brian. *Hope of the Early Church*. New York: Cambridge University Press, 1991.

Daniélou, Jean, SJ. *Platonisme et theologie mystique: Doctrine spirituelle de Saint Gregorie de Nysse*. Aubier: Editions Montaigne, 1944.

Dart, John. "Up Against Caesar: Jesus and Paul versus the Empire." *The Christian Century* (February 8, 2005) 20.

Davies, E. W. "The Morally Dubious Passages of the Hebrew Bible: An Examination of Some Proposed Solutions." *Currents in Biblical Research* 3 (2005) 197–228.

Davis, Ellen F. "Critical Traditioning: Seeking an Inner Biblical Hermeneutic." *Anglican Theological Review* 82 (2000) 733–51.

Davis, Mike. *No One Is Illegal: Fighting Racism and State Violence on the U.S.-Mexico Border*. Chicago: Haymarket, 2006.

Deal, Terrence E., and Allan Kennedy. *Corporate Cultures: The Rites and Rituals of Corporate Life*. New York: Basic, 2000.

DeGraaf, John, David Wann, and Thomas H. Naylor. *Affluenza: The All-Consuming Epidemic*. San Francisco: Berrett-Koehler, 2001.

Denning-Bolle, Sara J. "Gregory of Nyssa: The Soul in Mystical Flight." *Greek Orthodox Theological Review* 34:2 (1989) 97–116.

Dodd, C. H. *The Apostolic Preaching and Its Developments*. London: Hodder & Stoughton, 1936.

Doran, Robert. "Apocalyptic Thinking after 9/11: An Interview with Rene Girard." *SubStance* 37:1 (2008) 20–32.

Dostoevsky, Fyodor. *The Karamazov Brothers*. Translated by Ignat Avsey. New York: Oxford University Press, 1998.

Douglas, Mary. "Deciphering a Meal." *Daedalus* 101:1 (1972) 61–82.

Douglass, James W. *The Nonviolent Coming of God*. Maryknoll, NY: Orbis, 1991.

Dunstone, A. S. *The Atonement in Gregory of Nyssa*. London: Tyndale, 1964.

Edwards, Sarah A. "Christological Perspectives in the Book of Revelation." In *Christological Perspectives: Essays in Honor of Harvey K. McArthur*, edited by Robert F. Berkey and Sarah A. Edwards, 139–54, 281–86 [notes]. New York: Pilgrim, 1982.

Ehrman, Bart D. *Jesus: Apocalyptic Prophet of the New Millennium*. New York: Oxford University Press, 1999.

Eller, Vernard. *The Most Revealing Book in the Bible: Making Sense of Revelation*. Grand Rapids: Eerdmans, 1974.

Elliott, John. "Second Epistle of Peter." In *Anchor Bible Dictionary*, 5:282–87. New York: Doubleday, 1992.

Ellul, Jacques. *Apocalypse: The Book of Revelation*. New York: Seabury, 1977.

Evdokimov, Paul. "Eschatology: On Death, the Afterlife, and the Kingdom; the 'Last Things.'" In *In the World, of the Church: A Paul Evdokimov Reader*, edited and translated by Michael Plekon and Alexis Vinogradov, 11–35. Crestwood, NY: St. Vladamir's Seminary Press, 2001.

Falwell, Jerry. "The Myth of Global Warming." Sermon, Thomas Road Baptist Church, Lynchburg, VA, February 25, 2007.

Ferguson, Everett. "God's Infinity and Man's Mutability: Perpetual Progress According to Gregory of Nyssa." *Greek Orthodox Theological Review* 18:1–2 (Spring/Fall 1973) 59–78.

Finamore, Stephen. *God, Order, and Chaos: René Girard and the Apocalypse*. Paternoster Biblical Monographs. Eugene, OR: Wipf & Stock, 2009.

Fishbane, Michael. *Biblical Interpretation in Ancient Israel*. Oxford: Clarendon, 1985.

Ford, J. Massyngberde. "The Construction of the Other: The Antichrist." *Andrews University Seminary Studies* 33 (1995) 203–30.

———. *My Enemy Is My Guest.* Maryknoll, NY: Orbis, 1984.

Fornberg, Tord. *An Early Church in a Pluralistic Society: A Study of 2 Peter.* Lund, Sweden: CWK Gleerup, 1977.

Fretheim, Terrence E. "Is Anything Too Hard for God? (Jeremiah 32:27)." *Catholic Biblical Quarterly* 66 (2004) 231–36.

Friesen, Steven J. *Imperial Cult and Apocalypse of John: Reading Revelation in the Ruins.* New York: Oxford University Press, 2001.

Geljon, Albert-Kees. "Divine Infinity in Gregory of Nyssa and Philo of Alexandria." *Vigiliae Christianae* 59:2 (2005) 152–77.

Georgi, Dieter. "Who Is the True Prophet?" *Harvard Theological Review* 79 (1986) 100–126.

Gilbert, Martin. *The Day the War Ended: May 8, 1945—Victory in Europe.* New York: Henry Holt, 1995.

Gingerich, Ray, and Ted Grimsrud, editors. *Transforming the Powers: Peace, Justice and the Domination System.* Minneapolis: Fortress, 2006.

Gingerich, Ray. "Theological Foundations for an Ethics of Nonviolence: Was Yoder's God a Warrior?" *Mennonite Quarterly Review* 76:3 (July 2003) 418–35.

Girard, René. *Battling to the End: Conversations with Benoît Chantre.* East Lansing, MI: Michigan State University Press, 2010.

———. *Deceit, Desire, and the Novel.* Baltimore: Johns Hopkins University Press, 1965.

———. "Dionysus versus the Crucified." *Modern Language Notes* 99 (1984) 816–35.

———. "The Founding Murder in the Philosophy of Nietzsche." In *Violence and Truth: On the Work of René Girard*, edited by Paul Dumouchel, 227–46. London: Athlone, 1988.

———. *The Girard Reader.* Edited by James G. Williams. New York: Crossroad, 1996.

———. *I See Satan Fall Like Lightening.* Maryknoll, NY: Orbis, 2001.

———. "Is There Anti-Semitism in the Gospels?" *Biblical Interpretation* 1 (1993) 339–56.

———. "Nietzsche and Contradiction." *Stanford Italian Review* 6 (1986) 53–65.

———. *The Scapegoat.* Stanford, CA: Stanford University Press, 1986.

———. *"To Double Business Bound": Essays on Literature, Mimesis, and Anthropology.* London: Athlone, 1988.

———. *Violence and the Sacred,* Baltimore: Johns Hopkins University Press, 1979.

Girard, René, with Jean-Michel Oughourlian and Guy Lefort. *Things Hidden since the Foundation of the World.* Stanford: Stanford University Press, 1987.

Girard, René, with Pierpaolo Antonello and João Cezar de Castro Rocha. *Evolution and Conversion: Dialogues on the Origins of Culture.* New York: Continuum, 2007.

Gore, Al. *Earth in the Balance: Ecology and the Human Spirit.* New York: Penguin, 1993.

Got Questions Ministries. "How Should a Christian View Global Warming?" Online: http://www.gotquestions.org/global-warming.html.

Gregory of Nyssa. *Gregory of Nyssa: The Life of Moses.* Translated by Everett Ferguson and Abraham J. Malhebre. New York: Paulist, 1978.

Griffith, Lee. *The War on Terrorism and the Terror of God.* Grand Rapids: Eerdmans, 2002.

Grimsrud, Ted. "Against Empire: A Yoderian Reading of Romans." In *Peace Be with You: Christ's Benediction Amid Violent Empires*, edited by Sharon Baker and Michael Hardin, 120–37. Telford, PA: Cascadia, 2010.

———. *Embodying the Way of Jesus: Anabaptist Convictions for the 21st Century.* Eugene, OR: Wipf & Stock, 2007.

———. *God's Healing Strategy: An Introduction to the Bible's Main Themes.* 2nd ed. Telford, PA: Cascadia, 2011.

———. *Theology as If Jesus Matters: An Introduction to Christianity's Main Convictions.* Telford, PA: Cascadia, 2009.

———. *Triumph of the Lamb.* Scottdale, PA: Herald, 1987.

Grindal, Gracia. "Hastening the Day." *The Christian Century* (November 20, 1996) 34.

Gunkel, Hermann J. F. *Schöpfung und Chaos in Urzeit und Endzeit: eine Religionsgeschichtliche Untersuchung über Gen 1 und Ap Joh 12,* Göttingen: Vandenhoeck & Ruprecht, 1921.

Guyatt, Nicholas. *Have a Nice Doomsday: Why Millions of Americans are Looking Forward to the End of the World.* New York: Harper Perennial, 2007.

Hamerton-Kelly, Robert G. *The Gospel and the Sacred: Poetics of Violence in Mark.* Minneapolis: Fortress, 1994.

———. "Religion and the Thought of René Girard: an Introduction." In *Curing Violence,* edited by Mark I. Wallace and Theophilus H. Smith, 3–24. Sonoma, CA: Polebridge, 1994.

Hansen, James. "Why We Can't Wait." *The Nation* (May 7, 2007).

Harder, James M. "The Violence of Global Marketization." In *Teaching Peace: Nonviolence and the Liberal Arts,* edited by J. Denny Weaver and Gerald Biesecker-Mast, 179–93. Lanham, MD: Rowman & Littlefield, 2003.

Hardin, Michael. "Ecospirituality." Presented at COV&R, 2004. Online: www.preachingpeace.org.

———. *The Jesus Driven Life.* Lancaster, PA: JDL, 2010.

Harrington, Wilfred J. *The Apocalypse of St. John: A Commentary.* London: Geoffrey Chapman, 1969.

———. *Revelation.* Collegeville, MN: Liturgical, 1993.

Hart, David B. "The Mirror and the Infinite: Gregory of Nyssa on the *Vestigia Trinitatis.*" *Modern Theology* 18:4 (2002) 541–61.

Haussleiter, Johannis. *Victorini Episcopi Petauionensis Opera.* Leipzig, CSEL 49, 1916.

Hays, Richard B. *The Moral Vision of the New Testament—Community, Cross, New Creation: A Contemporary Introduction to New Testament Ethics.* San Francisco: HarperSanFrancisco, 1996.

Heide, Gale Z. "What Is New about the New Heaven and the New Earth? A Theology of Creation from Revelation 21 and 2 Peter 3." *Journal of the Evangelical Theological Society* 40:1 (1997) 37–56.

Heidegger, Martin. *Being and Time.* Translated by Joan Stambaugh. Albany: State University of New York Press, 1996.

———. *On Time and Being.* Translated by Joan Stambaugh. New York: Harper, 1972.

Heine, Robert, editor and translator. *Gregory of Nyssa's Treatise on the Inscription of the Psalms,* Oxford: Clarendon, 1995.

Hincapié, Marielena. "Aquí estamos y no nos vamos: Unintended Consequences of Current U.S. Immigration Law." In *Global Connections and Local Receptions: New Latino Immigration to the Southeastern United States,* edited by Fran Ansley and Jon Shefner, 89–127. Knoxville: University of Tennessee Press, 2009.

Hoffmann, Matthias Reinhard. *The Destroyer and the Lamb: The Relationship between Angelomorphic and Lamb Christology in the Book of Revelation.* Tübingen: Mohr/Siebeck, 2005.

Horsley, Richard. *Paul and Empire.* Harrisburg, PA: Trinity, 1997.

Howard-Brook, Wes, and Anthony Gwyther. *Unveiling Empire: Reading Revelation Then and Now.* Maryknoll, NY: Orbis, 1999.

Hurtado, L. W. "Revelation 4–5 in the Light of Jewish Apocalyptic Analogies." *Journal for the Study of the New Testament* 25 (1985) 105–24.

Ibarra, María de la Luz. "Buscando la vide: Mexican Immigrant Women's Memories of Home, Yearning, and Border Crossings." *Frontiers: A Journal of Women's Studies* 24 (2003) 261–81.

St. Isaac the Syrian, Bishop of Nineveh. *The Ascetical Homilies of Saint Isaac the Syrian.* Brookline, MA: Holy Transfiguration Monastery, 1985.

Jenson, Robert W. "Gregory of Nyssa, The Life of Moses." *Theology Today* 62:4 (2006) 533–37.

Jewett, Robert. *Mission and Menace: Four Centuries of American Religious Zeal.* Minneapolis: Fortress, 2008.

Johns, Loren L. *The Lamb Christology of the Apocalypse of John: An Investigation into Its Origins and Rhetorical Force.* Tübingen: Mohr/Siebeck, 2003.

Johnson, Chalmers. *The Sorrows of Empire: Militarism, Secrecy, and the End of the Republic.* New York: Metropolitan, 2004.

Johnson, Luke Timothy. *The Gospel of Luke.* Collegeville, MN: Liturgical, 1992.

Johnson, William. "Contemporary Native American Prophecy in Historical Perspective." *Journal of the American Academy of Religion* 64:3 (1996) 575–611.

Kaptein, Roel, with the co-operation of Duncan Morrow. *On the Way of Freedom.* Dublin: Columba, 1993.

Käsemann, Ernst. "An Apologia for Primitive Christian Eschatology." In *Essays on New Testament Themes.* Philadelphia: Fortress, 1982.

Keller, Catherine. *God and Power: Counter-Apocalyptic Journeys.* Minneapolis: Fortress, 2005.

Kelly, J. N. D. *A Commentary on the Epistles of Peter and Jude.* New York: Harper, 1969.

King, Martin Luther, Jr. "I Have a Dream." Online: http://usinfo.state.gove/usa/infousa/facts/democratic/38.het.

Kirkpatrick, David D. "The Return of the Warrior Jesus." *New York Times* (April 4, 2004) 4–1, 4–6.

Kirsch, Jonathan. *A History of the End of the World: How the Most Controversial Book in the Bible Changes the Course of Western Civilization.* San Francisco: HarperSanFrancisco, 2006.

Kirwan, Michael. *Discovering Girard.* London: Darton Longman & Todd, 2004.

Kittredge, Cynthia Briggs. "2 Peter." In *Postcolonial Commentary on the New Testament Writings,* edited by Fernando Segovia and R. S. Sugirtharaja, 404–12. New York: T. & T. Clark, 2007.

Klassen, William. "Vengeance in the Apocalypse of John." *Catholic Biblical Quarterly* 28 (1966) 300–11.

Knight, J. "The Enthroned Christ of Revelation 5:6 and the Development of Christian Theology." In *Studies in the Book of Revelation,* edited by Steve Moyise, 43–50. Edinburgh: T. & T. Clark, 2001.

Kraybill, J. Nelson. *Apocalypse and Allegiance: Worship, Politics, and Devotion in the Book of Revelation*. Grand Rapids: Brazos, 2010.

Kreider, Eleanor. *Communion Shapes Character*. Scottdale, PA: Herald, 1997.

Ladner, Gerhart B. "The Philosophical Anthropology of Saint Gregory of Nyssa." *Dumbarton Oak Papers* 12 (1958) 59–94.

LaHaye, Tim, and Jerry B. Jenkins. *The Glorious Appearing: The End of Days*. Carol Stream, IL: Tyndale House, 2004.

Laird, Martin. "Gregory of Nyssa and the Mysticism of Darkness: A Reconsideration." *The Journal of Religion* 79:4 (1999) 592–616.

Lampe, G. W. H. "The Testimony of Jesus Is the Spirit of Prophecy." In *The New Testament Age; Essays in Honor of Bo Reicke*, edited by William Weinrch, 245–58. Macon, GA: Mercer University Press, 1984.

Landau, Yehezkel. "The President and the Bible: What Do the Prophets Say to Our Time?" *Christianity and Crisis* (December 12, 1983).

Lawrence, D. H. *Apocalypse*. London: Penguin, 1960.

Laws, Sophie. *In the Light of the Lamb; Imagery, Parody, and Theology in the Apocalypse of John*. Wilmington, DE: Michael Glazier, 1988.

Lind, Millard. *Yahweh Is a Warrior: A Theology of Warfare in the Ancient Israel*. Scottdale, PA: Herald, 1980.

Lindsey, Hal. *The Late Great Planet Earth*. Grand Rapids: Zondervan, 1970.

López, Ann Aurelia. *The Farmworkers' Journey*. Berkeley: University of California Press, 2007.

Lossky, Vladimir. *The Mystical Theology of the Eastern Church*. Crestwood, NY: St. Vladimir's Seminary Press, 1957.

Louth, Andrew. "Eastern Orthodox Eschatology." In *The Oxford Handbook of Eschatology*, edited by Jerry L. Walls, 233–47. New York: Oxford University Press, 2008.

Ludlow, Morwenna. *Universal Salvation: Eschatology in the Thought of Gregory of Nyssa and Karl Rahner*. New York: Oxford University Press, 2000.

Luibheid, Colm, and Norman Russell. *John Climacus: The Ladder of Divine Ascent*. Mahwah, NJ: Paulist, 1982.

Maier, Harry O. *Apocalypse Recalled: The Book of Revelation after Christendom*. Minneapolis: Fortress, 2002.

Marshall, Christopher D. *Beyond Retribution: A New Testament Vision for Justice, Crime, and Punishment*. Grand Rapids: Eerdmans, 2001.

———. "The Violence of God and the Hermeneutics of Paul." In *The Work of Jesus Christ in Anabaptist Perspective*, edited by A. Epp Weaver and G. Biesecker-Mast, 74–105. Telford, PA: Cascadia, 2008.

Matter, E. Ann. "The Apocalypse in Early Medieval Exegesis." In *The Apocalypse in the Middle Ages*. Edited by Richard K. Emmerson and Bernard McGuinn, 38–50. Ithaca, NY: Cornell University Press, 1992.

McCann, J. Clinton. "The Hermeneutics of Grace." *Interpretation* 57 (2003) 5–15.

McClure, Robert, and Lisa Stiffler, "Federal Way schools restrict Gore film: 'Inconvenient Truth' call too controversial." *Seattle Post-Intelligencer* (January 11, 2007).

McDonald, Patricia M. "Lion as Slain Lamb: On Reading Revelation Recursively." *Horizons* 23 (1996) 29–47.

McEwan, Ian. *Enduring Love*. New York: Anchor, 1999.

McGuckin, John Anthony. "The Book of Revelation and Orthodox Eschatology." In *The Last Things: Biblical and Theological Perspectives on Eschatology*, edited by Carl E. Braaten and Robert W. Jenson, 113–34. Grand Rapids: Eerdmans, 2002.

———. *The Orthodox Church: An Introduction to Its History, Doctrine, and Spiritual Culture*. Malden, MA: Blackwell, 2008.

McKibben, Bill. *The Comforting Whirlwind: God, Job, and the Scale of Creation*. Grand Rapids: Eerdmans, 1994.

Meeks, M. Douglas. "Jürgen Moltmann's Systematic Contributions to Theology." *Religious Studies Review* 22 (April 1996) 95–105.

Mendenhall, George. "The Shady Side of Wisdom." In *A Light unto My Path: Old Testament Studies in Honor of Jacob M. Myers*, edited by Howard N. Bream et al. Philadelphia: Temple University Press, 1974.

Mendez Montoya, Angel F. *Theology of Food: Eating and the Eucharist*. Malden, MA: Wiley-Blackwell, 2010.

Meredith, Anthony. *Gregory of Nyssa*. New York: Routledge, 1999.

Metzger, Bruce. *A Textual Commentary on the Greek New Testament*. New York: United Bible Societies, 1971.

Migne, Jacques Paul, editor. *Patrologiae Graeca: S. Gregorius Nyssenus*. Vol 44. Paris: Vives, 1863.

Moessner, David P. *The Lord of the Banquet: The Literary and Theological Significance of the Lukan Travel Narrative*. Minneapolis: Fortress, 1989.

Moltmann, Jürgen. *God in Creation: A New Theology of Creation and the Spirit of God*. San Francisco: Harper & Row, 1985.

Moya, Paula M. L. "Postmodern, 'Realism,' and the Politics of Identity: Cherrié Moraga and Chicana Feminism." In *Feminist Genealogies, Colonial Legacies, Democratic Futures*, edited by M. Jacqui Alexander and Chandra Talpade Mohanty. New York: Routledge, 1997.

Moyise, Steve. "Does the Lion Lie Down with the Lamb?" In *Studies in the Book of Revelation*, edited by Steve Moyise, 181–94. Edinburgh: T. & T. Clark, 2001.

Murray, Robert. *The Cosmic Covenant: Biblical Themes of Justice, Peace and the Integrity of Creation*. London: Sheed & Ward, 1992.

Nabakov, Peter. *Native American Testimony*. Rev. ed. New York: Penguin, 1999.

Nemoianu, Virgil. "René Girard and the Dialectics of Imperfection." In *To Honor René Girard*, edited by Alphonse Juillard, 1–16. Stanford, CA: Stanford University Press, 1986.

Neville, David J. "Toward a Teleology of Peace: Contesting Matthew's Violent Eschatology." *Journal for the Study of the New Testament* 30 (2007) 131–61.

Neyrey, Jerome H. "The Form and Background of the Polemic in 2 Peter." *Journal of Biblical Literature* 99 (1980) 407–31.

Nicolet, Claude. *Space, Geography, and Politics in the Early Roman Empire*. Ann Arbor: University of Michigan Press, 1991.

Niditch, Susan. *War in the Hebrew Bible: A Study in the Ethics of Violence*. New York: Oxford University Press, 1999.

Niewiadomski, Jozef. "'Denial of the Apocalypse' versus 'Fascination with the Final Days.'" In *Politics and Apocalypse*, edited by Robert Hamerton-Kelly, 51–68. East Lansing: Michigan State University Press, 2007.

Noll, Mark. *The Civil War as a Theological Crisis*. Chapel Hill: University of North Carolina Press, 2006.

Noonan, Peggy. "A Separate Peace." *Wall Street Journal* (October 27, 2005).

O'Connell, Patrick F. "The Double Journey in Saint Gregory of Nyssa: The Life of Moses." *Greek Orthodox Theological Review* 28:4 (1983) 301–24.

Oakes, Edward T., and David Moss, editors. *The Cambridge Companion to Hans Urs von Balthasar*. New York: Cambridge University Press, 2004.

Olson, R. Dennis. "NAFTA's Food and Agriculture Lessons." *Peace Review: A Journal of Social Justice* 20 (2008) 418–25.

Page, Jake. *In the Hands of the Great Spirit: The 20,000-Year History of American Indians*. New York: Simon & Schuster, 2003.

Palmer, G. E. H., Philip Sherrard, and Kallistos Ware, editors and translators. *The Philokalia*. Compiled by St. Nikodimos of the Holy Mountain and St. Makarios of Corinth. 4 vols. (t.d.). London: Faber & Faber, 1979–.

Phelan, John E., Jr. "The Bible, Culture, and Mission." *The Covenant Quarterly* 66:2 (May 2008) 3–15.

———. "Revelation, Empire, and the Violence of God." *Ex Auditu* 20 (2004) 65–84.

Quam, Alvina, translator. *The Zunis: Self Portrayals*. Albuquerque: University of New Mexico Press, 1972.

Quispel, Gilles. *The Secret Book of Revelation: The Last Book of the Bible*. London: Collins, 1979.

Rad, Gerhard von. *Holy War in Ancient Israel*. Grand Rapids: Eerdmans, 1991.

———. "The Origin of the Concept of the Day of Yahweh." *Journal of Semitic Studies* 4 (1959) 97–108.

Rahner, Karl. "The Concept of Existential Philosophy in Heidegger." *Philosophy Today* 13 (1969) 125–37.

———. *Foundations of Christian Faith*. Translated by William V. Dych. New York: Crossroad, 1992.

———. "Theology and Anthropology." In *The Word in History*, edited by T. Patrick Burke. New York: Sheed & Ward, 1966.

Ramírez, Daniel. "Call Me 'Bitter': Life and Death in the Diasporic Borderlands and the Challenges/Opportunities for Norteamericano Churches." *Perspectivas: Occasional Papers* (Fall 2007) 39–68.

Reddish, Mitchell G. *Revelation*. Macon, GA: Smyth and Helwys, 2001.

Reiser, Marcus. *Jesus and Judgment*. Translated by Linda M. Malony. Minneapolis: Fortress, 1997.

Resseguie, James L. *Revelation Unsealed: A Narrative Critical Approach to John's Apocalypse*. Leiden: Brill, 1998.

Rhoads, David M. "Who Will Speak for the Sparrow? Eco-Justice Criticism of the New Testament." In *Literary Encounters with the Reign of God*, edited by Sharon Ringe and H. C. Kim, 64–86. New York: T. & T. Clark, 2004.

Richard, Pablo. *Apocalypse: A People's Commentary on the Book of Revelation*. Maryknoll, NY: Orbis, 1995.

Rieger, Joerg. *Christ and Empire: From Paul to Postcolonial Times*. Minneapolis: Fortress Press, 2007.

Roberts, Alexander, and James Donaldson, editors. *Nicene and Post Nicene Fathers: Series I & II*. 28 Vols. Peabody, MA: Hendrickson, 2004.

Rodriguez, Raul Humberto Lugo. "Wait for the Day of God's Coming and Do What You Can to Hasten It . . . (2 Pet 3:12): The Non-Pauline Letters as Resistance Literature."

In *Subversive Scriptures: Revolutionary Readings of the Christian Bible in Latin America*, edited by Leif Vaage, 193–206. Valley Forge, PA: Trinity, 1997.

Rossing, Barbara. "Alas for the Earth: Lament and Resistance in Revelation 12." In *The Earth Bible, Volume 5: The Earth Story in the New Testament*, edited by Norman Habel and Shirley Wurst, 180–92. Sheffield, UK: Sheffield Academic, 2002.

———. *The Choice Between Two Cities: Whore, Bride, and Empire in the Apocalypse.* Harrisburg, PA: Trinity, 1999.

———. "For the Healing of the World: Reading Revelation Ecologically." In *From Every Tribe, Tongue, People, and Nation: The Book of Revelation in Intercultural Perspective*, edited by David Rhoads, 165–82. Minneapolis: Fortress, 2005.

———. "Hastening the Day When the Earth Will Burn: Global Warming, Revelation, and 2 Peter 3." In *The Bible in the Public Square: Reading the Signs of the Times*, edited by Cynthia Briggs Kittredge et al., 25–38. Minneapolis: Fortress, 2008.

———. "Hastening the Day When the Earth Will Burn? Global Warming, Revelation, and 2 Peter 3." *Currents in Theology and Mission* 35:5 (2008) 363–73.

———. *The Rapture Exposed: The Message of Hope in the Book of Revelation.* 2nd ed. New York: Basic, 2005.

———. "(Re)Claiming *Oikoumene*? Empire, Ecumenism and the Discipleship of Equals." In *Walk in the Ways of Wisdom: Essays in Honor of Elisabeth Schüssler Fiorenza*, edited by Cynthia Briggs Kittredge and Melanie Johnson-DeBaufre, 74–87. Harrisburg, PA: Trinity, 2003.

———. "River of Life in God's New Jerusalem: An Eschatological Vision for Earth's Future." In *Christianity and Ecology*, edited by Rosemary Radford Ruether and Dieter Hessel, 205–24. Cambridge, MA: Harvard Center for World Religions, 1999.

Roszak, Theodore. *Unfinished Animal.* New York: Harper & Row, 1975.

Rowland, Christopher C. "The Book of Revelation." In *The New Interpreter's Bible*, edited by Leander Keck, 12:501–743. Nashville: Abingdon, 1998.

———. *The Open Heaven: A Study of Apocalyptic in Judaism and Early Christianity.* London: SPCK, 1982.

Rowland, Christopher, and Mark Corner. *Liberating Exegesis: The Challenge of Liberation Theology to Biblical Studies.* London: SPCK, 1990.

Russell, David M. *The "New Heavens and New Earth": Hope for the Creation in Jewish Apocalyptic and the New Testament.* Philadelphia: Visionary, 1996.

Sachs, John R. "Apocatastasis in Patristic Theology." *Theological Studies* 54:4 (1993) 617–40.

Saint Silouan the Athonite. *St. Silouan the Athonite.* Edited by Archimandrite Sophrony and translated by Rosemary Edmonds. Crestwood, NY: St. Vladimir's Seminary Press, 1991.

Sakharov, Nicholas V. *I Love Therefore I Am: The Theological Legacy of Archimandrite Sophrony.* Crestwood, NY: St. Vladimir's Seminary Press, 2002.

Sanders, James A. "The Ethic of Election in Luke's Banquet Parable." In *Luke and Scripture*, edited by Craig A. Evans and James A. Sanders, 106–20. Minneapolis: Fortress, 1993.

Schmemann, Alexander. *For the Life of the World.* Crestwood, NY: St. Vladimir's Seminary Press, 1982.

Schnelle, Udo. *The History and Theology of the New Testament Writings.* Translated by M. Eugene Boring. London: SCM, 1998.

Schüssler Fiorenza, Elisabeth. "The Phenomena of Early Christian Apocalyptic: Some Reflections on Method." In *Apocalypticism in the Mediterranean World and the Near East*, edited by David Hellholm, 295–316. Tubingen: Mohr, 1989.

———. *The Power of the Word: Scripture and the Rhetoric of Empire*. Minneapolis: Fortress Press, 2007.

———. *Revelation: Vision of a Just World*. Minneapolis: Fortress, 1991.

———. "The Words of Prophecy: Reading the Apocalypse Theologically." In *Studies in the Book of Revelation*, edited by Steve Moyise, 1–19. Edinburgh: T. & T. Clark, 2001.

Schwager, Raymund. *Jesus in the Drama of Salvation*. Translated by James G. Williams. New York: Crossword, 1999.

———. "The Theory of the Wrath of God." In *Violence and Truth: On the Work of René Girard*, edited by Paul Dumouchel, 44–52. London: Athlone, 1988.

———. *Must There Be Scapegoats?* Translated by Maria L. Assad. San Francisco: Harper & Row, 1987.

Schweitzer, Albert. *The Quest of the Historical Jesus: A Critical Study of Its Progress from Reimarus to Wrede*. Translated by W. Montgomery. 1906. Reprint, New York: Macmillan, 1968.

Sciarrino, Enrica. "A Temple for the Professional Muse." In *Rituals in Ink*, edited by Alessandro Barchiesi et al, 45–56. Munich: Franz Steiner, 2004.

Sheehan, Thomas. *Karl Rahner: The Philosophical Foundations*. Athens, OH: Ohio University Press, 1987.

Shuck, Glenn W. *Marks of the Beast: The Left Behind Novels and the Struggle for Evangelical Identity*. New York: New York University Press, 2005.

Silvey, Rachel. "Power, Difference, and Mobility: Feminist Advances in Migration Studies." *Progress in Human Geography* 28 (2004) 490–505.

Skaggs, Rebecca, and Thomas Doyle. "Lion/Lamb in Revelation." *Currents in Biblical Research* 7 (2009) 362–75.

———. "Violence in the Apocalypse of John." *Currents in Biblical Research* 5 (2007) 220–34.

Slater, Thomas B. *Christ and Community: A Socio-Historical Study of the Christology of Revelation*. Sheffield, UK: Sheffield Academic, 1999.

Smith-Christopher, Daniel. "The Book of Daniel: Introduction, Commentary, and Reflections." In *The New Interpreter's Bible*, edited by Leander Keck, 7:17–152. Nashville: Abingdon, 1996.

Smith, Daniel L. "Jeremiah as a Prophet of Non-Violent Resistance." *Journal for the Study of the Old Testament* 43 (1989) 95–107.

Smith, J. Warren. *Passion and Paradise: Human and Divine Emotion in the Thought of Gregory of Nyssa*. New York: Herder & Herder, 2004.

Sobrino, Jon. *Terremoto, terrorismo, barbarie y utopia: El Salvador, Nueva York, Afganistán*. San Salvador: UCA Editores, 2003.

Spivak, Gayatri Chakravorty. *A Critique of Postcolonial Reason: Toward a History of the Vanishing Present*. Cambridge, MA: Harvard University Press, 1999.

Standaert, Michael. *Skipping towards Armageddon: The Politics and Propaganda of the Left Behind Novels and the LaHaye Empire*. Brooklyn, NY: Soft Skull, 2006.

Stringfellow, William. *An Ethic for Christians and other Aliens in a Strange Land*. Waco, TX: Word, 1973.

Suro, Robert. "Remittance Senders and Receivers: Tracking the Transnational Channels." (2003). Online: http://pewhispanic.org/files/reports/23.pdf.

Swartley, Willard M. *Covenant of Peace: The Missing Peace in New Testament Theology and Ethics*. Grand Rapids: Eerdmans, 2006.

Sweet, John P. M. "Maintaining the Testimony of Jesus; the Suffering of Christians in the Revelation of John." In *Suffering and Martyrdom in the New Testament*, edited by William Horbury and Brian McNeill, 101–17. New York: Cambridge University Press, 1981.

———. *Revelation*. London: SCM, 1979.

Tannehill, Robert C. "Freedom and Responsibility in Scripture Interpretation, with Application to Luke." In *Literary Studies in Luke–Acts: Essays in Honor of Joseph B. Tyson*, edited by R. P. Thompson and T. E. Phillips, 265–78. Macon, GA: Mercer University Press, 1998.

Thiede, Carsten Peter. "A Pagan Reader of 2 Peter: Cosmic Conflagration in 2 Peter 3 and the *Octavius* of Municius Felix." *Journal for the Study of the New Testament* 26 (1986) 79–96.

Thomas, David Andrew. *Revelation 19 in Historical and Mythological Context*. New York: Peter Lang, 2008.

Tinker, George E. *Spirit and Resistance*. Minneapolis: Fortress, 2004.

Tori, Michael J. "Apokatastasis in Gregory of Nyssa: From Origen to Orthodoxy." *Patristic and Byzantine Review* 15 (1997) 87–100.

Torreblanca, Jorge. "Continuidad para el futuro del pueblo de Dios: Análisis exegético-estructual de Jeremías 52, 54 y 29." *Cuadernos de Teología* 23 (2005) 17–35.

Travis, Stephen H. *Christ and the Judgment of God*. Peabody, MA: Hendrickson, 2008.

Trites, Allison A. *The New Testament Concept of Witness*. New York: Cambridge University Press, 1977.

Tsirpanlis, Constantine N. "The Concept of Universal Salvation in Saint Gregory of Nyssa." In *Greek Patristic Theology: Basic Doctrines in Eastern Church Fathers*, 1:41–56. New York: Eastern Orthodox, 1979.

"Unlicensed to Kill." Online: http://www.fairus.org/site/News2?page=NewsArticle&id=16857&security=1601&news_iv_ctrl=1007.

Van Gogh, Vincent. *The Complete Letters of Vincent Van Gogh*. 3 vols. New York: Bulfinch, 2000.

Vattimo, Gianni. *Belief*. Translated by Luca D'Isanto and David Webb. Oxford: Polity, 1999.

Vlachos, Hierotheos of Nafpaktos. *Life after Death*. Translated by Esther Williams. Levadia, Gr.: Birth of the Theotokos Monastery, 1996.

Volf, Miroslav. *Exclusion and Embrace: A Theological Exploration of Identity, Otherness, and Reconciliation*. Nashville: Abingdon, 1996.

———. "The Final Reconciliation: Reflections on the Social Dimension of the Eschatological Transition." *Modern Theology* 16:1 (2000) 91–113.

Wainwright, Arthur W. *Mysterious Apocalypse: Interpreting the Book of Revelation*. Nashville: Abingdon, 1993.

Ware, Kallistos. "Dare We Hope for the Salvation of All?" In *The Inner Kingdom*, 193–215. The Collected Works 1. Crestwood, NY: St. Vladimir's Seminary Press, 2000.

———. *The Orthodox Church*. New York: Penguin, 1997.

———. *The Orthodox Way*. Crestwood, NY: St. Vladimir's Seminary Press, 1995.

Warrior, Robert Allen Warrior. "A Native American Perspective: Canaanites, Cowboys and Indians." In *Voices from the Margin: Interpreting the Bible in the Third World*, 3rd ed., edited by R. S. Sugirtharajah, 235–41. Maryknoll: Orbis, 2006.

Waters, Frank. *Book of the Hopi*. New York: Penguin, 1977.

Weaver, J. Denny. *The Nonviolent Atonement*. Grand Rapids: Eerdmans, 2001.

————. "Reading the Past, Present, and Future in Revelation." In *Apocalypticism and Millennialism: Shaping a Believers Church Eschatology for the Twenty-First Century*, edited by Loren Johns, 97–112. Kitchener: Pandora, 2000.

Whealon, John F. "New Patches on an Old Garment: The Book of Revelation." *Biblical Theology Bulletin* 11 (1981) 54–59.

Whisenant, Edgar C. *88 Reasons the Rapture Will Be in 1988*. Nashville: World Bible Society, 1988.

Williams, James G. *The Bible, Violence and the Sacred; Liberation from the Myth of Sanctioned Violence*. San Francisco: Harper & Row, 1991.

Wink, Walter. *Cracking the Gnostic Code: The Powers in Gnosticism*. Atlanta: Scholars, 1993.

————. *Engaging the Powers: Discernment and Resistance in an Age of Domination*. Minneapolis: Fortress, 1992.

————. *Naming the Powers: The Language of Power in the New Testament*. Minneapolis: Fortress, 1984.

————. "The New Worldview: Spirit at the Core of Everything." In *Transforming the Powers: Peace, Justice, and the Domination System*, edited by Ray Gingerich and Ted Grimsrud, 17–28. Minneapolis: Fortress, 2006.

————. *The Powers That Be: Theology for a New Millennium*. New York: Doubleday, 1999.

————. *Unmasking the Powers: The Invisible Forces that Determine Human Existence*. Minneapolis: Fortress, 1986.

————. *When the Powers Fall: Reconciliation in the Healing of Nations*. Minneapolis: Fortress, 1998.

Wood, John A. *Perspectives on War in the Bible*. Macon, GA: Mercer University Press, 1998.

Wybrew, Hugh. *The Orthodox Liturgy: The Development of the Eucharistic Liturgy in the Byzantine Rite*. Crestwood, NY: St. Vladimir's Seminary Press, 2003.

Yarbro Collins, Adela. "Appreciating the Apocalypse as a Whole." *Interpretation* 45 (1991) 187–89.

————. *Crisis and Catharsis: The Power of the Apocalypse*. Philadelphia: Westminster, 1984.

————. "Eschatology in the Book of Revelation." *Ex Auditu* 6 (1990) 63–72.

————. "The Political Perspective of the Revelation to John." *Journal of Biblical Literature* 96 (1977) 241–56.

————. "Revelation, Book of." In *Anchor Bible Dictionary*, edited by David Noel Freedman, 5:694–708. New York: Doubleday, 1992.

Yeatts, John R. *Revelation*. Scottdale, PA: Herald, 2003.

Yoder, John Howard. *Body Politics: Five Practices of the Christian Community before a Watching World*. Nashville: Discipleship Resources, 1994.

————. *The Politics of Jesus: Vicit Agnus Noster*. 2nd ed. Grand Rapids: Eerdmans, 1994.

————. *The Royal Priesthood: Essays Ecclesiological and Ecumenical*. Grand Rapids: Eerdmans, 1994.

————. "To Serve Our God and to Rule the World." In *The Royal Priesthood: Essays Ecclesiological and Ecumenical*, edited by Michael G. Cartwright, 127–40. Grand Rapids: Eerdmans, 1994.